Checking Back

Also by Neil D. Isaacs

All the Moves: a History of College Basketball
The Sporting Spirit: Athletes in Literature and Life
(co-editor with Robert J. Higgs)

Checking Back

A History of the National Hockey League

Neil D. Isaacs

W·W·Norton & Company·Inc·
NEW YORK

Copyright © 1977 by Neil D. Isaacs
Published simultaneously in Canada by George J. McLeod Limited, Toronto. Printed in the
United States of America.

Library of Congress Cataloging in Publication Data

Isaacs, Neil David, 1931–
Checking back.

Bibliography: p.
Includes index.
1. National Hockey League—History.   I. Title.
GV847.8.N3I82   1977   796.9′62′097   77–10482

ISBN 0 393 08788 3

1 2 3 4 5 6 7 8 9 0

Contents

Contents

Dedicatory Preface

Trusting that the statute of limitations applies, I confess that my first experience with pro hockey was as a scalper. In the middle and late forties an enterprising schoolboy in New Haven could earn some walking-around money by mingling with the crowds at Grove and Orange streets and (carefully, avoiding the ever-present plainclothesmen) selling tickets for the always-sold-out Eagles. I usually kept a seat for myself—that was part of the education of the compleat sports fan that was available to a New Haven boy. If it was not the best of both worlds, at least it was a representative selection. On one side was the sports crowd, on the other the sporting crowd.

One world extended from the pastoral opulence of Yale Bowl and Walter Camp Field to the Gothic splendor of Payne Whitney Gymnasium. If you were lucky you got to see Tom Harmon run back a punt through eleven men in blue, Glenn Davis play football *and* baseball, Clint Frank pass, Larry Kelly catch, Levi Jackson run, John Prchlik tackle, Paul Walker do everything, Bob Kiphuth's men swim, and Tony Lavelli gracefully score. It was a world that embraced Kaysey's and the Taft and the Old Heidelberg and J. Press and Barrie Ltd. and beautiful furred and scarfed women, a world of careless wealth and conspicuous self-satisfaction, where everything smelled fresh and clean, however much booze and chlorine was there.

The other world extended from the New Haven Arena to the Elm City Gym, and included Lip's and the Arena Grille and a Runyonesque bookie named Broadway Jonesy and bowling alleys and pool halls. If you were lucky you got tickets to the Eagles games and you saw some fights and wrestling matches and Bobby Riggs beat Jack Kramer by lobbing every other shot up into the lights. You learned a lot about odds and angles, and you learned to appreciate a harder kind of fun that stank of stale smoke and lime and cheap perfume and that echoed with crowd noises no less joyous for their brutality. If you were very lucky you got to rub shoulders with Nate Mann, one of Joe Louis's bum-of-the-month victims, and you got to talk boxing with Max Kogan, while watching his brother Julie, who could have been lightweight

11

Dedicatory Preface

champ if he'd been willing to play ball with Mike Jacobs. You learned about Battling Levinsky and Kid Sal Carabetta, and maybe, just once, you got to work out with Guglielmo Papaleo, who didn't need his stage name, Willy Pep, in New Haven.

In nostalgic gratitude for having breathed both of those worlds, for having had the encouragement and security of fine parents who gave me freedom in the one, and for inheriting the curiosity and spirit to dare the other, I dedicate this book, with love,

to my son Daniel,

who has grown in different worlds and with quite other tastes, but has found his spirited way to an independent development and continues to grow along with our admiration for him.

Acknowledgments

For a wide variety of assistance on this project, thanks are due to the following: The Library of Congress, where most of the work was done; the Inter-Library Loan Division of McKeldin Library at the University of Maryland; Esther Isaacs and Mory Isaacs, for help in research; Don Ruck, Milt Schmidt, Abe Pollin, Peter O'Malley, Pierce Gardner, and Chip Campbell, for generous cooperation; Ellen Levine and Eric Swenson, for establishing and keeping open the vital lines of communication; Charlie Rutherford, for trying in vain to get the author on skates; and Eddie Jeremiah, for unknowingly suggesting the title of this book with the litany he chanted constantly to the Dartmouth hockey team, "CHECK BACK CHECK BACK CHECK BACK."

Bibliographical Note

Of the fifteen shelves of books on hockey in the Library of Congress, several deserve special mention here.

Among reference books, *The Trail of the Stanley Cup,* Vol. I, by Charles L. Coleman, is indispensable to research on the period before 1918. More recent works which I found useful are John Devaney and Burt Goldblatt, *The Stanley Cup;* Zander Hollander and Hal Bock, *Complete Encyclopedia of Hockey;* Gary Ronberg, *Hockey Encyclopedia;* and Robert A. Styer, *Encyclopedia of Hockey.* The researcher is advised to cross-check frequently among these until he is confident of specific areas of reliability. The annually updated *National Hockey League Guide,* is, wherever applicable, the most reliable of all.

Among books by regulars on the hockey beat, I found the following to be helpful: Gerald Eskenazi, Foster Hewitt, Brian McFarlane, Andy O'Brien, Scott Young, and the prolific, omnipresent Stan Fischler.

From the rest I would select four as especially good reading: Frank Boucher (with Trent Frayne), *When the Rangers Were Young;* George ("Punch") Imlach (with Scott Young), *Hockey Is a Battle;* Frank J. Selke (with H. Gordon Green), *Behind the Cheering;* and George Sullivan, *Face-Off: A Guide to Modern Ice Hockey.*

PART *I*

In the Beginnings

As the National Hockey League approaches the sixtieth anniversary of its founding, it is well to remember that the history of hockey extends back further than sixty years before 1917. Since history, unlike epic, is not supposed to begin in the middle of things, this first brief section of four chapters will sketch a rough picture of the game up to that inaugural season.

One purpose of this section is to provide a broad context in which the initiation of the NHL seems almost incidental. That in turn will provide an appreciation of both the original floundering and the subsequent accomplishments of the league. Another purpose is to show how many of the lines of development that distinguish the NHL, particularly in its early years, have their beginnings before its founding, sometimes far afield. Finally, a sense of the nature of the game, rooted in its ancient history, will provide some background for understanding many of the continuing problems of the league.

This section, then, discusses vital changes, developments, and refinements of hockey that either had already taken place or had at least been initiated before the NHL was organized. It had alrady turned radically from an outdoor sport for amateur sportsmen to an enclosed world of professionalized spectacle. Its violent excesses had already aroused indignant protests from voices of civilized and legalized propriety. The appeal to spectators' tastes had become prevalent, with a resultant polarization between players and management.

Meanwhile, the techniques and rules of the game had evolved in a pattern of steady improvement. It had become by 1917 a faster, more exciting, more challenging, but more disciplined game than it had been at the turn of the century. Trends toward continued progress were clearly established. And it had done all that while protecting the integrity of the game as represented by its basic element—the scoring of a goal.

1

The Name and Nature of the Game

So obscure is the word *hockey* (also *hockie, hawky, hawkey*) that the OED simply confesses that its origin and etymological form are unknown. A more dramatic demonstration of that obscurity is a fanciful folk-etymology: French explorers sailing up the St. Lawrence in 1740 saw the Iroquois hitting a hard ball with sticks and heard them punctuating their game with shouts of "*Ho-gee*," (which they translated, "It hurts"). That legend—invented, according to Frank Boucher, by the Rangers' original PR man, Jack Filman—has wide currency. But there is more credibility in the theory that the game takes its name from the stick and that the stick was called "hockey" after the shepherd's crook or staff, which is *hoquet* in Old French.

An identical word (also *hawkey* and *horkey*), equally obscure, was the name for the feast at harvest time in the eastern counties of England, from about 1555. Though there is no apparent connection between the two, there is at least a common sense of joy and abandon. Indeed, the earliest known occurrence of the first word is testimony to that sense of the second: in 1527, "The horlinge of the litill balle with hockie stickes or staves" was included in a list of forbidden sports in the Galway Statutes. John Bunyan, the seventeenth-century author of *Pilgrim's Progress*, had his own progress as a Christian, according to Macaulay, impeded by the sin of playing hockey on Sunday.

Cognate and similar games—bandy, hurley, and lacrosse—also take their names from the sticks used to play them. The stick was the salient feature, apparently, but the related idea of a feast remained in close association, as when the traditional "bandy" between Bury Fen and Willingham was followed by a traditional English "randy" through the early nineteenth century.

The maneuvering of a ball—by hand, by foot, by implement—is probably one of the oldest of athletic ideas, and it remains by far the most widespread. In some forms it is a static, stately activity, in some an elaborate and rhythmic ritual, and in others an exercise in purposeful speed and controlled violence. Perhaps they all have their places, as Thoreau said in his *Journal* on April 24, 1859, sounding like Ecclesiastes:

Checking Back

> There is a season for every thing, and we do not notice a given phenomenon except at that season. . . . Boys fly kites and play ball or hawkie at particular times all over the state. A wise man will know what game to play today, and play it. We must not be governed by rigid rules, as by the almanac, but let the season rule us. The moods and thoughts of man are revolving just as steadily and incessantly as nature's. . . . You must live in the present, launch yourself on every wave, find your eternity in each moment.

There is no record that Thoreau ever played hockey, but he apparently thought more highly of it than the statutory fathers of Galway. More important, he describes the kind of spirit that fills and inspires the play of the game.

How the idea of hockey was first combined with the idea of skating on ice is unknown. The Irish have, on occasion, played an ice version of hurling since the eighteenth century. Englishmen played bandy on ice as early as 1813. Long before we began to keep records the Iroquois, whose *baggataway* became lacrosse, were playing their "hockey in the air" on winter ice. But since people have been skating for at least twenty-five centuries, it would be surprising if the stick-and-ball game had not somehow been combined with the speed-on-ice idea long before March 3, 1875, when the term *ice hockey* was first recorded, describing the game played by two teams of McGill students at the Victoria Skating Rink.

The combination was a natural, so that on one level this history tells how "ice hockey" has preempted the name "hockey" while "hockey" has come to be called "field hockey."

In trying to describe the nature of the game, it is well to begin with the final major distinguishing element—the skating—and move back to others. It is the skating that with its speed and grace provides both the aesthetic pleasure for audiences and the exhilaration for players. Bruce Kidd and John Macfarlane, in *The Death of Hockey,* call it one of the most sensual of sports and quote Eric Nestorenko: "Some nights you just go. You can't stop. The rhythm gets to you, or the speed. You're moving, man, moving, and that's all." That, in turn, suggests two quite different things: that the skating is a way of transcending self, beyond feeling the personal satisfaction of performing up to the fullest achievement of excellence—a basic tenet of sport—to a kind of oneness with action and movement that is at the heart of certain Eastern ways and arts (Zen, tai chang, aikido); and that the skating makes hockey the most self-centered and individual of team sports.

Bobby Hull has said that the body contact is a *personal* thing, so that the fights are more personal too. But he has also said that he sometimes hates the game "because of the way it *changes* a man." It may change *a* man, but it certainly does nothing to change Man. It is a game that celebrates the elemental pleasure of violent contact. King Clancy said, "If you don't mix it in hockey

. . . if you don't run into fellows and try to knock them down—you're missing a big part of the game. This was the bit I enjoyed most." Thus, for Punch Imlach, "the soul of a hockey game is a tough man who never backs up." But that would also be a soul with a poor plus-minus record.

The significance of individual play has never been lost on those who study hockey or on those who simply enjoy it. It produces what Chandler Sterling calls "sheer unpredictability of movement and action" in a sport where "classical plays and classicized behavior [are] incapable of being developed" and what Kidd and Macfarlane call the "magic" of "unlimited dramatic possibilities." It also produces a degree of audience involvement unparalleled in team sports (excepting only the programmed mayhem of roller derby) and very close to the fan identification of boxing and wrestling. The contact and the fights, physically close to spectators and spotlighted among isolated players, stimulate a blood lust. Stan Fischler cites a psychoanalytical view that the fights allow fans to act out fantasies, particularly where violence is part of everyday life in lower-class urban society.

If there is a class element, there may also be a nationalistic element. Scott Young speaks of hockey's appeal in the "combination of blood, sweat and beauty. Perhaps these qualities in juxtaposition have an extra meaning for a nation that still is engaged in pushing back its fierce and beautiful frontiers." Keith Magnuson has gone beyond class and nation to the notion of tribe:

> It is actually nothing but a gutsy, brutal, brawling world, the roughest and least forgiving sport. And it's easy to sense this blood lust on the ice bringing the roaring crowds to their feet, which in turn drives participants to even greater heights. . . . There's something tribal about it, primitive really. . . . Survival and supremacy are the keys, as a number of us seem to regress into our brute natures.

In the period prose of 1910, Arthur Farrell, a Hall of Fame player and one of our earliest hockey authors, called hockey "a game for men; essentially it is a game for the youth. It needs strong, full-blooded men. Weaklings cannot survive in it, the puny cannot play it, and the timid have no place in it. It is, perhaps, the greatest game that man can play unaided. It possesses all the spice of polo without the necessity for calling upon the animal kingdom." Two decades later, Conn Smythe's notorious dictum, "If you can't beat them outside in the alley, you can't beat them inside on the ice," seems on the contrary to call upon the animal kingdom in mankind.

Hockey is rooted, nurtured, and triumphant in violence. Its inevitability is compounded: not only is the stick a weapon, but the skates are sidearms; not only is bodychecking necessary, but the use of stick and shoulder and elbow and head and hand and even skate to facilitate checking is artfully developed.

Checking Back

Enclosing the playing surface adds a new dimension of boards and glass to the physical and psychological rigidity of the frozen surface. Further enclosure with the noise and increasingly rabid presence of fans does the rest.

Fischler lists the conditioned reflex of kicking or hitting back, the myth of might, and the image of machismo as built-in elements of the violence. But perhaps the most significant element is the ratio of violence to speed. In hockey, such a premium is put on skating speed, and such a preponderance of the sport's distinctiveness resides in its speed on skates, that there is almost a precise equation taken from physics or mechanics to multiply the incidence of violence by the increased speed in an enclosed arena, surrounded by hard surfaces. Beyond the playing area, the rink is often enclosed by another violence-producing element, a mob of frenzied spectators. The blood on the ice and the blood-lust in the stands feed upon each other.

Given such a climate, it is not surprising that hockey has produced an ethic that celebrates the Germanic and Stoic virtue of playing on despite injuries. The idea is to hide pain, not display it. Ken Dryden has observed that anyone who "puts on the big act" (playing to the crowds to dramatize wounds) is ostracized in NHL dressing rooms for violating the unwritten code, and he cites Serge Savard's skating off the ice on a broken leg and Bobby Baun's playing two periods of a Stanley Cup game with a broken ankle.

If all these factors stress the individual nature of hockey, it must not be forgotten that it is also a team sport and that at its best the team play triumphs. Farrell, writing almost a decade before the NHL's organization, said, "The secret of a team's success is combination play, in other words, unselfishness. It means the giving of the puck to a player of one's own side who is in a better position to use it than the man who first secures the rubber. It is the science of mutual help." With the changes in rules to allow forward passing, the importance of team play grew. All of the great hockey teams in its history have been distinguished by great combinations: lines, or even lines with defensemen. But even when that thesis is stressed, the distinctive and individual quality of goaltending forms an apposite antithesis.

Ironically, what is best in hockey—team play—has contributed to what is worst in it—deliberate violence. The brutality has become calculated as an instrument of winning. Putting out for the team means defending teammates, retaliating for teammates, and even exercising aggression as a deterrent to opponents. Contemporary coaches speak openly of physical intimidation as a strategy for winning hockey—a significant change but perhaps a logical progression from the willingness to mix it up that earlier characterized a hockey player's attitude toward violence. It is one thing to be the only sport that *tolerates* fighting as "part of the game," and quite another to *encourage* fighting as a tactical necessity for winning.

The original values of hockey resided in its nature as an activity for amateur sportsmen—a game that produced an inordinate degree of satisfaction for the participants. But it very soon became professionalized: it became a way of life for participants and a separate world on exhibition for spectators. In the resulting transvaluation, a special class of relatively uneducated, relatively unreflective, relatively animalistic mesomorphs was cultivated. And that special breed of hockey players catered to and was in turn glorified by a populace that reveled in the speed, the grace, the violence—in short, the instinctive nature—of the game. For a hockey fan, an aesthetic response begins and ends as a gut reaction.

In the wake of a contemporary trend toward athletics for athletes, a quest to restore hockey's original values has been undertaken. Bruce Kidd and John Macfarlane lament that the "hockey player, the most influential athlete in [Canada], could encourage more people to discover how good it feels to participate in sport. Instead, he reinforces the belief that sport has no intrinsic worth." And W. R. McMurtry, Q.C., in his *Investigation and Inquiry into Violence in Amateur Hockey,* recognizing the significance of sport in society, preaches remedial reform:

> Sport, and particularly hockey, need not be a symptom of a sick society. It can be an effective instrument to improve the social conditions. It can be a positive educational force—a model—to instil values such as cooperation, personal discipline, tolerance and understanding—a catalyst to promote fellowship and mutual respect among individuals and peoples—a celebration of speed, courage, and finesse. Rather than a decisive force, fueled by calculated animosities, it can and should be a bond between participants, with a shared commitment to excellence, and the common love of a game, hockey, which perhaps more than any other can give one a sense of physical exhilaration and sheer joy of participation.

But McMurtry's context is amateur hockey, and the simple truth is that amateur hockey throughout most of this century has been a reflection—however diluted—of professional hockey. Values would have to change in social, economic, educational, and philosophical terms before the ideal fulfillment of athletic potential envisioned by McMurtry could take place.

If ever. Perhaps what we are talking about is a change in human nature. If there is a special pleasure in the speed of skating, there is also pleasure in watching it. If there is a special sensual satisfaction in delivering a well-timed bodycheck, there is also satisfaction in seeing and hearing it. If there is special pride of achievement in a patterned sequence of passes, there is also appreciation by anyone who follows the moves. Most of all, if there is a special elation in scoring a goal in hockey, there is also a special elation in beholding it. Perhaps no other occasion in any sport gives quite so much simultaneous and shared joy to player and fan as a goal in hockey. No matter how achieved, no matter what the context, a hockey goal evokes an orgasmic response that at once sends us deeper than thought within our nature and lifts us out of ourselves.

2

Sources, Analogues, and Pioneers

It is impossible to pinpoint the age of hockey. The basic idea of the game—advancing a ball with a curved stick while an opponent tries the same in the opposite direction—is at least twenty-five centuries old. A bas-relief from the wall of Themistocles, unearthed in Athens and housed in the British Museum, shows two men facing off with sticks and ball. It has been dated at about 478 B.C., and since skating was known in the Greek mountains in the fifth century B.C. it is not unreasonable to suppose that ice hockey, in a primitive form, is that old. Yet fifteen centuries before *that*, if we can accept the deciphering of certain stone tablets in Persia, a kind of field hockey was played in Ur of the Chaldea around 2000 B.C.

Skating in Scandinavia, perhaps a by-product of skiing, also seems twenty-five centuries old, with skates fashioned from shank or rib bones of oxen, elk, and reindeer. But a development of ice hockey from field hockey seems a preferable theory to the notion that as long as there was ice skating there may have been ice hockey. I cannot hope, however, to trace a direct line of influence and transmission. The discovery of an ancient ball court at Chichen-Itza in the Yucatan and an ancient Aztec ball-and-stick game should teach us, if nothing else, that certain recreational concepts—like other cultural commonplaces—may well be universal and require no explanation of unique invention and subsequent adoption. The most I can do, then, is provide in rough chronological order the evidence of hockey's historical existence, without constructing a scenario of linear development.

The Romans, from the second century on, played a game using crooked sticks and a leather ball stuffed with feathers, a *pagnica*. The Latin name *cambucca* for both the game and the stick is of uncertain date, but was used in England in the reign of Edward III. The analogous Irish game of hurley is probably older than that, since there is a firm tradition that the losers of a match were sacrificed. Several fourteenth-century evidences of hockey are extant: a stained-glass window at Gloucester from about 1335, a pair of silver cruets engraved with crossed curved sticks and a ball, and a British Museum manuscript with a drawing of two bandy players. The game was evidently so popular during that time that Edward III, concerned over the diminishing supply of trained archers, fined landowners for allowing it to be played on their property. From this, a folk etymology "bandy ball" from "banned ball" has been created, but occurrences of *bandy* are too late to support it; the commonly accepted source is the French *bander* in the sense "to bandie at Tennis," which is supported in sixteenth-century usages.

The words *hurling, hurley, hockey, bandy, shinty,* and *shinny* were all used in the British Isles by 1600, but none of the occurrences refers to a game played on ice. In Holland, however, the canals had been used for skating since the Middle Ages, and there are paintings of bandy from Belgium, Luxembourg, and Holland in the sixteenth and seventeenth centuries. An engraving by Romein de Hooghe (1645–1708) depicts a *kolven* player; at least a generation earlier is "Winter Landscape" by Henrick Auercamp (1585–1634), now in the Rijksmuseum in Amsterdam, depicting a game of *hut kolven* that looks for all the world like ice hockey. By 1662 skating, if not *hut kolven,* had come to London, because Pepys records in his diary for December 1, "on canal in St. James Park, where first in my life did see people skiding in the skeetes, which is a very pretty art."

To the village of Bury Fen, in the marshlands of Cambridgeshire, belongs the oldest continuing tradition of ice hockey. As early as 1813 Bury Fen men were playing bandy on the ice. In 1827 they played a team from Willingham on the Old West River, and the bandy was followed by a randy. Shortly before his death in 1891, the old captain, William Leeland, told C. G. Tebbutt how the team,

> accompanied by the entire adult population of Bury Fen, skated up the main river one wintry day and defeated Swavesey and Over; how they skated along the Old West River and lowered the colors of Willingham and Cottenham; and how on the frozen wash between the Bedford rivers, they played for and won a keg of ale and legs of mutton at the expense of Sutton and Mepal; and how on their own Fen, besides winning return games with each of these teams, they also beat Chatteris, Somersham, and St. Ives.

The team never lost throughout the nineteenth century, winning two exhibition matches at the Crystal Palace in 1860 and all of their exhibitions on a tour of the Netherlands in 1890–1891.

By then, however, ice hockey was already so firmly rooted in Canada that almost all theories of origins argue variously for how and where the game started there. Indeed, French explorers in 1740 had found the Iroquois playing a stick and ball game in the St. Lawrence Valley. English garrisons had imported bandy and shinny by the 1830s. Arthur Farrell suggested that the latter name came from the frequent danger to which a player's shins were exposed in the game of wild swinging over a large field, but the accepted etymology is from *shinty* for "shin t'ye," "shin ye," "shin you," and "shin your side." The one basic rule, common to all those sports, is summarized in the phrase "shinny on your own side," which has been generally taken to refer to the requirement of identifying two teams in a more or less free-for-all scrambling game. But surely it really means that hockey, like many other team sports, has been from the beginning an on-sides game.

Fragmentary evidence of shinny on the ice comes from the 1830s and from 1846, but the earliest clear reference is to 1855, on the basis of which Kingston was awarded the site of the Hall of Fame of the Canadian Amateur Hockey Association over the claims of Halifax and Montreal. The Royal Canadian Rifles at Tete-du-Pont Barracks cleared snow from the ice in Kingston Harbor in 1867 and played an organized game with skates, sticks, pucks, and goal posts. The English garrisons at Halifax were playing a somewhat organized form of shinny in 1870, and transferred soldiers carried the game to Quebec and Ottawa. By then the enclosed Victoria Skating Rink in Montreal had been in operation for several years. It was there that lacrosse was played on the ice in 1874 and that on March 3, 1875, two nine-man teams of McGill students played what was called "ice hockey" for the first time.

When the game was described by the McGill University *Gazette* in 1877, the word *checking*, borrowed from lacrosse, was used for the first time. And when W. F. Robertson and R. F. Smith codified the first set of rules at McGill in 1879, there were other borrowings. Robertson used terminology from field hockey which he had observed on a trip to England, and they transferred many of its rules to ice, incorporating rudiments of lacrosse and polo, while the "on-sides" aspect allegedly was borrowed from rugby. The following winter there was class competition at McGill; hockey was on its way toward institutionalization.

By 1881 McGill had one formal hockey club and the Victoria Rink had another. By 1885 there was an organized league at Kingston. A further step toward institutionalization was taken in 1886, when the Amateur Hockey Association of Canada was formed. There were five member clubs: the Quebecs, the Ottawas, and three from Montreal: the Victorias, the Crystals, and the Montreals. About three years later, the Victoria Hockey Club of Winnipeg was organized, but the game had moved south before it went west.

The McGill rules of Robertson and Smith were in force, calling for no body-checks, a face-off when the puck went behind the goal, a two-hour limit, nine players, and a referee. But a significant change took place at the winter carnival in Montreal in 1886, just two years after the inaugural carnival had elicited a formal statement of rules: only seven men were available for one team. The seven-man game proved to be such an improvement that it became the standard for the next quarter-century. The names of the seven positions (goalkeeper, point, cover point, rover, right wing, centre, left wing) were borrowed from English soccer.

With no forward passing allowed, the prohibition against bodychecking was gradually relaxed, since it was the best defensive weapon. Another rule that came in time to be honored in the breach was a prohibition against hitting—as opposed to pushing—the puck forward. Exactly when the typical bandy or shinny ball was changed to a flat disk, and how it came to be called a *puck*, are not known. Various apocryphal stories of accident and design are unconvincing, but both the implement and the name were established by the early 1880s. The stick was lengthened for two hands (a great improvement over the shepherd's crook or the lower branches of pollard willow trees used at Bury Fen) and the blade flattened, as an early premium was placed on stick-handling. The value of constant action was recognized by enclosing the area with 40-inch sideboards. And the surface itself was much reduced, with minimum dimensions of 58 by 112 feet.

As in Buddy Hackett's Chinese menu, no substitutions were allowed, except for injury, but the time of the games was reduced to an hour, with a ten-minute intermission between thirty-minute halves. The size of the goal was reduced to six feet by four (nets were attached in 1900 at the suggestion of Francis Nelson), but the goalie was required to stay on his feet. The idea in hockey, from the start, has been to make scoring difficult and make it significant. The crucial nature of a goal was recognized by appointments of goal umpires, whose decisions at first could not be overruled.

This was the game that T. L. Paton, a goalkeeper from Montreal and first Stanley Cup–winning goalie in 1893, described to J. Massey in Toronto in 1887. Massey promptly wired to Montreal for eighteen sticks, a puck, and copies of the rules. Before the turn of the century, several monumental developments had already taken place: expansion to the United States, provisions for large audiences, professionalism, and the donation of a cup by Lord Stanley. The implications of those developments are still actively being realized.

Malcolm G. Chace and Arthur E. Foote, two tennis players from Yale, brought the game of hockey from Montreal to New Haven in 1893, at about the same time that the Elis were also pioneering collegiate basketball. During this same season, C. Shearer, a Johns Hopkins student from Montreal, formed a team in Baltimore and then imported a team from Quebec to play it. The results of the match are not recorded, but the significance of hockey's appeal as a spectator sport in the United States cannot be overemphasized. Throughout its subsequent history, the actual play of the great Canadian game of ice hockey has responded to its entertainment appeal south of the Dominion's borders.

Entertainment appeal was inherent in the Canadian game. Already in the early 1890s, professional teams were barnstorming on a profit-sharing basis in the central provinces, and before the decade was over Montreal had an arena at Wood Avenue and St. Catherine's Street with seats for 4,300 and room for perhaps another 4,000 fans. It was still ostensibly an amateur sport, however, and it was in that sporting spirit that Frederick Arthur, Baron Stanley of Preston, G.C.B., younger son of the fourteenth Earl of Derby, sixth Governor-General of Canada, donated the trophy that still bears his name. It was his great-grandfather, the twelfth Earl, who founded the Derby stakes in 1780. Probably no other family has ever had its name associated so prominently with major events in two sports. The connection between hockey and racing, thus coincidentally begun, came to have larger significance in later years.

At his brother's death in 1893, Lord Stanley retired from Canada to succeed as sixteenth Earl of Derby. At his death in 1908, his estate was estimated at close to four million pounds sterling, but he is best known for the ten pounds he spent for the Stanley Cup. It was to be "a challenge cup to be held from year to year by the champion hockey club of the Dominion." He appointed Sheriff John Sweetland and Philip D. Ross of Ottawa to act as trustees and suggest conditions of competition, but he designated the Montreal Club, champions of the Amateur Hockey Association of Canada, to be awarded the Cup for 1893. The Cup was not to be retired but to remain open for challenge, under conditions to be determined by the trustees.

The first playoff series occurred in 1894 because of a four-way tie in the Amateur Hockey Association. Quebec withdrew in a wrangle over home ice, and Montreal beat the Victorias and then Ottawa to retain the Cup. Before the following season was over, however, the Cup ceased to be the exclusive preserve of the AHA. The trustees accepted the challenge of the Queens University team to play Montreal. When the Victorias won the league championship, Montreal was put in the position of defending the Cup on behalf of their AHA rivals, but despite the diminished incentive they won an easy 5–1 victory.

During the course of the 1896 season, the Victorias accepted a Cup challenge from the Winnipeg Victorias, losing the trophy to the West in a 2–0 defeat at Montreal. The Winnipeg goalie, G. H. Merritt, wore white cricket pads, setting a style that caught on immediately and that has been carried on with modifications leading to the present mattress pads. But after winning the AHA championship again, the Victoria club recaptured the Cup before the following season, beating Winnipeg 6–5 in an exciting come-from-behind win before a sellout crowd in the Winnipeg rink in December. They retained the

Checking Back

AHA championship in 1897 and accepted a Cup challenge from the Ottawa Capitals, champions of the Central Canada Association. For the first time a series—best two of three games—was to decide the winner prior to the next season in December. But the Victorias won the first game so easily, 14–2, and the match attracted so little attention, that the rest of the series was abandoned. The Victorias then went through their season undefeated in eight games and retained the Stanley Cup without a challenge. On this dominant team, three of the four forwards—Cam Davidson, Bob McDougall, and Graham Drinkwater—were among the top six goal scorers in the league; the point Hartland McDougall and the cover point Mike Grant also got into the scoring; and the goaltending was divided between Gordon Lewis and Frank Richardson.

The last season before the turn of the century saw some patterns and precedents established that were to blight the sport for years to come. For the second time, the petition of the Ottawa Capitals for membership in the AHA was considered. This time it was accepted. Quebec, the Victorias, and Ottawa then withdrew from the league. When the council declined to reconsider, Montreal withdrew as well. The delegates of these four clubs then met at the Windsor Hotel and formed the Canadian Amateur Hockey League. McGill applied for a franchise but withdrew in favor of the Shamrocks, the new name taken by the old Crystals in 1896. The new league had the same clubs, nearly the same rules of play, but a new council.

It also had a champion, the Shamrocks, who lost only the opening game to Ottawa. The Victorias defended the Cup successfully during the season by beating Winnipeg, 2–1 and 3–2. The first game was won on a last-minute rink-long dash by Drinkwater; the second ended prematurely. The provocative elbow of the Winnipeg rover Tony Gringas brought a slashing response from Bob McDougall's stick. Gringas's injury brought McDougall a two-minute penalty, but Winnipeg thought that too slight and left the ice. J. Findlay, the referee, followed them off, returned to say he had been insulted, and left for home while eight thousand fans continued their clamor. Coaxed back by officials over an hour later, Findlay forfeited the game to the Victorias when Winnipeg still refused to play.

The Victorias lost the championship (and Cup) on March 1, when the Shamrocks beat them, 1–0, in a game marked by open wagering of thousands of dollars among the eight thousand people crowded into the arena. Two weeks later the Shamrocks easily put down a Cup challenge from Queens University, 6–2, led by Harry Trihey and Arthur Farrell, and the century ended with the Irish in firm control of the Earl of Derby's legacy. Other legacies to hockey may be embodied in the figure of Fred Chittick, the Ottawa goalkeeper. In 1898, Chittick sat out a game against the Victorias because he hadn't received his share of complimentary tickets to the game. The following season, Chittick was refereeing a Montreal-Quebec game when Montreal refused to play the last twelve minutes. They claimed that he was too drunk to handle the game, but when charges and countercharges were aired in the press in the following weeks (and when Chittick had been replaced in the Ottawa goal), the first public attention was drawn to allegations that amateur players were getting paid to play.

That was hockey as the nineteenth century ended: a game of color, excitement, striking action on the ice and in the stands, clever maneuvering in the club and league offices, and a tradition of open challenges for the cherished emblem of supremacy. It was a game for seven men on a side, playing without substitution for two half-hour periods on a rink at least 112 by 58 feet. The puck was a solid inch of vulcanized rubber, 3 inches in diameter; the sticks could not be more than 3 inches at the widest part; the goal posts were 6 feet apart and 4 feet high. Goaltenders had to stay on their feet, skaters had to stay behind the puck at all times, and no offensive player could be closer to the goal than the puck. The referees' decisions were final except for umpires' decisions about goals. Of these rules, all have been changed in the twentieth century except for the size of the goal, the stick, and the puck.

3

Coming of Age in the Twentieth Century

The United States took the lead in acknowledging hockey as a professional sport, but the teams organized there were staffed with Canadian players. If men were to be paid for playing hockey, the payers wanted the best players for their money. Writing in 1898, J. A. Tuthill observed, in his *Ice Hockey and Polo Guide,* that "three winters ago Chicago, Minneapolis and Detroit were about the only scenes of the game's activity, but last winter wherever ice could be found, out of doors or inside, East and West, ice hockey was being played." He added that Baltimore was "the most enthusiastic ice hockey city in the country." Yet the first pro teams were formed away from these metropolitan centers of hockey interest.

The first was the creation of Dr. J. L. Gibson, a dentist in Houghton, Michigan, who imported Canadian players to form his Portage Lakes team in 1903. Soon nearby Calumet had a pro team, and then there were teams in Sault Ste. Marie on both the Michigan and the Ontario side, the Canadian Soo team being the first acknowledged professional team in the Dominion. One of Pittsburgh's four teams was also admittedly professional. In February 1904, in two games between Pittsburgh and the Soo, because of an injury to Charlie McClung, both teams played with only six men on the ice. Not only was the six-man game faster and more spectacular, it was also less expensive—by one salary—and soon became the crowd-pleasing and owner-pleasing rule for pro hockey.

The first professional league was the International Professional Hockey League, organized for the 1904–1950 season, with the American teams listed above. Of the Canadian players in the league, Pittsburgh had two of the best-known: Charlie Liffiton from the CAHL champion Montreals, the Little Men of Iron who had regained the Stanley Cup from Winnipeg; and defenseman Hod Stuart from Quebec, who eventually returned to the Canadian league with the Wanderers in 1907, accepting a cut in salary but better working conditions. Stuart was probably the first attacking defenseman in the game. Lester Patrick, who is often given that credit, particularly for a famous performance with the Brandon team against Ottawa in 1904, himself names Stuart. Another claimant is Ottawa's Harvey Pulford, but perhaps Rod Flett, who scored for the Winnipeg Victorias in Cup play against the Wanderers, should also be considered. In any case, the two-way defenseman was one of the major strategic bequests of this decade.

The Toronto Argonauts innovated another lasting development in defensive play in 1906. By the simple change of lining up alongside each other instead of one behind the other, the point and coverpoint became the left and right defensemen. Just as basic and equally significant was the venturesome innovation of Frank Stocking, the Quebec goalkeeper. He preached the advisability of going out from the goal to meet a solo breakaway. Though he had little success himself in practicing what he preached, his successor in the Bulldogs' nets, Paddy Moran, was one of the decade's best. In 1905, however, Moran was the victim of a unique event when his opponent, Fred Brophy, left the Westmount goal, rushed the length of the ice with the puck, and scored. Brophy scored five other goals that season, in four games as a forward, but his penchant for skating didn't help his goaltending record of fortynine goals against in his six games in (and out of) the nets. Brophy repeated his feat against the Victorias a year later, but his goals-against average wasn't much improved.

In self-defense and aggravation, Fred C. Waghorne invented the modern face-off about the turn of the century. Instead of placing the puck between opposing sticks as in lacrosse, he simply dropped it. Having used this method with some success in Brantford and neighboring hockey towns in southwestern Ontario, Waghorn introduced it to the NHA where it was officially adopted in 1903. He also introduced the use of bells instead of whistles that often froze to referees' tongues or lips. The whistle didn't come back until heated rinks came in. Also in 1903, the rules changed to allow referees to overrule goal umpires, a measure necessary to centralize the controlling authority in a game. Authority was continually challenged in many ways through this decade.

The major issue of the period was amateurism versus professionalism. From 1895, when the Shamrocks assimilated and replaced the Crystals, despite the reorganization of the league in 1899, the member clubs remained constant for almost a decade. In 1904, however, Ottawa withdrew during the season in a dispute over games starting late. That was the first season for a new league, the Federal Amateur Hockey League, formed primarily for James Strachan's Wanderers, who had raided Montreal for its stars. The FAHL's three other teams were the Capitals, Cornwall, and the Nationals, who featured rookies Didier Pitre and Jack Laviolette, but the Wanderers lost no games. Ottawa joined the FAHL for the following season, but the Capitals could not compete in the same city, and they withdrew. Brockville and Montagnards were awarded franchises, making a five-team league, because the Nationals had been admitted to the CAHL along with Westmount. Ironically, the Wanderers' CAHL application was rejected with the pronouncement that the league intended to remain purely amateur.

A year later the CAHL disbanded and reorganized as the Eastern Canada Amateur Hockey Association. Ottawa and the Wanderers came over from the FAHL. The Victorias, Quebec, Montreal, and the Shamrocks were retained. Westmount was out, however, and so were the hapless Nationals, who had won no games, defaulting most, even with Joe Cattarinich in goal. Smith Falls and the Ottawa Vics replaced the departed leaders in the FAHL; but the league had been permanently weakened, even though undefeated Smith Falls, with Percy LeSueur in goal and Art Ross at forward, played well in a Cup challenge against Ottawa.

The hypocrisy was confronted but perpetuated in 1907 when the ECAHA ruled that teams must list the players who were paid and those who were simon-pures. In 1909, the league's last year before yet another reorganization, the word *Amateur* was dropped from the title when Montreal and the Victorias resigned, leaving four all-pro teams. Meanwhile, the first admittedly all-professional league in Canada had been formed in 1907, the Ontario Professional League with Toronto, Berlin (Kitchener), Brantford, and Guelph. The OPL had its first season in 1908. Professional in many ways, that league considered travel expenses when awarding franchises to neighboring communities and was called the Trolley League. The leading scorer of the leading team was the Maple Leafs' Newsy Lalonde, who also scored two goals against the Wanderers in a strong Cup challenge.

Problems with the innate violence of the game, destined to haunt it throughout its history, came to a head during this period. Friction on the Ottawa team in 1906 over the captaincy resulted in Harvey Pulford's two black eyes before the start of a Cup match against Queens University. In 1907 Fred Chittick was assaulted by fans after refereeing a Cup match. In 1908 Joe Hall was expelled from the Manitoba League for rough play and was promptly signed to play a couple of games for Montreal.

During a Wanderers-Ottawa game in 1907, matters got out of hand. Baldy Spittal used his stick like an ax on Cecil Blachford's skull, Alf Smith used his like a bat in catching Hod Stuart across the temple, and Harry Smith used his like a war club in breaking Ernie Johnson's nose. Those descriptions all have the hometown team as victims, but since the Wanderers won the game, 4–2, there remains some suspicion that Ottawa got as good as it gave in what the Montreal *Star* called "the worst exhibition of butchery" among "hockey brutalities." Montreal justice prevailed, however, as Spittal and Alf Smith were tried, fined twenty dollars and costs, and put on probation for a year.

Serious injury was less common than one might expect, perhaps because of the short schedules, but it was also inevitable. The FAHL had been troubled with squabbles throughout the 1907 season. Morrisburg, admitted after the defection of Ottawa and the Wanderers, couldn't win a game. The Montagnards led the league, but under protest because they used H. Baxter and J. Brennan of the ECAHA Shamrocks. Ordered to replay a Cornwall game, the Montagnards chose instead to resign from the league. The Ottawa Vics meanwhile protested a loss to Cornwall on the same grounds: J. Degray and Owen McCourt had also played for the Shamrocks.

McCourt, however, was the league's leading scorer, with sixteen in eight games, including seven in one game against Morrisburg, and he was on the ice for the rematch on March 6. Early in the second half, McCourt tangled with Art Throop, sparking a brawl, and left the ice with a bloody head wound, apparently from the stick of Charles Masson. He lost consciousness and died the next morning. A coroner's inquest not only ordered Masson held for trial but also recommended severe legislation against violence by hockey players and spectators. Masson was charged with murder, but the presiding magistrate reduced the charge to manslaughter. When some witnesses testified that other sticks than Masson's had earlier reached McCourt's head, Judge Magee acquitted the defendant.

These incidents draw attention both to the rough nature of the play and to the problems of players jumping teams and teams jumping leagues. The issue of money was complicated by issues of honor and power and machismo. There was also the Cup, a symbol that produced more than its share of squabbles in this period. In 1900 the Shamrocks defended the Cup against Winnipeg, as Harry Trihey scored seven of their eleven goals in the three close games. Tony Gingras led the losers, who won the opener, 4–3, only to lose, 3–2 and 5–4. The Shamrocks also defended successfully against the outclassed Halifax Crescents that year. A year later Winnipeg finally won it in two games, although the defending Shamrocks finished third to Ottawa and the Victorias in the CAHL.

Winnipeg defended successfully against the Toronto Wellingtons in 1902, but then lost two of three to CAHL champion Montreal. The 1903 rematch saw Winnipeg skaters all equipped with tube skates, but the new equipment didn't save them from being trounced, 8–1, in the first game, with Jimmy Gardner dominating play and Art Hooper scoring four times. The second game went to twenty-seven minutes of overtime tied 2–2, when the mayor of Westmount refused to allow the game to continue into Sunday. The trustees ruled that the game would continue Monday, but club officials overruled the idea because they feared poor attendance for an event that could end very briefly with a Montreal goal. Winnipeg won the replay, 4–2, only to lose the Cup, 4–1, in the third game, despite the absence of Gardner, whose collarbone had been broken in the tie. In effect Montreal won the 1903 Cup for Ottawa, winners in a two-game playoff series (total goals to count) over the Victorias for the CAHL title. Russell Bowie and Bert Strachan managed to earn a 1–1 tie in the first game, but Ottawa—with Frank McGee, Pulford, and the three Gilmour brothers, Siddy, Dave, and Billy—whipped them, 8–0, in the second. Ottawa then easily defended against the challenging Thistles of Rat Portage (Kenora).

Though Ottawa had resigned from the CAHL, the trustees awarded them the right to defend the Cup in 1904. They successfully took on Winnipeg and then the OHA champion Toronto Marlboros. Against the FAHL champion Wanderers a game ended 5–5, but the challengers refused overtime with Dr. Kearns as referee and then insisted on a rematch in Montreal. Trustee Ross ruled that Ottawa could choose the site. The defenders then took on Brandon, the Manitoba and Northwestern League champion, featuring the attacking-point play of Lester Patrick, and they retained the Cup, 6–3 and 9–3.

A year later Lester and his brother Frank were both playing for the CAHL Westmount team along with rookie Art Ross, another rushing defenseman. Perhaps the presence of Patrick and Ross was what inspired goalie Fred Brophy to dash down the ice with the puck, but in any case Westmount finished tied for fourth. Victoria led the league but could not agree to terms for the challenge, and so the CAHL was again shut out of Cup play. Ottawa, FAHL champions, defeated Dawson City, 9–2 and 23–2, and then Rat Portage, 4–2 and 5–4, after losing the first game, 9–3, retaining the Cup for the third straight year.

The Yukon team had traveled four thousand miles to play for the Cup, taking more than three weeks via dog sled, boat, and train to reach Ottawa for their challenge. They had little chance or skill to defeat the Silver Seven, but they seemed to get their money's worth of enjoyment both on and off the ice. Actually, it was Colonel Joe Boyle's money, about three thousand dollars from that successful Klondike prospector. An asterisk in the record books should give Boyle and the Dawson City safari due credit for Frank McGee's fourteen goals in the second game, eight in a row in 8 minutes 20 seconds, three in 90 seconds, four in 140 seconds.

The Thistles, on the other hand, were worthy opponents, led by Tommy Phillips, who has been called the most accurate shooter of all time. He used to practice shooting from twelve to eighteen feet into a tin can placed eight or ten inches above ice level. He scored five times against Dave Finnie as Rat Portage made Ottawa look bad on slick ice. But in the second game, with McGee back from an injury and the ice wet and soft and slow, perhaps flooded and salted by Ottawa partisans, and with Phillips shut out by the rough and ragged play of Alf Smith, Pulford, McGee, and company, Ottawa prevailed, 4–2. The deciding game was won 5–4, McGee's third goal winning after Phillips's third had tied it.

The Silver Seven was the great team of the era, but they featured more than seven players during that three-year dynasty. Bouse Hutton shared goaltending with Finnie; Jim McGee and Charles Spittal spelled Pulford and Art Moore on defense; and at forward were Frank McGee, Harry Westwick, Percy Sims, Alf Smith, Hamby Shore, Frank White, Horace Gaul, and Siddy, Dave, and Billy Gilmour. But in the second half of the decade, Ottawa was challenged and dethroned by the Wanderers.

Before the 1906 season ended, Ottawa successfully defended the Cup against challenges from Queens University and Smith Falls, champions respectively of the OHA and the Federal League. Alf and Harry Smith scored fifteen goals in two games against the former, while Frank McGee had fifteen in the four games himself. McGee was virtually alone in being able to beat the Smith Falls goalie, Percy LeSueur, who less than two weeks later was in the Ottawa nets. When the ECAHA season ended, however, Ottawa and the Wanderers had tied. The playoffs—two games, total goals to count—became a Stanley Cup match. Led by Ernie Russell, Ernie Johnson, Pud Glass, and Lester Patrick, the Wanderers whipped Ottawa, 9–1, at home. Back in Ottawa, with LeSueur replacing Billy Hague, the result was very nearly reversed. Harry Smith's fifth goal made the score 9–1, equaling the match with ten minutes to play, but Lester Patrick scored twice to clinch the Cup for the Wanderers. The Governor-General personally congratulated Harry Smith for his valiant effort and had his own hat hit by Ernie Johnson's stick in a scuffle along the boards.

The new dynasty lasted through 1908, except for a brief tenure by the up-start Thistles. The Wanderers defended successfully against New Glasgow at the end of 1906 (Patrick and Glass scoring eleven of their seventeen goals, while Riley Hern was outstanding in goal), before being upset a month later. It was Tom Phillips's shooting and Art Ross's aggressive play at point that won for Kenora, but the Wanderers won the rematch in March after going through their league schedule undefeated. Bickering continued over the constant shifting and borrowing of players, and the edicts of acting Cup trustee William Foran were persistently ignored.

In 1908, though Stuart had died in a swimming accident and Patrick had gone west, the Wanderers signed Art Ross away from Brandon and repeated as champions in a better-balanced league. The Victorias were led by perennial scoring champion Russell Bowie; the Shamrocks were improved with the return of Pitre and Laviolette from the International Professional League; Quebec had Charles, Joe, and Rocket Power; and Ottawa introduced Cyclone Taylor on defense. Cup challenges from the Ottawa Vics and Winnipeg were easily put down, and then the Wanderers faced the Toronto Maple Leafs in a single game. Newsy Lalonde and Bruce Ridpath kept it close, but the champions prevailed. Before the calendar year ended there was one more challenge, from Edmonton, the Alberta champions who had earlier beaten the Manitoba champions to reign in the West. The ringers on the challenging squad included Les Patrick, Didier Pitre, Tom Phillips, and Bert Lindsay in goal, but still the Wanderers won, 7–3 and 6–7. When they lost the Cup in 1909 it was because they lost the ECHA championship, by one game, back to Ottawa.

Of all the action during that period, perhaps the development with the greatest long-range impact was a little-noted rule change for the ECAHA in 1907: "After a puck strikes a goalkeeper, the rebound can be played by a member of his team without being declared offside." As innocuous as it sounds, it was in fact revolutionary. It was the first modification of the doctrinaire on-sides structure of the game, and it led ultimately to further recognition of the positive virtues of the forward pass.

4

False Starts, True Guidelines

The period from 1910 to 1917 in hockey seems to support the psychohistorical view that in times of unrest the greatest developments are likely to take place. Those years saw in hockey great turmoil, great expansion, and great change, not to mention great pettiness on a variety of matters.

The Wanderers' franchise had been bought by P. J. Doran, who owned the Jubilee Rink in Montreal. The other ECHA owners preferred games to be played at the Westmount Arena on Wood Avenue, with its larger seating capacity, so they simply voted the old league out of existence on November 25, 1909, and formed a new Canadian Hockey Association, with franchises awarded to Ottawa, Shamrocks, Quebec, Nationals, and All-Montreal (a newly organized club for the Wood Avenue arena). The cost of a franchise was a thirty-dollar initiation fee plus an annual twenty-five-dollar subscription. Forcing the Wanderers out was a short-sighted maneuver, but what proved to be less wise was turning down the application of J. Ambrose O'Brien for a franchise in silver-rich Renfrew.

Less than two weeks later, while the CHA was meeting in Room 135 of the Windsor Hotel, down the hall in Room 129 the National Hockey Association of Canada was formed, the result of J. Gardner's proposal to O'Brien. Gardner, the Wanderers' general manager, suggested a league consisting of his team and the existing clubs in Cobalt, Haileybury, and Renfrew, plus an all-French team in Montreal. O'Brien, who had been laughed at by the CHA, determined to make the NHA work, and his family interests gave financial support to the three mining-community clubs and to Les Canadiens as well.

When the smoke cleared from the bidding for players, it was plain that the NHA had won the war, another victory for descendants of the high kings of County Clare. Indeed, the Renfrew team itself, representing a community of 7,360 souls, was called the Millionaires and had Bert Lindsay in goal, with Cyclone Taylor and the Patricks all skating at an unprecedented three thousand dollars each. With five teams in two leagues in Montreal alone at the start of the season, the market was more flooded than the ice ever was; the dissolution of the CHA was inevitable. Within three weeks, Ottawa and the Shamrocks were absorbed by the NHA. All-Montreal and Quebec disbanded. The Nationals were offered Les Canadiens' franchise but bitterly refused: after standing by Ottawa in the struggle with the Wanderers, they now spitefully withstood going with the winds of change. Besides, they had lost all four games they played.

The better players from the lost teams found fitter employment in the surviving league, and the play throughout the season was more spirited than ever. Les Canadiens operated with O'Brien money but with Jack Laviolette as manager, besides playing point. Didier Pitre came over from the Nationals, and other Frenchmen were forwards Ed Decarie, Art Bernier, and Skinner Poulin. Lalonde, at rover, was their star, but he finished the season with Renfrew as the Millionaires tried to buy their way to a title. The Canadiens, on the other hand, finished last, Joe Cattarinich in goal averaging almost eight against. Their fortunes improved beginning in their second season when they signed Georges Vezina.

Renfrew, despite M. J. O'Brien's largesse, could do no better than third place. The Wanderers beat them twice and they split with Ottawa, but for their money the Millionaires provided a wealth of excitement. In a game with the Shamrocks, for example, Frank Patrick fought with Joe Hall, cutting him over both eyes. Hall, perhaps blinded with blood as he later claimed, hit the judge-of-play Red Kennedy; it cost him one hundred dollars and a two-game suspension. Cyclone Taylor had boasted in Percy LeSueur's presence that he could score skating backward through the Ottawa defense (Fred Lake and Hamby Shore). Taunted by the Ottawa fans, Taylor played an outstanding game, but never got a clear shot on goal. Ottawa won, 8–5, in a ten-minute overtime. In the return match, however, with the league standings all settled and the Ottawa players reportedly celebrating before the game, Renfrew bombarded LeSueur with seventeen goals, including one by Taylor late in the game when he took a pass from Lester Patrick, turned his back while skating at full speed, and flipped the puck into a corner of the net. Lalonde had six goals in that game, and another nine against Cobalt three days later; he won the scoring title with thirty-eight in eleven games. Ernie Russell of the champion Wanderers had thirty-one in twelve games.

The Wanderers regained the Stanley Cup from Ottawa, as Ottawa had taken it from them, by beating them in the league race. Ottawa had successfully put down challenges from Galt and Edmonton during the season, and then the Wanderers defeated Berlin in March. Now for the first time they also won the O'Brien Cup, donated to honor the NHA champion.

Before the start of the 1911 season the NHA was reduced to five teams, as owners and cities continued the game of musical franchises. But the contraction could not be taken as a sign of diminished interest in pro hockey. Quite the contrary, it was a period of continued expansion. Arthur Farrell reported in 1910 that "Canada no longer has a monopoly of the sport. The United States have the fever, and ice hockey is now a recognized winter sport where a few years ago it was unknown. Rinks are springing up everywhere, and even their greatest capacity cannot accommodate the enthusiastic attendances." Meanwhile in Canada the pro leagues proliferated. The Maritimes had a circuit including New Glasgow, North Sydney, Moncton, and Halifax. In Saskatchewan a league included Moose Jaw, Prince Albert, and Saskatoon. The Ontario Professional League had two divisions, the Eastern including Port Hope, Belleville, Trenton, and Picton, the Western encompassing the old Trolley League with Berlin, Galt, Waterloo, and Brantford. After the NHA reorganized, the Timiskaming League had Cobalt, Haileybury, and New Liskeard. Perhaps most important of all, the Patricks organized their own league on the Pacific Coast, with Vancouver, Victoria, and New Westminster. Still later there was a Western Canada League with Edmonton, Calgary, Regina, and Saskatoon.

The contributions of the Patricks and their Pacific league, both to the period and to the long-range development of hockey, were many and significant. Organized with three teams for the 1912 season, they drew most of their players from the East, including Ernie Johnson, Walter Smaill, Skinner Poulin, Tom Phillips, Don Smith, Harry Hyland, and best of all, Newsy Lalonde. This raiding improved the contracts of hockey players everywhere, but these blessings were mixed with the many disputes precipitated by the jumping. In toto, the three Patrick franchises operated with a total of twenty-three players, and the personnel pool was strained by the determinations to use players as officials and to retain the rover position.

The Patricks' support of seven-man hockey was uncharacteristically reactionary, motivated in part by competition with the NHA. They accused their old employers of advocating six-man hockey just to save money. The NHA was itself indecisive about the rule. It played six in 1912 but in 1913 proposed to play the second half of the season with seven. After only eight games in February the rover was dropped for good. The Patricks eventually came around in 1916 and even the conservative OHA in 1918.

In every other way the Patricks worked for constructive change, opening up the game to improvement, to speed, to new ideas, and their innovations were ultimately accepted everywhere. From their baseball experience they borrowed the notion of numbers on uniforms and programs. In 1914 they adopted blue lines dividing the ice into three zones with forward passing allowed within each zone. They beat the NHA to the development of individual scoring records based on assists as well as goals. They pioneered the deferred penalty system and the kicking of the puck under certain conditions. They had the first league all-star team in 1914, chosen by chief referee Mickey Ion. They accepted the eastern innovation of three twenty-minute periods, which tended to produce faster play throughout a game. They introduced a left-handed shooter on the right wing. And they changed the rules for goaltenders.

Though goalies had been required to stay on their feet, they would often "accidentally" fall to the ice in stopping a shot. Clint Benedict, the first accomplished flopper, actually had a better average than Vezina. In 1914 there was a two dollar fine for the first offense of deliberately lying down, a major offense for subsequent punishments. The Patricks had already done away with that hypocrisy, and in time the flopping goalie became universally accepted. But the PCHA also protected goalies within a designated area.

In economic terms, the Patricks' vision was most perceptive. In organizing their little league they foresaw the virtues of investing in rinks with artificial ice—the first in Canada—and the implications of this development are obvious, particularly in terms of their expansion southward to include Portland and Seattle. Financial success, in part the result of facilities that could rely on good conditions for play and watching it, in turn brought a loosening of substitution rules: substitution on the fly (perhaps introduced first in the East), and then substitution of entire forward lines as units. More than any other single idea, that latter one in time resulted in the greatest achievements of artistry in hockey as a team sport.

In political terms, too, the Patricks changed hockey by challenging and modifying its power structure. Their challenge to the winners of the NHA for the Stanley Cup was more than a matter of a sporting proposition. It took the form, in time, of a formalized structure of postseason playoffs, in which the Western champion and the Eastern champion would face off for the Cup. They had maneuvered themselves into a position of such strength that that proposal became for a while the de facto rule, though its assumptions simply ignored the trustees and their charge.

In 1914 the Victorias came east to play a series with Toronto, without bothering with a formal challenge for the Cup, but lost three straight games. In 1915 the New Westminster franchise moved to the United States and became the Portland Rosebuds, but they finished second to Vancouver (without any help from Citizen Kane). Vancouver, however, thoroughly dominated Ottawa in a formal proceeding, and the Patricks (Frank's team, Lester's league) had brought the Cup to the Coast. The Canadiens regained it from the Rosebuds in a best-three-of-five series in 1916, but a year later, after Ottawa lost a playoff to the Canadiens, the Canadiens then lost the Cup not just to a team from the PCHA, but to a team in the United States, the second-year Seattle Metropolitans.

Meanwhile, the eastern hockey establishment, the NHA, continued its turbulent way forward—and backward and sideward. In 1911 two of the O'Brien teams changed hands, Haileybury going to the Canadien Athletic Club, which exercised its rights to the name "Les Canadiens," and Cobalt going to Quebec interests. The O'Brien franchise in Montreal, which had used the Canadiens' name, was kept in the league but without a team, presumably to be operated in Toronto in a year. With the dissolution of the Shamrocks there remained a five-team league, with only one O'Brien club operating, the Creamery Kings in Renfrew. Ottawa, with an offense that produced 122 goals in sixteen games, paced by Marty Walsh, Cubby Kerr, Ridpath, and teenager Jack Darragh, led the league and defended the Cup against Galt and Port Arthur. Percy LeSueur, however, was outplayed in goal by young Vezina, the Chicoutimi Cucumber, up for the Canadiens. There seemed no relief from the violence, particularly with the Cleghorn brothers, Odie and Sprague, on the ice for Renfrew and Art Ross still swinging a mean stick for the Wanderers. But there was no diminishing the artistry of Canadiens Pitre and Lalonde, who was also a lacrosse superstar.

The O'Briens withdrew completely in 1912. Both their idle franchise and the Renfrew Millionaires were made available for Toronto interests. But when the Toronto arena was not completed in time, a four-team league operated. The Canadiens' Vezina again led the goalies, and Ottawa's Skene Ronan led the scorers (Lalonde had gone to Vancouver); but it was Joe Malone who led Quebec to the title and the Cup, defending against Moncton as Jack McDonald scored nine in two games. In a bid to stimulate competitive spirit and gate receipts in Montreal, the Canadiens were supposed to use only French players while the other teams were to use none. Ethnic rivalry was thus consciously added to the natural elements for mindless conflict.

With the new arena ready in Toronto, bringing artificial ice to the NHA, the Blueshirts and the Tecumsehs entered the league. An inaugural exhibition game, played there in December, had spectacular effects. Lalonde, back from the West for the Canadiens, dumped the Wanderers' Odie Cleghorn into the boards. Brother Sprague Cleghorn retaliated, high-sticking a twelve-stitch gash over Newsy's eye. Cleghorn was brought up for assault, but he was fined only fifty dollars when Lalonde testified he didn't mean it. Later, Joe Hall drew some fines, but no blood, in an assault on a referee. Joe Malone edged teammate Tommy Smith for scoring honors; Clint Benedict debuted as a brilliant goalie in four games; and Quebec won the league, defended the Cup against Sydney of the Maritime Professional League, and then lost a postseason exhibition series to Victoria.

The Tecumsehs were renamed Ontarios but stayed in the cellar for 1914, but the Blueshirts tied the Canadiens for the title, beat them in a two-game

Checking Back

playoff, and took three straight from the Victorias in a postseason series. A year later, E. J. Livingstone, the new Ontarios' owner, changed their name to the Shamrocks, but not their luck, finishing just one game ahead of the Canadiens, who had dropped to the cellar. Like old times, Ottawa—with Benedict allowing only 65 goals in twenty games—and the Wanderers—scoring 127 goals, led by Gordon Roberts, Hyland, the Cleghorns, and Brownie Baker—tied for the league lead. In the playoff, Benny allowed only one goal in two games, but Ottawa then went west and lost the Cup to Vancouver. Among Ion's all-star selections that year, among the familiar names of Johnson, Patrick, Taylor, Mickey Mackay, and Eddie Oatman, appeared that of Frank Nighbor for the first time.

In 1916 Livingstone made a grasp for power by buying the other Toronto franchise, but the league would not allow him to operate both teams in the city and ordered him to sell the Shamrocks. Involved in a vigorous player-war with the expanded PCHA, Livingstone had some of his problems solve some others. He staffed the shorthanded Blueshirts with some of the Shamrocks and disbanded the latter team, but his new team still finished last. The Canadiens came from last in 1915 to the title, and as usual Pitre, Lalonde, and Vezina were the stars. The series with Portland was the first Stanley Cup classic. The Rosebuds, fresh from a transcontinental train ride, shut out the Canadiens, 2–0, in the first game, but lost, 2–1, in the second, each team winning under the other's rules. That was reversed in the third and fourth games, 6–3 and 6–5, and then Vezina outdueled Tommy Murray in nets for a 2–1 win and the Cup in a six-man game on March 30, the latest date so far for hockey playoffs and the start of a continuing trend.

Two scandalous stories remain to be told from the pre-NHL era, the episodes from the eternal management-versus-player saga, and organized hockey's response to World War I. From the beginnings of professionalism in hockey, players had moved freely and frequently from team to team, gradually improving their salaries as arena and club owners steadily gained in profits. The first signs of serious trouble appeared before the 1911 season. The following letter to the editor from Art Ross, which appeared in the Montreal *Herald* on November 25, sums up the situation nicely:

> For some little time now the newspapers, especially the Herald, have been handing it to the hockey player. It seems to me about time somebody took up the cudgels on behalf of the players, who, after all are not asking for any princely salaries, but who do object to doing all the work and getting a small portion of the gain, as they will likely do if they go into the clubs on the $5,000 salary limit basis. Hockey players have been compared to professional baseball players, but the comparison is unjust. The hockey season is comparatively short, and the majority of players engaged as professional players hold other positions also. While

playing hockey they run the risk of injury and probable loss of time, in addition to suffering a certain amount of distraction, which is almost bound to effect the prospects of advancement in business. All these things have to be taken into consideration in assessing the value of a professional hockey player. Hockey isn't a gentle pastime—not as it is played among the big teams. If it were, people wouldn't go to see it and there wouldn't be any need for salary limits, because there would be no paid players. With the possible exception of football, which after all only lasts one month, hockey is the most strenuous game I know.

The promoters, I see, claim that they will uncover a lot of stars from the bushes if the older players insist on standing out. To do this the promoters will have to go into the amateur field. Do they think they will get many of the amateurs to abandon their good standing, to cut themselves off from any other game except lacrosse, for a paltry $500 or less? And remember these bush stars might not make good at that, but their amateur standing would be gone just the same.

During a period of four years my own salary as a professional hockey player has varied from $1,000 to $2,700, the amount I got from Haileybury last season. But I would gladly give back all I have made as a professional player to regain my amatuer standing, and there are a good many other professionals who feel the same way I do.

But once a man has become a professional, he naturally places the highest value he can on his skill. The pros of to-day who are standing out against the salary limit aren't asking for any princely salaries, but merely what their skill is worth as revenue producers.

The contention of the promoter is that a $5,000 salary limit is necessary to make both ends meet. Now the Wanderers have paid on the average from $10,000 to $14,000 a year in salaries since they first started in the pro game. Ottawa has paid from $10,000 to $25,000 and yet Wanderers and Ottawa have never been in the hole. As a matter of fact, they have or should have made money.

All the players want is a fair deal. Personally, I am taking no active part in the matter just now, but if necessary will do what I can for the cause. The players are not trying to bulldoze the N.H.A., but we want to know where we get off at.

At about the same time, club owners began to assert their right to sell players to other clubs. Ottawa wanted to be compensated for Walter Smaill, who was jumping to the Wanderers, and Renfrew for Lalonde, who had already jumped to the Canadiens. Bruce Stuart, Ottawa's captain, was a leader in a threat by players to form their own league. The five thousand dollar limit for a whole squad was not, finally, enforced, nor even the porposed compromise of eight thousand dollars, and the season went on.

The following year, when the owners tried to control the dispersal of talent at Renfrew's dissolution, some players balked, and their position was strengthened by competitive offers from the Patricks. But the PCHA itself acted as a syndicate in assigning players to their three teams. Despite mutual raiding among the pro leagues, owners recognized their common interest in controlling players, and in 1914 they began formally to recognize "rights of other leagues." Art Ross was again active in threatening a players' league, but he and other holdouts eventually signed contracts for the season. Waivers were explicitly not recognized as part of the NHA structure. But by the 1915 season, Ross was "suspended from organized hockey" for his efforts in opposing an announced six hundred dollar-per-player limit. The threatened rival league never materialized, but neither the salary limit nor the Ross suspension could be enforced.

With the PCHA expansion for 1916, an open bidding war between the two major leagues developed, with all players regarded as free agents and fair game. Salaries rose accordingly and several players finished the NHA season after playing out the PCHA schedule. Cy Denneny, who fought through the season with Lalonde and Joe Malone for the scoring title, precipitated the next crisis when he took a job in Ottawa during the off-season. He refused to report back to Toronto and was suspended. Ottawa offered a trade for Benedict, but Livingstone wanted Nighbor or a cash deal for $1,800.

The players began to rally to Denneny's support, talking heretically about forming a union and suggesting a fixed "transfer fee" in case of a legitimate change of residence. But matters were settled by a deal closed on January 31: Denneny to Ottawa for Sammy Hebert and $750, a record deal. By that time, however, attention was focused on more sensational matters. A larger war was going on.

Many hockey players had enlisted in the army, and some were already overseas. Several, however, remained in Ontario with the 228th Battalion, the Northern Fusiliers, and they were admitted to the NHA as a sixth team under the management of Captain L. W. Reade. Patriotism was also displayed by Sam Lichtenheim, the same owner who had hired detectives to check on the Wanderers' off-ice moves in 1915, who announced that only married men and munition workers would play for his team; but the line-up was virtually unchanged. Livingstone, however, succeeded in keeping Gordon Keats—now a sergeant in the 228th Battalion—in a Toronto uniform.

The soldiers won their first four games, but were beaten by the Canadiens, Ottawa, and the Wanderers, and finished the first half of a divided schedule in third place. In the second half they had lost twice before being ordered overseas, and there followed a furor much louder than the time in 1915 when Harry Mummery reported a bribe offer from gamblers for Quebec and the Canadiens to lose to Toronto. Eddie Livingstone vigorously urged his own ideas about how to finish the season. Not only was he rejected, but over his anguished shouts the other directors decided to "balance the schedule" by dropping his team and dividing his players. Meanwhile, it came to light that not all the Fusiliers' players had been bona fide soldiers. Eddie Oatman, on leave from Portland, had been paid to play, and Gordon Meeking, who was discharged as medically unfit, claimed he'd been promised a share of gate receipts.

The hockey itself seemed of secondary importance during the season, though there was a high incidence of scoring and fighting. Frank Nighbor, the greatest poke-checker and hook-checker ever, tied for the scoring title with 41 goals in nineteen games, including 5 in the last one against Quebec when Joe Malone, who had scored 8 against the Wanderers three days earlier, was shut out. Only Benedict played well in goal, with a 2.8 average, while Vezina and the rest allowed 4 or more per game. The Canadiens and Ottawa, winners of the two halves of the schedule, played for the title, and that time Vezina edged Benedict by a single goal in the two games.

The Canadiens then went west to play for the Cup against the PCHA champion Seattle Metropolitans, winning the first game, 8–4, under western rules as Pitre scored four times. But that was the best they could do. Seattle won the next three games, two under eastern rules, as Bernie Morris and Frank Foyston accounted for seventeen goals while Harry Holmes held the Canadiens to just one per game. Newsy Lalonde, generally considered the best of the era, did not have a good series, and the Stanley Cup—preempted for the PCHA-NHA playoff—was taken from the Dominion for the first time. But greater changes lay just ahead, among them the new league which was to be called the National Hockey League, and again it was Eddie Livingstone who played a leading dramatic role.

PART *II*

Fortune's Fleeting Darlings

For the first quarter century of the NHL's existence, the one constant was change. The size of the league waxed and waned like phases of the moon, and the rules of play were altered like a flock of urban pets. Dynasties, if they can be called that, ruled as long as Latin American juntas and fell as fast as Italian governments. Cities played musical franchises with the teams, and players went from team to team almost as often as coaches and managers went in and out of office. Great stars flashed on the scene like novae and faded like the streakers of last year's quadrangles. Combinations of stars kept in cohesive lines were even rarer.

Yet a line of development—however meandering—may be traced throughout this period. The first great expansion to the United States produced financial resources far beyond anything hockey had experienced before. The NHL buried its rivals, assumed hegemony of the hockey world, and took permanent possession of its symbol, the Stanley Cup. An elaborate structure of minor leagues, amateur and professional, evolved to feed the NHL, alone at the top of the pyramid. While the rules of play evolved radically, they nevertheless maintained the essence of action in the game, and they resisted the pinball-machine syndrome of escalating scores in other sports by hanging on to the precious integrity of the goal.

A few teams retained their unique identities. A few managers and coaches left long-range brands on their teams. A few players managed to outskate the turns of fortune's wheel. And a very few lines stayed together long enough to characterize whole styles of play. Those most blest of the fleet and fleeting darlings of hockey's fortunes are featured in this section, as its eleven chapters take us through the many changes of the period. It is the period when hockey seems often to get lost, only finally to find and define itself.

5

Mr. Livingstone Presumes

Too much did Livingstone presume. The other owners, according to one of their number, were "fed up with Eddie Livingstone shaking his fist under everybody's nose" at every meeting. The cavalier manner in which the NHA had resolved its second-half scheduling muddle after the Fusiliers' disorderly withdrawal in 1917—by dropping Toronto and dispersing its troops throughout the league—signaled the extent of the league's disaffection for the contentious Toronto lawyer. Livingstone came to the NHA bitterly offering his players for sale to the highest bidder, thus threatening to take the league's only artificial ice out of play.

But the lawyer should have known that there was clear precedent, in 1906 and again in 1909, for dealing with an unwanted francise: simply vote the old league out of existence, reorganize as a new league, and award the franchise at issue to new management. Perhaps Livingstone did anticipate such a move, because a rumor circulated after the November 9 meeting that he had sold his franchise to the Toronto Arena directors and that the Arena manager, Charles Querrie, would manage the hockey club. At the next day's meeting it was not clear whether J. F. Boland, representing the Toronto franchise as one of the five continuing NHA interests, was acting for Livingstone or for the Arena management.

The November 17 meeting produced the announcement that Quebec would not operate a team for the 1918 season because of the lack of fan support. M. J. Quinn, however, continued to represent the Quebec franchise at subsequent meetings. Presumably he retained the privilege of reentering the league at a later date, and speculation in the press argued that the development made formation of a new league unlikely.

A meeting on November 22 gave signs to the contrary. Only Sam Lichtenheim, Quinn, George Kennedy, and Tommy Gorman, representing Wanderers, Quebec, Canadiens, and Ottawa, were present. Eleven days less than a year before the Armistice ended World War I, the NHA owners were still looking for a way to satisfy their hostilities against Livingstone. Their historic decision was probably made that day, but it was not made official until four days later.

On November 26, 1917, at the Windsor Hotel in Montreal as usual, the National Hockey League was formed. Franchises were awarded to Ottawa, Canadiens, Wanderers, and Toronto. The new league adopted the NHA constitution with virtually no change in the rules (a determination that did not survive the first season). Frank Calder, a transplanted British soccer player who had been the NHA secretary, was elected both president and secretary of the NHL. The spiritual presence of the dormant Quebec franchise was acknowledged by having Quinn named "honorary president."

Tommy Gorman called it a "great day for hockey," and the whole group rejoiced that Livingstone had been purged. Elmer Ferguson, who had succeeded Calder as sports editor of the Montreal *Herald* and was the only reporter on the beat at the Windsor, got the following remark from Lichtenheim: "We didn't throw Livingstone out; he's still got his franchise in the old National Hockey Association. He has his team, and we wish him well. The only problem is he's playing in a one-team league." The news of the new league hardly caused shock waves through the Dominion. Canadians would remember 1917 for giving them the income tax, not the NHL.

The Quebec players were divided so as to balance the league in terms of the 1917 standings. The Wanderers got Jack McDonald, Dave Ritchie, George Carey, and Jack Marks. The Canadiens got Joe Malone, Joe Hall, and Walter Mummery. Toronto got Harry Mummery. And Ottawa got Rusty Crawford, who moved over to Toronto late in the season. It is not recorded whether Quebec received the two hundred dollars a player that had been requested—if anything. When the franchise reentered competition two years later, all those players were returned. Perhaps future rights to the players was sufficient recompense for Quebec.

Peace seemed as remote in Europe as in the Toronto Arena. Livingstone battled on. Jimmy Murphy had been named manager of the team but had resigned at once in favor of Querrie. Like Lalonde a lacrosse star, Querrie determined to rule with a firm hand, posting the following rules in the Arena dressing room:

1. First and foremost do not forget that I am running this club.
2. You are being paid to give your best services to the club. Condition depends a lot on how you behave off the ice.
3. It does not require bravery to hit another man over the head with a stick. If you want to fight go over to France.
4. You will not be fined for doing the best you can. You will be punished for indifferent work or carelessness.
5. Do not think you are putting over something on the manager when you do

anything you should not. You are being paid to play hockey not to be a good
fellow.
6. I am an easy boss if you do your share. If you do not want to be on the square
and play hockey, turn in your uniform to Dick Carroll and go at some other
work.

Yet in a matter of days Querrie resigned, saying he could not tolerate the constant interference of Mr. Livingstone. If this was a power play, it was successful. The name of Livingstone as an enemy was enough to rally many friends. A
week later, Querrie was in full control, with authority to hire and fire players
as well as instruct and fine them. He exercised his new cachet by signing
Harry Holmes to tend goal, a move that led to the league championship and
the Stanley Cup at the end of his first season.

Livingstone abandoned guerrilla warfare in favor of legal maneuvering before the next season could start. He managed to convene a meeting of the
defunct NHA in September, determined to operate another franchise in
Toronto. Lichtenheim moved the suspension of the NHA, seconded by Kennedy, and carried with the single and vocal opposition of Livingstone. Quebec
was represented by Quinn at the meeting and the Ontarios by Tom Wall. Afterward, Percy Quinn of Toronto met informally with Kennedy and Gorman,
discussing purchase of the Quebec franchise.

Within days, Percy Quinn and Eddie Livingstone were reported to be planning a suit against the Arenas, the Canadiens, Ottawa, and the NHA, alleging
a payoff from the Arena Gardens of Toronto for Ottawa's and the Canadiens'
votes on suspension. The threat was defused, however, when the NHL voted
to approve Percy Quinn's purchase of the Quebec franchise, on the condition
that he—not Livingstone—operate the club. Subsequently his down payment
of six hundred dollars was forfeited when he failed to complete the transaction.
Meanwhile, the Toronto Arena was pronounced unavailable for teams with no
NHL franchise, a preventive measure taken to ward off symptoms of a new
league to be organized by Livingstone and Percy Quinn.

Livingstone attacked on another front, now ostensibly supported by the
Brunswick Balk Collender Company, owners of twelve of the Canadiens' fifty
shares. He hoped that the association would reactivate by a vote of 162–138,
counting fifty from dormant Quebec, fifty from the defunct Ontarios, fifty from
his own exiled Torontos, and twelve from the newly involved Brunswick Company. President Calder delayed the proceedings by ordering back payments to
the treasury before a meeting could be convened, but meet they did on
December 11. The arguing resolved nothing, but when the Brunswick repre-
sentatives walked out with those of the Canadiens, Ottawa, and the Wanderers, the dead NHA was finally laid to rest.

Two years later Livingstone tried again, hoping to organize a "Canadian

Checking Back

Hockey Association," with teams in Hamilton and Cleveland and two in Toronto. But that hope too was dashed, in part by the NHL shift of Quebec to Hamilton, and Livingstone's days in the hockey courts were over. By uniting against a common enemy, the infant NHL had found a strength that overcame several separate weaknesses; the debt that the league owes Mr. Livingstone can only be paid, ironically, in the pages of its history.

That history begins, as this chapter suggests, with little promise of success and less of longevity. Professional hockey was as weak in eastern Canada as it had been in a decade. The quality of play had not risen, fan interest had fallen, and inner conflicts weakened the few surviving clubs. Perhaps only the determination of the owners and Calder to thwart Livingstone kept the NHL going in its first few years, and it was business as usual for a while. But then, when along with new players, new rules, and new management blood came new and broader horizons, the NHL rose to assume its role as the single, dominant, ruling force in hockey.

6

Business as Usual

The league was brand new in 1918, but the brand of hockey had barely changed. The NHL began with names and faces and styles familiar to the NHA and in part to the PCHA and even to the long-gone ECHA. Cyclone Taylor had blown out west, dominating the scoring race in the Patricks' league, but most of the customary stars were still on hand: Malone, Lalonde, Pitre, Hall, and Laviolette with the Canadiens; Cy Denneny, Jack Darragh, Eddie Gerard, and Frank Nighbor with Ottawa; Art Ross with the Wanderers; Corbett Denneny, Reg Noble, and Harry Mummery with the new Toronto entry. Benedict, Holmes, and Vezina retained their accustomed places in the nets, but Benedict was so accustomed to and adept at falling to the ice that the rule against it was changed during the season; the old rule was no longer enforceable. The Cleghorns sat out the season, Odie because of wartime responsibilities and Sprague with a broken leg. In his frustration, Sprague high-sticked his wife with a crutch, but the assault charge was dismissed and no Cleghorn served a single recorded penalty that year.

Lichtenheim's Wanderers were in trouble. After beating Toronto in their opener they couldn't win a game and couldn't draw spectators. Before the league could meet to hear the owner's pleas for help, things got suddenly worse. On January 2 the Westmount Arena was destroyed by fire, the Wanderers and the Canadiens each losing a thousand dollars' worth of equipment besides their home ice. Les Canadiens moved to the Jubilee Rink despite its small capacity (3,250 seats), but Lichtenheim refused Hamilton's invitation to host the rest of the Wanderers' schedule.

The Canadiens won the first half, Toronto the shorter second half with only three teams competing. Malone scored forty-four goals in twenty games, while Taylor in Vancouver had thirty-two in eighteen. When Vancouver upset Seattle in the PCHA playoff, the two scorers should have shot it out in the Stanley Cup series, but the Canadiens came a cropper in their playoff with the Arenas. Lalonde was the leading scorer in the series but served so many penalty minutes that Toronto prevailed. The Arenas won the Cup three games to two in

Checking Back

Toronto. The two games Vancouver won were played under western rules, with seven-man sides, and Taylor led all scorers with nine goals.

When the Western Canada Hockey League was organized for the 1922 season—with Edmonton, Calgary, Regina, and Saskatoon—the six-man game was adopted, and a year later the PCHA finally dropped the rover position. Pioneers in almost every other rules development, the Patricks had resisted that particular improvement for eleven years.

The six seasons from 1919 to 1924 produced many minor changes, but everything seemed to stay the same. The three-team alignment continued through the 1919 season, but the Quebec franchise was reactivated for 1920, while the Toronto management sold the Arenas (for two thousand dollars) and then bought the right to reorganize as the St. Patricks (for five thousand dollars, on time). Quebec moved to Hamilton the following year and was given a little help with personnel from the other teams, but dwelt in the cellar throughout the period. A change in management for Ottawa in 1924 accompanied the team's move to a new auditorium with ten thousand seats. The Canadiens had already moved, in 1920, to the Mount Royal Arena—and not any too soon, because the Jubilee Rink burned down that season.

In October 1921, George Kennedy's widow put the Canadiens up for sale. In the auction, President Calder himself represented an Ottawa group and Tom Duggan was bidding for himself and the Mount Royal Arena Company. The winning offer, however, came from Cecil Hart, representing his partner in a Cleveland race track, Leo Dandurand, and Joe Cattarinich. The price was $11,000, a profit of $3,500 over Kennedy's 1910 purchase. Hart became coach and Dandurand manager, with Cattarinich and Louis Letourneau providing financial management. It was they, in 1924, along with the organizational leadership of Senator Donat Raymond, who financed, arranged, and designed the finest facility for hockey up to that time, The Forum, built for $1,250,000 and still in use.

Despite changes in management and location and number of franchises, the teams played a fairly constant schedule—twenty-two games in 1918, eighteen in 1919, twenty-four from 1920 to 1924—and despite changes in personnel the teams were fairly constant in style of play. Ottawa, Toronto, and the Canadiens were the dominant teams during the period, two of them playing off for the NHL championship every year and the winner going on to take the Stanley Cup each time but one.

The one exception was 1919, when the NHL playoff was extended to four out of seven, the Canadiens beating Ottawa four games to one. On this team Lalonde was the scoring and spiritual leader, not to mention serving most penalty minutes. Perhaps right wing Pitre, with his flashy skating and flowing long hair, typified the team's color. Laviolette, the bone-crushing, stick-handling defenseman, had retired after the 1917 season, but Hall and Bert Corbeau were there, Louis Berlinquette skated on Newsy's left, and the substitutes included Jack McDonald, Billy Couture, and Odie Cleghorn. But the heart of those Canadien teams was in its nets.

Georges Vezina rarely led the league or the playoffs in goals-against average, had only twenty shutouts in fifteen full seasons, yet is considered by many the greatest goalkeeper in history. The NHL award to top goalie bears his name, but ironically it is awarded on purely statistical criteria. Vezina dominated by his determination and fighting heart, not statistically. Through fifteen years he never missed a regularly scheduled or playoff game. His face cut by a puck and his eye slashed "so that it seemed to be popping out of his head" (according to Red Dutton), he still refused to leave the ice. Vezina's career ended in 1925 when he collapsed in the nets and had to be carried from the ice. Six months later he was dead of tuberculosis and ulcers and complications.

Seattle in 1919 had edged Vancouver in the PCHA and was prepared to host the Canadiens. In the first and third games, with rovers on the ice, Seattle won, 7–0 and 7–2, with Frank Foyston scoring three and then four goals. Les Canadiens won the second game, 4–2, with eastern rules, Lalonde scoring all their goals, but the fourth game ended, 0–0, after 100 minutes of overtime. Harry Holmes and Vezina were perfect in nets, and Hall and Cully Wilson excited the crowd with their physical defensive play. The fifth game, four days later, was strangely lackluster. Players skated lethargically and checked perfunctorily. Hall retired sick. Down 3–0, the Canadiens were led back by Lalonde and finally tied the score. After 15 minutes, 57 seconds of overtime Odie Cleghorn scored from the right wing, and the Canadiens had finally won a game with a seven-man team.

But the series went no further. Hall had influenza and a high fever. Lalonde, McDonald, Berlinquette, and manager Kennedy all were confined to bed. Joe Hall never recovered, dying within the week. The other players made it back to play again, but their boss never completely regained his health. He died in 1921.

Ottawa, Cup winners in 1920, 1921, and 1923, had remarkable teams. In goal, Benedict consistently led in goals-against average. In five NHA seasons and nine NHL seasons, including nine playoff years, his overall average was 2.8—and that's without the wide pads and huge mitt. Defensemen were Sprague Cleghorn, Eddie Gerard, and George (Buck) Boucher. Cleghorn, one of the few skaters of his time with the power consistently to split two opposing defensemen, played only the 1919 and 1920 seasons with Ottawa; three games into 1921 he was dropped and moved over to Toronto. Tom Gorman had got him from San Lichtenheim for nothing except the $8.50 to bring him and his wife to Ottawa after his broken legs had led to the Wanderers' owner's disenchantment with him. He was expendable now in Ottawa because Boucher and Gerard were the league's most effective tandem in shutting down the opponents and protecting a lead.

Boucher skated at left wing in 1920, but when he moved back to defense, Ottawa assembled one of the greatest of early forward lines. Frank Nighbor at center was perhaps the best ever at both ends of the rink. Always a consistent high scorer, he was also, as Bill Roche puts it, a "one-man team in defensive forward work." Skating backward, smoothly menacing with his stick, he would poke-check and hook-check to break up attack after attack. Before the 1923 season the league legislated against concentration of forwards on defense: great players are often honored by the rules passed to control them when other players can't. The first winner of the Hart Trophy (1924), he also won the Lady Byng Trophy the first two years it was awarded (1925, 1926). In 1923 he played six consecutive complete games—360 minutes without substitution at center. On his left wing was Cy Denneny, who was not only the sturdy police-man of the line but also Ottawa's all-time leading scorer.

At right wing was Jack Darragh or Punch Broadbent. Darragh, a left-handed shooter, broke in the same night as Vezina in 1910 and scored against him. After scoring Cup-winning goals in 1920 and 1921, he retired from hockey during the 1922 season, when the Senators failed to retain the Cup. But he returned for the 1923 championship. The next year was his last: he died of peritonitis at thirty-three. Elbows Broadbent, the other right wing, was also a prodigious scorer, twenty-five goals in sixteen consecutive games in 1922 when he tied Toronto's Babe Dye, the cocky right-winger whose bullet shots scored in eleven straight games in 1921 and 1922, for the scoring title with thirty goals. One other player for Ottawa must be mentioned here, King Clancy, who broke in as a substitute in 1922; his career and accomplishments will be featured later.

The Senators may have dominated the scene for that short period, but Frank Patrick for one was hard to convince. In 1923 Ottawa came west to regain the Cup and warmed up with a scrimmage at Calgary. Playing under wraps on Gorman's orders, they lost, 5–0. Patrick anticipated a Vancouver sweep over the weakened easterners and, hoping to insure a gate for at least five games, suggested that the Vancouver-Ottawa winner play Edmonton, the WCHL champion. Gorman accepted, and though never branded as hustlers, Ottawa dispatched the Millionaires in three games out of four. Patrick now called them the greatest team he'd ever seen, and they went on to take two straight from Edmonton, 2–1 in overtime and 1–0, with Denneny and Broad-bent scoring the winning goals.

A year earlier it had been brother Lester whose sporting generosity may have cost the Millionaires the Cup. Vancouver led two games to one when

Toronto requested that Eddie Gerard replace the injured Harry Cameron. Patrick accepted, perhaps because there was no objection to Vancouver using Victoria's Eddie Oatman. Patrick himself was actually Victoria's manager during the regular season. With Gerard anchoring the defense, Toronto won the fourth game, 6–0. Then, with Cameron back, they held on to the Cup for the NHL in a 5–1 victory in the final game. Gerard declined any pay, saying, "You don't owe me a cent, I've had a lot of fun," but the grateful St. Pats gave him a diamond pin.

Sporting gestures were not uncommon, although the persistence of violence on the ice bred repeated instances of brutality, injury, and revenge. When Sprague Cleghorn joined brother Odie on the Canadiens, it seemed that they carried on a vendetta against Ottawa. In one game in 1922 the Cleghorns put Gerard, Nighbor, and Denneny out for the next two games—Gerard with a slash over the eye, Nighbor with a charge that damaged his elbow on the ice, and Denneny with a butt-end to the face.

In 1923 Bert Couture got into the act. After Denneny opened the scoring in the first playoff game, Couture simply cracked him over the head with his stick, the cut and concussion taking him out of the game, the match penalty taking Couture out as well. With the Canadiens down 2–0 near the end, the frustrated Sprague cross-checked Lionel Hitchman in the face, and they too were gone for injury and penalty. Leo Dandurand didn't wait for the league or the courts to act against his overaggressive defensemen; he suspended them from the remaining playoff game. Veterans Malone and Pitre rose to the occasion and led the Canadiens to a 2–1 victory in Ottawa, but the goal by Denneny—still dizzy from Couture's stick—earned the edge in the series for the Senators and the trip west for the Cup.

Sprague had simply taken upon himself the chief mauler's mantle that had been worn for the Canadiens by Newsy Lalonde. Indeed the two had tangled many times in the past, though they professed to like each other. When Sprague almost killed Lalonde with his stick one night in Toronto and was booked for assault, Newsy showed up in court, bandages and all, to plead for him and helped him get off with a small fine. It was Sprague who had welcomed King Clancy to the league in 1923. Clancy had tricked Cleghorn into passing the puck to him. As he skated off the ice at the end of the period, there was a friendly tap on his shoulder. He turned into a punch that knocked him cold.

That was the first year in the last eleven that Lalonde was not in the Canadien red, white, and blue. Indeed, he had worn the old Canadien uniform with the green maple leaf in 1910 and 1911. But now Dandurand had traded him to the Saskatoon Sheiks for an unproven amateur, Aurel Joliat. Lalonde played on and also managed in the WCHL, where among his protégés were the Cook brothers. Sprague Cleghorn, too, tried his hand at management after finishing his career with Boston, though he was less successful at it than brother Odie. Sprague's colorful ways seem to typify an attitude of total mindlessness. He and Howie Morenz used to drop cannon firecrackers under police cars in the midst of traffic jams in Montreal, just for fun. A final glimpse into the nature of this character comes from his days as manager of Providence in the Canadian-American League. The team had a black trainer, Pinky Lewis, and the Hotel Adelphi in Philadelphia was reluctant to allow him to register. But Cleghorn insisted, arguing spiritedly that the clerk had never before seen a genuine "Canadian Arctic Indian."

The simultaneous departure of Lalonde and arrival of Joliat marked a changing of the guard in Montreal, and the early era of the NHL ends as the new era of the Canadiens begins. The rules of play had seen many minor changes. Only the 1920 move permitting goalies to pass the puck forward in the defensive zone had significant implications for the future. The NHL had established a consistent, though still narrow, measure of dominance over the western leagues. But in the process of proving it, the playoff system for the Stanley Cup had begun to grow in complexity, evolving menacingly toward the elaborate second-season tournament of the present era.

An occasion of far-reaching significance occurred in March 1923. A young reporter gave the first radio broadcast of a hockey game. Foster Hewitt's approach was perfectly suited to the occasion, his high-pitched climax—"he shoots . . . he scores"—capturing the intensity of the moment and the appreciative imagination of listeners. In time, "Hockey Night in Canada" became a phenomenal media success, and the subsequent sports-media relationships owe a large debt to the happy and lasting radio marriage of Hewitt and hockey. When Hewitt came to pick his all-time all-star six, only Eddie Gerard had preceded him in hockey, though Shore, Joliat, and Bill Cook were waiting in the wings.

The era ended, as it had begun, with as much acrimony as good feeling. Morenz was signed and then reluctantly pressured into playing for the Canadiens. Sprague Cleghorn went on hurting people, especially in Senator uniforms, and being denounced and suspended, while Lalonde was carrying on the tradition in the WCHL. Regina's Amby Moran went to jail for assaulting a policeman. The Canadiens took the NHL playoffs from Ottawa, Morenz and Joliat leading the way, and then Dandurand bickered with Frank Patrick over the Cup playoff arrangements. In the events, Vancouver took the PCHA playoff from Seattle, Calgary the WCHL playoff from Regina. Calgary then earned a bye by beating Vancouver two games to one. The Canadiens prevailed over Vancouver, 3–2 and 2–1, Bill Boucher scoring both goals in the deciding game, and over Calgary 6–1 and 3–0, with Morenz, Boucher, and Joliat each scoring in both games.

The Candiens held the Stanley Cup, but as the NHL passed into a new era for the 1925 season, it became the Candiens' distinction to lose the Cup outside the league for the last time. Ironically, or prophetically, they also literally lost the Cup almost as soon as they won it this time. Fêted and honored all over Montreal, they were on their way to Dandurand's home to continue celebrating. As the story goes, Vezina, Cleghorn, and Sylvio Mantha were in a Model T which stalled going up Cote St. Antoine Road in Westmount. Out to help push the car, Cleghorn left the trophy on the curb, and there it stayed for an hour before the forgetful champions realized they had left it.

7

South of the Border: The Cup Taken Over

In 1924 the National Hockey League may have been tempest-tossed, but it was certainly neither tired nor homeless. Yet like millions of other emigrants, Candian professional hockey was drawn to the United States by the promise of gold-paved streets all leading to the arenas. In the West, the Patricks had long since begun to tap the markets in Seattle and Portland. Ironically, the financial impetus lent to the eastern hockey establishment by expansion southward led to the end of the Patricks' league as competitively big-time.

The first step across the border was a natural one toward Boston, which had long been a good hockey town. The Boston Arena had exhibited a Wanderers-Ottawa series in 1910, and Conn Smythe had regularly brought in his University of Toronto teams to play Harvard and Boston University before sellout crowds. Boston was ready for the NHL, and the NHL was ready to expand, but this first United States venture was rather timidly undertaken, accompanied by another new team close to home.

Leo Dandurand sold half of the Canadiens' territorial rights to the Canadian Arena Company (James Strachan and Donat Raymond) for fifteen-thousand—no part of which went to the Ottawa, Hamilton, and Toronto clubs. The Maroons would be Montreal's second team in the league, and presumably if that city could have two the United States could have one—at the same price. The franchises were considered to have no value in 1918 but had tripled the 1920 price of five thousand.

Charles F. Adams was the man in Boston with the money and the enthusiasm to put NHL hockey regularly into the Boston Arena, rebuilt after a 1918 fire. Montreal's Thomas J. Duggan had options for two United States franchises and easily persuaded Adams to buy one of them; the new owner realized his fantasy of having the brown and gold colors of his grocery chain decorate a sextet on skates. The Bruins did very poorly on the ice that first year, but very well at the turnstiles, and with Art Ross in control they were certain to reward their faithful fans soon.

Duggan's salesmanship was then turned toward New York and William V.

Dwyer, better known among the bootlegging trade as Big Bill. With the help of sportswriter Bill McBeth, Duggan sold Dwyer on the idea of bringing an NHL team to New York. And then Duggan and Dwyer sold Tex Rickard the idea of putting hockey into his new Madison Square Garden.

Big Bill didn't acquire just a franchise; he bought a whole NHL team for $75,000. Hamilton had led the league in 1925, but the players struck for bonus money before they would play in the playoffs. President Calder had acted decisively, barring the players from the playoffs, declaring the winner of the Toronto-Canadiens series the champions, and then simply awarding the franchise and all its rights—including players—to the Americans.

By the time the 1926 season began, the New York Americans had company in breaking into the league, the Pittsburgh Pirates, with Odie Cleghorn representing them on the board. For five years the Pirates struggled with diminishing success and crowds, but that first year they were a surprising third in the league with many holdovers from the Yellow Jacket squad of the United States amateur league, including Lionel Conacher, Hib Milks, Duke McCurry, Harold Darragh, and Roy Worters in goal. Of course the main focus of attention was New York, where the NHL premiered on December 15, 1925 before sixteen thousand in furs and diamonds or black tie. Mayor John F. Hyland dropped the puck for the first face-off between Billy Burch and Howie Morenz, and the Canadians skated to a 3–1 win.

Dwyer believed he had a commitment from Rickard that there would be no other NHL team in New York. But he had nothing in writing, and for a promoter like Rickard that meant the door was open, especially with Colonel John S. Hammond urging him to put a house team on the home ice of the Garden. Eventually, by having their rental fees steadily raised on them, the Americans would be put out to Brooklyn and then to pasture by the upstart Rangers.

The pivotal year in this period of expansion and consolidation was 1926–1927. Of the six teams that would survive through the "closed circuit" era, three came into the league at this time, and with the Bruins formed a majority of United States clubs. Within a few years, hockey was the major winter sports attraction in those four major cities: New York, Chicago, Boston, and Detroit. The American markets had escalated the demand and the price on hockey talent, and the western leagues were feeling the squeeze. There was additional economic pressure in the West from a widespread feeling that the spacious rinks should be used for storing grain.

Six teams operated in the WCHL—Edmonton, Saskatoon, Victoria, Regina, Calgary, Vancouver—during the 1925 season. The PCHA had folded when Seattle withdrew, and Vancouver and Victoria were accepted in the WCHL, both strengthened by some Seattle players. Some of the disgruntled Hamilton players came west, including Corbett Denneny, and Eddie Shore was a rookie forward for Regina. Victoria went on to beat Saskatoon and Calgary in the western playoffs and then took on the Candiens, who had also been third in their own division. Harry Holmes continued his brilliant play in goal, Frank Fredrickson and Jack Walker led the scoring, and the Cup went outside the NHL for the last time.

In one last franchise shift, Regina went to Portland for the 1926 season, but it was a swan song for an independent major league in the West, now called the WHL. Outstanding players were being lured east by the larger salaries, though the Patricks vainly tried to argue that the golden reports were fake. Victoria beat Saskatoon and then Edmonton in the playoffs, Holmes continuing his goals-against average of less than two. Surprising Pittsburgh had extended Montreal in the NHL playoffs, but the Maroons went on to beat Ottawa for the championship.

Alex Connell had debuted in Ottawa's goal in 1925, leading with 7 shutouts but only tying for third in goals-against average. His second season was incredible, 15 shutouts in 36 games and a 1.2 average. He once recorded 6 consecutive shutouts. Ottawa finished first in the standings by virtue of this defensive master, but in the playoffs two goals in two games were enough for the Maroons to win. Ottawa got only one, by Clancy, and Montreal went on to win the Cup in a return match with Victoria, three games to one, with 2 shutouts for Benedict.

This was the last "challenge" year for the Stanley Cup. The NHL was growing in franchises, prestige, financial success, and American dollars. Frank Patrick announced that all WHL players except those on Saskatoon were available for sale. With the decline of the West, all the WHL players might have severely depressed the market. But boom conditions prevailed in the East, and the competitiveness among the new teams—accompanied by the success-fueled expansiveness of the NHL as a whole—simply drove prices higher.

The franchise fee was now fifty thousand dollars. Paddy Harmon wanted a team in Chicago and laid fifty one-thousand dollar bills on the table before the board. The assembled NHL governors collectively swallowed hard, but they had already accepted another bid with only twelve thousand dollars cash by a group led by Jack Hardwick, a former Harvard football All-American, and Major Frederic McLaughlin, a polo-playing coffee tycoon. The Detroit franchise went to Colonel Charles Hughes, competing with four other groups. And to Rickard went a second New York franchise, a team that was called Tex's Rangers (first by George Daley of the *Herald-Tribune*) before it had any players.

Rickard was the perfect character to set off the NHL cast with an extra dimension. Just in his own person he projected an image that was almost a cartoon version of the league's power structure. His biography, told by his third (or fourth) wife to Arch Oboler, reads like an episodic dime-store melodrama. Tex was a cowhand, a marshal of Henrietta, Texas, and a proprietor of a merry-go-round in Dallas before heading for the frontier. He made his first fortunes prospecting for gold and gambling in the Yukon and the Klondike, always moving on at the appropriate time. After an unsuccessful venture in a South African diamond mine, he struck it rich again and again in Nevada—in gold, silver, saloons, and the promotion of prizefights.

The million-dollar gate in boxing became a reality because Rickard grasped the power of the press to promote a sporting event (by definition, an athletic competition that was interesting enough to excite spirited wagering). He promoted the Gans–Battling Nelson fight in Goldfield and then the Johnson–Jeffries fight in Reno, which he refereed himself. Back east, the Willard–Moran fight gave Tex a new thirty thousand dollar stake, which he promptly doubled by betting on Wilson to win the presidential election. Next he took the Dempsey-Willard fight to Toledo and then brought Dempsey and Carpentier to Jersey City.

Rickard played the press like a puppeteer in drawing attention to his spectacles. But to protect the sporting proposition involving the glamorous Frenchman, he banned reporters from Carpentier's training camp. He knew that any observant sportswriter would see that there wasn't the slightest threat to Dempsey. So he dealt with the fourth estate by means of press releases and planted leaks, flacking away at suggestions of secret punches and the like, thus providing a precedent for latter-day operators like George Allen, John Wooden, and Richard Nixon.

Back in Jersey City, he matched Lew Tendler and Benny Leonard, proving that it didn't take heavyweights to excite the ticket-buying and betting public, but his last major fight promotion was Dempsey-Firpo in the Polo Grounds. By that time Rickard had survived a cattle venture in Paraguay, had gained control of the old Garden with the help of John Ringling, and had become incidentally interested in hockey as a supporting sideline in plans for the new Madison Square Garden. At his death in 1929, Rickard was promoting plans for dog-racing, horse-racing, and gambling-casino facilities in Miami Beach. Those were the appropriate associations for professional hockey as it impressed itself on the American sporting scene—racing, fighting, gambling spectacles, but with a lot of flash and a touch of class. It was a world in which the new Ranger center, Frank Boucher, would live at Big Bill's Forrest Hotel and rub shoulders with Damon Runyon, Legs Diamond, and Dutch Schultz.

The image-makers in New York promoted hockey any way they could, and the potential for violence was prominent. Paul Gallico described it in the *News* as "a fast, body-contact game played by men with clubs in their hands and knives lashed to their feet . . . almost a certainty that someone will be hurt and will fleck the ice with a generous contribution of gore. . . ." In an attempt to appeal to the ethnic population, the Rangers' flacks Bruno and Blythe tinkered with players' names: Lorne Chabot became Chabotsky or Shobotsky and Oliver Reinikka was Ollie Rocco in press releases. When the Rangers opened before another black-tie crowd, with Boucher facing off against Nels Stewart of the Maroons and Lois Moran dropping the first puck, Tex's marquee read, WORLD'S BEST MEETS WORLD'S WORST TONIGHT IN GARDEN.

None of it was true, not even the rap on the home team, but it was all attention-grabbing PR. The fact of the matter was that Conn Smythe had assembled a first-rate hockey club before being fired by Colonel Hammond before the season started, and in the event the Rangers beat the Maroons, 1–0. But the important thing in Rickard's scheme of things was publicity. Tex's Rangers continued to get preferential coverage, climaxed in 1936 when the good gray *Times* reported a Stanley Cup game against the Americans as front-page news.

The 1927 season presented a ten-team NHL, divided into Canadian or International and American Divisions. New York's Americans played with the Canadiens, Maroons, Ottawa, and Toronto in the one, while the Rangers, Boston, Chicago, Detroit, and Pittsburgh made up the other. In the playoffs, second-place Montreal and Boston played third-place Canadiens and Chicago two games each, total goals to win. The survivors, the Canadiens and Boston, then played the division leaders, Ottawa and the Rangers, in similar series. Then the two winners, Ottawa and Boston, played a best-of-five series for the title.

Ottawa, by winning the NHL championship playoff, won the Stanley Cup as well. The NHL had assumed permanent proprietary rights to the trophy, but in the defunct challenge system they had discovered the box-office bonanza of postseason competition. Thus the playoff system was coopted into the structure of the league's championship play, and the postseason tournament idea was sold to a public that continues to buy it as it continues to proliferate throughout the sports world. In the eyes (and pockets) of many, that has been hockey's major contribution to contemporary sports.

The Rangers and the Americans had the Garden as home ice, and soon the Bruins had a Garden of their own. When they moved from the Boston Arena to their new North Station home on November 20, 1928, instead of the social occasion for dinner-dressed patrons, there was a mob scene and riot. The Boston fans took very seriously the fact that not all of them could get tickets for the event; hockey was bread and butter and beer to them, not caviar and champagne, and they reacted accordingly.

In Detroit the team was called the Cougars and played home games at Olympia Stadium. For one hundred thousand dollars the management had bought the WHL Victoria Cougars, with Jack Walker, Clem Loughlin, Art

Duncan, Frank Foyston, and Frank Fredrickson, and they continued to play as Cougars, though the Detroit habitat seemed to take the bite out of them. A change to Falcons carried them no higher, and new management put the Red Wings name and a flying wheel insignia together in 1933. But throughout their flights and flops they have remained at Olympia.

In Chicago Major McLaughlin's Black Hawks also acquired a number of WHL players and in 1929 he gave them a new home in the Chicago Stadium. In the same year the St. Louis Arena was completed, but it wasn't until 1934 that Frank Ahern sold the Ottawa franchise to bring NHL hockey into St. Louis. The moves to the United States were not unqualified successes. That temporary disruption of minor-league hegemony in St. Louis lasted only a year. The Pittsburgh franchise lasted five years, moved to Philadelphia for a single season, and then folded. And the Americans gave up the ghost after a last-gasp shift to Brooklyn. But through phases of contraction and expansion, of competition and exclusivity, the presence of the NHL in the United States has remained firm and on occasions even dominant.

Aside from the struggle for St. Louis, there were other skirmishes with the American Hockey League. In 1928 the AHL seemed to pose a genuine threat and was warring with the NHL for players. Tom Shaughnessy, fired as manager of the Black Hawks, took over the Chicago Shamrocks, and that AHL team began to draw crowds of ten to fifteen thousand. Finally, in 1931, the upstart league submitted a formal challenge for the Stanley Cup. The trustees refused; the days of challenges had receded past reclaiming. No other league had the temerity to challenge the NHL for its symbol of dominance, though other forms of challenge have in time materialized.

8

Cooking with Boucher

No expansion team, then or since, in any professional sport, ever attained championship quality so fast as Tex's Rangers. Colonel Hammond had hired Conn Smythe to assemble his team, and the result was a remarkable display of shrewd judgment, energetic scouting, and convincing salesmanship. For a total of $32,000, thirty-one players had signed with the Rangers, including Taffy Abel, Ching Johnson, Frank Boucher, Muzz Murdoch, Bill and Bun Cook, Billy Boyd, Paul Thompson, Reg Mackey, Oliver Reinikka, and goalies Hal Winkler and Lorne Chabot. In their first season the Rangers led the American Division but were eliminated by the Bruins in the Cup semifinals.

It was the best of times for expansion. The coincidental folding of the Western Hockey League made a substantial player pool available. Indeed, it was the first time in hockey history that all the best players skated in one league. It was a time of such promise, such golden opportunity, that Major McLaughlin could be terribly upset by the third-place finish of his Chicago Black Hawks (with Dick Irvin, Ducan MacKay, George Hay, and Rabbit McVeigh) in their first year, 1927, and elimination by the Bruins in the first round of the playoffs.

The story goes that the major summoned manager-coach Pete Muldoon to his office and told him, "This club is good enough to finish in first place."

"You're crazy," said the coach.

"You're fired," said the brass.

And then the angry Irishman, turning back before he left, threw this last shot: "I'm not through with you. I'll hoodoo you. This club will *never* finish in first place."

And they didn't, for forty years.

It has recently been reported that the whole incident, the Curse of the Muldoon, was the invention of Jim Coleman, who was touched in desperation by his Muse just before a deadline for the Toronto *Globe and Mail*. But if it is apocryphal, it has been a part of NHL legend long enough to be told. Besides, the debunking may just be a process of myth-making for a sportswriting legend, and there is no way to verify the incident either way. The point is that whether or not it happened, the hockey world believed it had, and it is thus a party of its history.

Muldoon was not the first managerial casualty of expansion hockey. That was Smythe, who was replaced before the squad he'd assembled ever played a game in earnest. It seems that Hammond was uneasy about entrusting the valuable new franchise to an untested amateur, and one of the game's dominant figures, Lester Patrick, was just as available as the many men who had played with and for him in the West. The incident that triggered the change was typically trivial; it should probably be regarded not as the cause but the occasion of the shift. Ironically, it sent Smythe back to Toronto and initiated a far more dramatic hockey saga.

What happened was that Baby Dye was put up for sale by the St. Pats, with a fourteen-thousand-dollar price tag, and went to Chicago. Hammond was furious with Smythe, especially when he couldn't reach him by phone in Toronto. Smythe had taken his first evening off in weeks and gone to dinner and the movies with his wife, and when Hammond got through to him, Smythe proudly retorted that Dye was "not the type of player we need" and couldn't make his team. Hammond called Barney Stanley, the Hawk coach, who said Smythe must be crazy and that this proved how little he knew about hockey. Then came the crucial remark: "How can you keep him when Les Patrick is available?"

Hammond summoned Smythe to a meeting but Patrick was already in the picture by the time they met. Hammond paid off Smythe with $7,500, though Rickard later made it an even $10,000.

Smythe's judgment of the team he had put together as Rangers proved accurate almost at once, though Patrick's management should not be belittled. The original Rangers were together only two years, but in the second year they won the Stanley Cup. After five years, only five of them remained, and by the time they won their second Cup, in 1933, it was Patrick's Rangers who beat Smythe's Leafs, but the dominant force in that series was still the line of the Cook brothers and Boucher that Smythe had assembled.

The center was Frank Boucher, who had played under Frank Patrick for four years in Vancouver. His brother Bob had a season with the Canadiens in 1924; his brother Bill had seven NHL seasons, scoring twice for the Canadiens in a 1924 Cup game against Vancouver when Frank scored too; and his brother Buck had fifteen NHL seasons on his way to the Hall of Fame as a defenseman, having led Ottawa to the Cup in 1923. But Frank was the best of the brood, considered by many the greatest center ever.

Boucher was sold first to Boston from Vancouver in the 1926 reassignment of WHL players, and only then to the Rangers—a transaction that he himself learned a month after the fact. He had modeled his skating after Didier Pitre and his checking after Frank Nighbor, even using sixty-three–inch sticks for hook-checking and poke-checking. A 1925 rule put a limit of fifty-three inches on stick length, but Boucher's effectivness was not limited. With his intelligence, guile, and unselfishness, he was an ideal centerman for a line with great shooters on the wings and on a team that was to develop a wide-open style of offense. With an almost uncanny ability to handle an upright puck on his stick and to use a flip pass, he was a perfect match for the brothers Cook, who had come over from Saskatoon, where they had benefited from Newsy Lalonde's coaching.

Bill Cook was a big, strong skater and a deceptive stickhandler, but best of all an accurate shooter who could either fire away quickly or delay until a goalie had made a move and left an opening. He has been rated with Richard and Howe among the greatest right wings ever. Brother Bun (for Frederick) at left wing was the one who kept them moving and kept them laughing, and he is given by most the dubious distinction of having invented the slapshot. Together, they blended into a line of checkerboard passers, a cohesive unit with great speed.

They skated together for ten years and made the playoffs in the first nine. When Mac and Neil Colville and Alex Shibicky took over as first line for the Rangers, it was their combined speed alone that earned comparison with the Cooks and Boucher. One of their innovations was the drop pass, a dangerous maneuver unless linemates have complete confidence in each other's position. Before practice once, Bun suggested a variation of the play—a drop pass followed by a screened shot through the legs of the passer. Boucher thought it was a good idea, and they went out to try it on the ice. When the opportunity came, Bun took the puck across the line, dropped the pass to Boucher, and continued toward the goal with his legs spread. But just as Boucher was about to shoot, he looked up to see Bun's head looking back at him upside-down through his legs. He just wanted to see the play work, Bun said. But the line never tried it again. One season Bun was in a terrible shooting slump, every shot going high for inexplicable reasons. The slump ended in Duquesne Gardens in Pittsburgh, where Bun finally knocked out the red goal light, and then he went back to aiming at the nets.

The Cook line scored the first Ranger goal in the Garden against the Maroons (Nels Stewart, Babe Siebert, Bill Phillips, Reg Noble, Dunc Munro, and Clint Benedict). It came at 18:37 of the second period, the only goal of the game, a flip shot by Bill on a pass from Bun. The sports headline for the *Times* that day, November 16, 1926, was the AAU approval of Charley Paddock's 9.5-second record in the one-hundred-yard dash, but a crowd of 13,000 turned out for the charity hockey game. As described by Seabury Lawrence in the *Times*, the game they saw was distinguished by a record number of penalties, referee Lou Marsh using a dinner bell instead of a whistle and apparently enjoying its sound, and also by the play of a goalie named "Shobotsky." The Rangers went on to a successful first season, winning the American Division, only to lose to the second-place Bruins in the Cup semis.

In 1928, however, that result was reversed, in part because the Ranger defense, particularly Ching Johnson and Taffy Abel, played up to the level of their forwards. American-born, 250-pound Abel concentrated on defense but avoided penalty minutes. The veteran Johnson had his greatest-scoring and most-penalized season but played every minute that he wasn't in the penalty box. Ching's involvement with hockey is symbolized by an Eastern Hockey League incident where he was officiating at age fifty. When a Washington Lion player broke in alone on the New York Rover goal, linesman Johnson reverted to defenseman Johnson and nailed him with a crunching body-check. "Instinct, I guess," was what the retiring official said, and it was with that same instinct that he scored a goal in his first season while out on his feet.

Bill Cook lost his goals and points leadership to Morenz in 1928, but Boucher won the first of his seven Byng Trophies (including four in a row). In the American Division the Bruins won twenty games with Winkler in the nets, while the Rangers, Pirates, and Cougars won nineteen each. During early February the Rangers went 341 minutes and 42 seconds, including four full games, without scoring a goal, then turned around to shut out four straight opponents, Chabot going through a 297-minute-42-second-stretch without allowing a goal. Ties put Detroit out of the playoffs, Pittsburgh in third place, and New York in second behind Boston, though the Rangers were the most prolific scorers in the division. By Pittsburgh's choice, both games of the first round were played in New York, the Rangers winning by a total of six goals to four after a 4–0 shutout in the first game.

After a 1–1 tie with the Bruins, the Rangers disappointed Boston's expectations of a second try at the Cup with a 4–1 win on the same day that the Maroons upset Les Canadiens and Vezina-winner George Hainsworth in Montreal. Unfortunately for the Rangers, the circus was booked into Madison Square Garden and hockey was locked out, so they faced the unlikely prospect of beating Montreal with every game played on Maroon ice. The opening game held no surprises, Dutton and Phillips beating Chabot while Benedict shut out the Rangers, but the second game provided one of hockey's most dramatic incidents.

The first period was scoreless. At the four-minute mark of the second period, Nels Stewart broke free for an open shot on Chabot, but it caught him in the eye, knocking him out not just for the moment but for the series. Patrick sent word to Maroon manager Eddie Gerard that he would like to substitute Alex Connell, the Ottawa goalie, who was in the stands. He expected no problem, since such courtesies were customary, and especially since he had allowed Gerard himself to substitute for the Toronto St. Patricks in the 1922 Cup finals against Patrick's Vancouver team. But Gerard's response was, "Hell no, you can't use Connell."

Assuming that Gerard just didn't want to go against one of the game's greatest goalies, Patrick then requested Hugh McCormick of the London, Ontario, team in the Canadian Professional League, who was also in the stands. Gerard sent Patrick into a rage with his answer: "Forget it. Play goal yourself." The Maroons had carried a spare goalie all season and weren't about to let the Rangers off easy. In the dressing room, Frank Boucher suggested that the silver-haired forty-five-year-old manager accept Gerard's challenge, and Patrick said finally, "I will, by God, I will." He put on Chabot's equipment, asked Odie Cleghorn, now the Pittsburgh coach, to take over for him behind the bench, and went into the nets.

The Rangers went out to protect their leader, playing aggressive, checking defense throughout the second period, though Patrick was called on to make scrambling saves against Russ Oatman, Bill Phillips, Jimmy Ward, and Babe Siebert. The game remained scoreless. As the third period started, the inspired Rangers managed to score. Bill Cook split Dutton and Munro and got the puck past Benedict. Then they went into a defensive shell, but at 14:20 Stewart trickled a long shot through the tiring Patrick's legs. In the overtime, the Rangers went on the attack, figuring that the longer the game went on the more vulnerable Lester would be. At seven minutes, Ching Johnson went behind the Maroon cage, wrestled the puck away from Benedict, who was trying to cover it, and passed to Boucher in front of the goal. Frank sent it home before Benedict could recover. Patrick was carried off the Forum ice by the happy Rangers while the Montreal fans gave him a standing ovation.

With President Calder mediating, the Maroon management agreed to let Joe Miller, the Amerks' goalie, substitute for Chabot. Miller was known as "Red Light" in the Garden, with the second worst goals-against average in the league, but perhaps he too was inspired by Lester's performance. Stewart and Siebert beat him as Benedict recorded a second shutout in the next game. But once again the Rangers came back. In Game 4 it was Miller who got the shutout while Boucher's second-period goal won it.

In the final game, skating short-handed toward the end of the first period, the Rangers had Boucher carom a face-off past Munro, deke Dutton out, and beat the left-handed Benedict on his left side. With only five minutes left in the game he repeated the maneuver, and though Phillips later scored on a pass from Siebert, the Rangers were on their way home with the Stanley Cup.

The championship was a great personal triumph for Patrick but hardly the watershed of his career. When called to the Rangers he had already accomplished much in hockey and was ready to retire to California after the demise of his western league. Then for thirteen years he coached the Blueshirts, earning the respect of the hockey world for his leadership and of his players for his comradeship—in strong contrast to the martinet Conn Smythe. In the first eight seasons of all-star teams selections, 1931–1938, Patrick was named as coach seven times. He was succeeded as coach by Frank Boucher, but continued to manage the team until 1946, when he became a vice president.

In the four seasons 1929 through 1932 the Rangers finished second, third, third, and first in the American Division. They made the playoffs each year, losing to Boston in the finals, to the Canadiens in the semis, to the Black Hawks in the semis, and to the Maple Leafs in the finals. Boucher won the Byng in the first three seasons and led in assists in the first two. Meanwhile Patrick was developing a solid farm system, which was to produce Davey Kerr, Art Coulter, Babe Pratt, Alex Shibicky, the Colville brothers, and his son Muzz. By the time they won their second Cup in 1933, only Boucher, the Cooks, Johnson, and Murray Murdoch remained of the original Rangers. Murdoch was the iron man of the squad: over eleven seasons he played 508 league games and 55 playoff games.

They also developed a legion of loyal fans, beginning in this golden age of sport, including the Duke and Duchess of Windsor, Humphrey Bogart, and Lucy and Desi. Boucher remembers his wife getting all excited about sitting near George Raft and Jack LaRue, when Raft turned around and recognized him, saying, "Say, ain't you Bushy?" The Rangers of this era, under Patrick's indulgent management, were a colorful group with great appeal for the crowds. They partied as they played, in wide-open style, and it was a rare losing streak that would make captain Bill Cook announce that they were all on the wagon until they won.

Of the original goalies, Winkler went early to Boston, and then Chabot to Toronto. John Ross Roach was in goal for four years, but Patrick unloaded him after the Stanley Cup fiasco of 1932. Andy Aitkenhead, the Glasgow Gobbler, was his replacement, and a Cup-champion goalkeeper in 1933. Earl Seibert and Ott Heller had been obtained from Ottawa in a trade for Leo Bourgault, and Babe Siebert, Art Somers, and Cecil Dillon from the Maroons. Butch Keeling was another notable addition, despite a memorable incident in Patrick's railroad compartment after a party in Hull, following a game in Ottawa. Patrick awoke to the sound and sight of Keeling pissing on the floor, and he shouted, "Butch, Butch, what the devil are you doing?" Keeling put his finger to his lips and said, "Shh, don't wake Lester." The next day Patrick asked Boucher if he knew that Keeling was a sleepwalker.

The heart of the team, however, was still the Cooks and Boucher. Though

Checking Back

the Rangers finished only third in the four-team division in 1933, they led all teams in scoring. Bill Cook was the goal and points leader and Boucher the assist leader. The format for the playoffs had been altered for this season. The two first-place finishers were to play each other three out of five, the winner to play for the Cup against the winner of a four-team tournament (second-place finishers and third-place finishers to play two-game series, total goals to count). The Rangers beat the Canadiens, 5–2, 3–3; the Detroit Falcons beat the Maroons, 2–0, 3–2; and the Rangers beat the Falcons, 2–0, 4–3. Then they waited for Toronto and Boston to finish their series.

The Bruins had won the first game, 2–1, on a Marty Barry goal at 14:14 of overtime; the Leafs the second on a Busher Jackson goal at 15:03 of overtime; Boston the third, 2–1, on an Eddie Shore goal at 4:23 of overtime; and Toronto the fourth, 5–3, in the only game decided in sixty minutes of play. The fifth game was a defensive marathon. Through four overtime periods there were no goals. Calder suggested a coin toss to decide the winner, but the Leafs' fans wouldn't tolerate what the players were willing to accept. It was two in the morning and almost five minutes into the sixth overtime period (104:46) when Ken Doraty put the puck past Tiny Thompson. Eighteen hours later the Leafs were on Madison Square Gerden ice to face the rested Rangers.

It was to be the only Cup game in New York because the circus was due to parade into the Garden, and the Rangers made the best of it. Bun Cook scored first on assists from Boucher and brother Bill, and New York went on to win, 5–1, Dillon scoring twice and feeding Murdoch once. Four days later in Toronto, the Leafs still looked tired. Doraty scored first for them, but goals by Heller, Bill Cook, and Siebert beat them, 3–1. They recovered by the third game to win, 3–2, and then held the Rangers scoreless through three periods of the fourth game but failed to score themselves. In the overtime, Ching Johnson was in the penalty box for raising his hand above his shoulder, a rule that was in effect only that one year. Then Clancy went off for the same offense, and with the Leafs skating three against four, Bill Cook took a pass from Keeling to win the Cup at 7:34, beating Chabot—who never had to be called Shobotsky in Toronto.

9

The Forward Pass and the Surging Shore

The process that began in 1907, and came into the NHL in 1920 with the rule allowing goaltenders to pass the puck forward in the defending zone, was completed in 1929, the year that the Boston Bruins won their first Stanley Cup. In that year, forward passing was permitted in all zones. The previous season, forward passing had been allowed in defending and center zones. The emphasis on speed in the game was increased, at the same time that goalies' pads were trimmed from twelve to ten inches across. The NHL had thus substantially altered the on-sides nature of the game—at its basic level designed for players—to a wide-open game that would please spectators even more.

Many of hockey's most influential leaders—Eddie Gerard, Frank Calder, Conn Smythe, and Art Ross—preached primarily the text of speed. The new rules made these preachers seem like prophets, though their influence upon the rules themselves made it a self-fulfilling prophecy. The forward pass changed styles of play by bringing up the defense, by creating a situation where five men in the attacking zone is fundamentally sound on offense and where the defense can be sound only to the degree of speed in effective forechecking and backchecking when the puck changes hands.

Given the new style and new emphasis on speed, the new freedom of substitution brought about a growth in squads from eight or nine skaters to fifteen. The idea was developed by Odie Cleghorn of Pittsburgh and Dick Irvin of Chicago: three fast lines skated in short shifts with roughly equal time, and two pairs of defensemen alternated. But the increased speed did not mean a decrease in hitting, as is clear in the ascendancy of the Bruins at the precise time that forward passing was opened up.

Boston hockey may be epitomized in a number of incidents and characters, but in general the Bruins (like the Maroons) seemed to specialize in big, battering players. Yet at the same time, their first championship team developed, in Red Dutton's words, a "set attack and fixed set of plays . . . the greatest passing combination ever in modern NHL . . . a group of men which for short accurate passing was nothing short of brilliant."

Checking Back

The finesse implicit in Dutton's praise would seem to have been out of place in Boston. The Boston Arena was the place where, in the Bruins' first season, a fan threw a monkey wrench on the ice, just missing Charlie Querrie on the Toronto bench. Querrie had it silver-plated, inserted a clock, and presented the appropriate symbol to Art Ross. And Boston Garden, when it opened in 1928, was where the fans staged a riot—in contrast to the black-tie opening in New York's Garden. There simply weren't enough seats, even though 17,500 got in (3,000 more than capacity) to see the Canadiens beat the Bruins, 1–0, on Sylvio Mantha's goal and Hainsworth's shutout.

Charles Adams's choice of Art Ross to run his team was indicative of the kind of hockey the Bruins were to play. A rugged defenseman himself over fourteen seasons with Westmount, Brandon, Kenora, Haileybury, the Wanderers, and Ottawa, Ross was even a fighter as an official. Cooper Smeaton remembers a night in Toronto when Ross and Minnie McGiffen were arrested for assaulting each other during a game and how he himself had to take on a fan who accused him of holding McGiffen so Ross could hit him. Ross skated at 190 pounds, and skated hard, most notably in tandem with Sprague Cleghorn for Montreal.

In 1907 Ross, borrowed from Brandon, had helped the Kenora Thistles win the Stanley Cup from the Wanderers, but when Montreal regained it two months later Ross was not allowed to play. By the 1908 season he was in the Wanderers' uniform, scoring eight goals in ten games for the ECAHA champions, and scoring four times in five Cup games while getting his name inscribed a second time. Twice more he played for Cup challengers but never won again as a player. His best scoring year was 1912 for the Wanderers, sixteen goals in eighteen games, but he was such a complete player that in 1914 when Montreal had goaltending problems, Ross began to practice in the nets. Moving over to Ottawa in 1915 he beat out Hamby Shore for a starting position but was back in Montreal in 1917 for his last two seasons.

As a manager Ross was a surprising choice. He had long been a management foe, threatening from time to time to organize a players' union or a league that players would control, and as playing manager he had been unsuccessful at Haileybury back in 1910. Yet he was Adams's choice, manager and coach for the Bruins and governor on the NHL board. His players, mostly PCHA and WCHL veterans, had a dismal first year, finishing a distant last and unable to find a goalie. They improved to fourth in 1926, mainly because of improved defense with Sprague Cleghorn, bought for five thousand dollars from the Canadiens, and Lionel Hitchman. But the big change came in the following year. His name was Eddie Shore, the embodiment of Art Ross's idea of a hockey player—only better than Ross had ever been himself.

Shore was called the Babe Ruth of hockey, but he was also compared with

Ty Cobb for his ability to arouse hatred in opponents and for the competitiveness that drove him to win over anyone in his way. For more than thirteen seasons he was the soul of the Bruins. He came to Boston in a seven-man CARE package from the West, for fifty thousand dollars, including Duke Keats and Frank Boucher. Boucher, of course, was dealt to the Rangers before the season began, and Keats ended the year in Detroit, but the rest became the nucleus of the team that finished first in the American Division's first year of play, only to lose in the playoffs to the Rangers.

The following season was the first year of unlimited forward passing in all zones and the first Stanley Cup for the Bruins. The new rules were supposed to increase offense, but it turned out to be the year of the goalies (though it is no doubt coincidental that it was the second year of the new goal nets, designed by none other than Art Ross). In Montreal, Canadien Hainsworth recorded twenty-two shutouts in forty-four games, allowing a total of 43 goals against for a 0.98 average. In New York, the Amerks' Roy Worters won the Hart Trophy (MVP) with a 1.2 average, and in Boston, the Bruins were the only team in the league to average more than 2 goals a game. The ultimate difference in the Bruins' success was the debut of Tiny Thompson, who was soon being acclaimed as the greatest goalie in the game. His rookie year produced a 1.2 average, a league title, and a Stanley Cup.

Thompson's brother Paul was a reserve on the Cup-holding Rangers but eventually was sent to Chicago in 1931 because he wanted more ice time—a cry that became more and more commonplace with the larger squads but was not heard from goaltenders for another three decades. Tiny's defense had veterans Cy Denneny in his last NHL season and Hitchman, young George Owen, and Shore. Veteran Bill Coutu, who was supposed to be a defensive mainstay, had been knocked and skated off the team by Shore's performance in training camp before the 1927 season, though the clash almost cost Shore an ear. As forwards, Ross had assembled a flashy new unit, the "Dynamite Line" of Cooney Weiland, Dit Clapper, and Dutch Gainor, with Harry Oliver and Perc Galbraith as the main reserves.

The playoff rules were changed because neither first-place finisher in 1928 had been around for the Cup finals. This time the Bruins played the Canadiens in a best-three-of-five series. Boston won three straight, Thompson shutting out the Habs twice, while Hainsworth, allowing only four goals in three games, couldn't get a win. In the other playoffs, Toronto beat Detroit, and the Rangers beat the Americans (Worters was superb, Roach perfect, as the only goal in two games was scored by Keeling at 29:50 of overtime) and then Toronto (Boucher scoring the winning goal at 2:03 of overtime), to set up the first Stanley Cup finals between United States teams. Clapper and Gainor scored in the first game in Boston, Oliver and Bill Carson in the second in

Checking Back

New York, where Keeling got the only Ranger goal of the series. Boston had put down the upstart New Yorkers and were the NHL champions five years after they had brought the United States into the league.

In the 1930 season, for the only time in its history, the NHL failed to resist the pinball-machine syndrome that has afflicted most other major team sports besides soccer. It deliberately tried to increase scoring. The forward-passing rules of 1929 had seemingly had the opposite effect, so the new season started with players allowed to cross the blue line before the puck. The puck-carrier, once across the line, could then pass ahead to goalhangers. The goals-per-game average suddenly was more than double the previous season. The chief beneficiary was Boston, where Weiland was getting at least a goal a game. The off-sides rule was reinstated in midseason, but at the season's end Weiland had forty-three goals and thirty assists, Clapper another forty-one goals, both benefitting from Gainer's stick-handling.

The Bruins scored 179 goals, 38 more than the Maroons. With Thompson's 2.2 winning the Vezina by a wide margin over Chicago's Chuck Gardiner, Hainsworth, Benedict (who used a mask for a while after breaking his nose), Connell, and Chabot, Boston's amazing record of thirty-eight wins, five losses, and one tie is understandable. They went fourteen games without a loss and then twenty-three games without a loss. Again the Bruins won the championship series, three to one over the Maroons, but this time, when the Canadiens beat Chicago and the Rangers to qualify, the Cup was returned to Montreal in a two-game series, 3–0 and 4–3, dominated by Morenz.

Boston's regular-season record fluctuated radically after this—first in 1931, last in 1932, first in 1933, last in 1934, first in 1935, second in 1936 and 1937, and first in 1938. But their playoff record was consistent. When they qualified, they failed to win a single series in those eight years. Frank Patrick replaced Ross as coach for two years, but it didn't help. Thompson won the Vezina in 1933, 1936, and 1938, but it didn't help. Shore won the Hart in 1935, 1936, and 1938, but it didn't help. The Bruins had become a team for all seasons but postseasons. When they broke that jinx in 1939, the team had been totally remade, if not reformed. From the 1929 Cup-winners, Clapper and Weiland remained, Dit as defenseman-policeman and Cooney strictly as a reserve, while only Shore played on in his accustomed role.

Eddie Shore's career as a player was marked by incidents, anecdotes, and exploits that made him a legendary rogue hero. Fischler has named him to his all-time dirtiest-toughest team, yet few but the most diehard modernists fail to put him among the all-time greatest defensemen. He is said to have earned 978 stitches on 80 wounds in his nineteen years of hockey, not to mention a nose broken fourteen times and a jaw fractured five times. He is also said to have backed down from a fight only once, when King Clancy, with whom he'd had many a scuffle, had checked him into the boards one night. Shore bounced back automatically with a mitt raised in anger, but Clancy grabbed it and pumped it up and down, saying, "Hello, Eddie, and how are you tonight?" Another set of reflexes took over. Shore mumbled, "I'm pretty good and how are you?" Clancy had blarneyed his way out of another licking.

Of the many Shore stories, a few must be told here about the four-time MVP, seven-time first all-star. Colonel Hammond tried to buy him once for five thousand dollars and a second-string player. Charles Adams wired back his answer: YOU ARE SO FAR FROM SHORE YOU NEED A LIFE PRESERVER. Shore himself needed a life preserver, so eagerly did he seem to provoke disaster. On home ice he skated through the warmups with a flowing gold cape. Disdaining the puck, he glided regally around the rink with his long stride while fans cheered and fanatic enemies snarled. Once play started, there was the constant expectation of a clash, a brawl, an open wound, or at least a penalty. But the game was also distinguished by his patented offense. He would carry the puck himself into the attacking zone, shoot it off the end boards, fight the opposing defensemen for possession, and pass to one of his forwards in position for a shot on goal.

Shore thrived on feuds, often forcing opposing stars to concentrate on him first and the game second. Canadien Babe Siebert was one regular opponent. In 1928, just before the end of a game, Siebert caught Shore's already bloodied face with his stick. Shore hit the ice and was unconscious for fifteen minutes. He suffered a broken nose, three cracked teeth, and two black eyes along with the concussion. But the next night he was back on the ice for another hockey game.

An even better demonstration of his compulsive drive to play took place the following season. Shore's cab was held up by a traffic accident, and the train to Montreal left as Shore was running down the platform hoping to jump on the last car. The next train wouldn't get to Montreal until after game time, and all air travel was canceled because of a sleet storm, but a friend offered the use of limousine and chauffeur. They left Boston at 11:30 P.M., driving through the January storm very slowly, but still skidding. Shore took the wheel himself, had tire chains put on at a service station, and drove on through New Hampshire. The blizzard blocked his vision and froze the wiper blades, so Shore removed the top half of the windshield. At 5:00 A.M. he had to get a new set of chains at a construction camp.

By 3:00 P.M., Shore turned the wheel back over the the chauffeur and tried to catch a nap, but as soon as he closed his eyes the big car skidded into a ditch. Shore hiked a mile to hire a team of horses from a farmer and finally had the car pulled back onto the road. At 5:30 he staggered into the lobby of the Windsor Hotel, eyes bloodshot, face frostbitten and windburned, fingers stiff

Checking Back

as claws, "in no condition for hockey," according to Ross. Shore ate a steak dinner and decided to nap briefly before the game. After an hour, Clapper and Weiland couldn't wake him until they splashed water in his face.

Shore demanded to play. Almost himself, he cross-checked Hooley Smith to the ice for the game's first penalty, and the two-minute rest apparently helped. In the second period, he scored on a rink-long solo dash. In the third he drew another minor penalty but played the rest of the game without substitution. The Maroons, beaten 1–0 by a shorthanded Bruin team, had been stranded by the archetypally rough Shore.

In April 1933 Shore was a crucial figure in one of hockey's most famous games, but this time in the unusual role of goat. It was the deciding game of the Stanley Cup semifinals against Toronto. The exhausted teams had played scorelessly through the game and five overtime periods. Four minutes into the sixth overtime, Shore, who had played most of the 164 minutes, delayed a pass to Joe Lamb in order to bring about a face-off for the deliberate off-sides so that there could be a line change. But Andy Blair anticipated the play, intercepted the puck, and passed to Ken Doraty, who scored at 4:47. Thompson and Chabot between them had stopped more than two hundred shots, and referee Odie Cleghorn had waved off three apparent goals earlier, before this one ended the game—at Shore's expense more than Thompson's.

Shore brooded about this bitter loss, and the bitter rivalry between Boston and Toronto was fueled by the on-going feud between their antipathetic bosses, Ross and Smythe. The following season Shore started very slowly, delayed by a contract dispute and poor training, but an impending visit of the Maple Leafs to Boston Garden on December 12 caused him to announce that he had decided to go back to work in earnest. Ahead early in the game but short-handed because of penalties to Blair and Hap Day, Toronto was trying to kill the time with Red Horner and Clancy on defense and Ace Bailey performing his specialty of ragging the puck. After over a minute, Bailey shot the puck down the ice, and Shore came roaring back with it.

The rush was stopped by Clancy (though some reporters credit a board check by Horner) as the King tapped the front of Shore's skates with his stick so that the Bruin defenseman dropped to his knees and slid ten feet along the ice. By the time he got up, Clancy was already up ice with the puck, and Horner and Bailey were at the Toronto blue line. Probably mistaking him for Clancy because they had exchanged positions in the play, Shore hit Bailey at full speed, catching him across the kidneys with his shoulder and sending him to the ice in a backward somersault.

Bailey lay on the line with his head turned sideways, his legs twitching. Horner tried in vain to straighten his head and then headed for Shore, saying, "Why the hell did you do that?" Shore's smile brought a right uppercut from

Horner that knocked him flat, cracked his head, with blood pooling out in a three-foot halo. Charlie Conacher joined Horner to hold off the gathering Bruins, but the apparent severity of the injuries seemed to take the fight out of everyone else. Shore was soon back on his feet and the ice, but Bailey hovered near death for eight days, his skull fractured and his brain hemorrhaging. Two operations pulled him through.

In February the first NHL all-star game was played, a benefit for Ace Bailey whose playing days were over. The crowd held its breath as Shore was introduced and skated over to Bailey, who was dressed in a long overcoat and dark glasses, a steel plate in his head. They shook hands as the crowd cheered, but the meaningful scene had been acted out in the dressing room the night of the accident. Shore had come in to say "I'm sorry, Ace. I didn't mean to hurt you." And Bailey, eyes glazed and complexion gray, had managed to answer, "That's all right, Eddie. It's all part of the game."

Shore kept right on fighting. In the 1939 playoffs with the Rangers, he tangled with Phil Watson, catching his neck with his stick. Murray Patrick went after him, Shore swung at Muzz, but the former Canadian heavyweight champion took him out with a combination that squashed his face. That was Shore's last full season with Boston. He bought the American Hockey League's Springfield Indians, ran them as playing manager, and played home games for the Bruins. But Ross then sold him to the New York Americans and he helped the Amerks into the playoffs. On six consecutive nights he played six games, three in each league.

Memories of the Ace Bailey incident probably kept Shore from being a charter member of the Hall of Fame in 1947, but a year later his undeniable qualifications as a player were duly honored. When he sold the Indians to Jack Kent Cooke after twenty-five years, his $42,000 investment was worth a cool $1,000,000. He had run his team as he had played the game, with a vengeance, and whatever the consequences in terms other than pragmatic, that way had paid off. It is the kind of hard-nosed integrity that may tell us more about hockey than anything else.

10

Conn's Games and Gardens

When Colonel Hammond decided that the valuable group of hockey players assembled by Conn Smythe had better be turned over to someone else to manage and coach, he inadvertently set off a chain of events that would make Smythe one of the most important forces in the NHL for four decades. To say that he *changed* the character of the league would be misleading, because in many ways Conn Smythe typified the league. He was a sportsman and a gambler. Next to hockey he loved horses, and when football offered a sporting proposition he loved football too.

His attitude toward players was that of a rigid authoritarian, and his manner in general that of a martinet. The chain of command led directly to him, and it seemed that he could never tolerate even the possibility of insubordination. Perhaps that was why he made a practice of dealing off established stars and bringing up promising young players. And he coined the line that has been taken as the unofficial motto of the National Hockey League: "If you can't beat them outside in the alley, you can't beat them inside on the ice."

Yet it would be wrong to say that Conn Smythe was typical. He was, if anything, singular. His single-minded determination was so apparent as to appear obsessive or compulsive. He took calculated dares, and rarely did his combination of shrewdness and boldness let him down. So forceful an antagonist was Smythe that he provoked polarized relationships with players and managers and whole organizations, and so determined an antagonist was he that any squabble was likely to become an enduring feud.

Frank Selke, in his autobiographical *Behind the Cheering,* remembers first encountering Smythe in 1914 as captain of the University of Toronto Varsity Juniors: "He was good, and . . . he knew he was good." But a year later it took Selke's brother-in-law, featherweight boxer Bert Ayerst, to pinpoint the significant quality in a prophetic remark: "Smythe is the brains of his Toronto team. When he's out of the lineup, they're all disorganized."

In 1916, a twenty-year-old junior officer in the Fortieth Battery, Conn Smythe organized and managed a team entered in the Senior Series of the

Ontario Hockey Association. The other managers felt they had duped him into accepting the first four games of the season as his home games, because games after New Year's were always better attended. But patriotic Toronto fans sold out the arena for all the games of the Battery team. The day before the fourth home game, Smythe learned that the unit was going overseas in a few days. He then checked the Battery treasury and bet the whole, almost seven thousand dollars, on his team against the Toronto Argonauts. With more than their honor riding on the game, the Battery team upset the Argos by several goals. The whole unit celebrated the Christmas season sumptuously with its enriched treasury, and they went overseas soon after, leaving the other managers with open dates on their home ice.

Overseas, Smythe won the Military Cross, transferred to the Royal Flying Corps, and was shot down on a reconnaissance flight. He was a prisoner of war for fourteen months, attempted twice to escape from the Germans, did some time in solitary confinement, and played so much bridge that he'd never play again. But those adventures were merely incidental interruptions of his hockey career, and he returned from the war to coach the varsity teams at the University of Toronto, while also succeeding in a sand-and-gravel business. His Senior team, the Varsity Grads, won the Allen Cup in 1926, and went on to the Olympic championship, but without Conn, who was busy elsewhere. Meanwhile, he had also backed Selke's reorganization of the Marlboro Club in the Juniors.

The amateur championship of 1926 marked Smythe's triumphal departure into professional hockey. His brief tenure with the Rangers was conspicuously successful, as has been described above, but it was his summary dismissal that determined his future course. He set his spirit on two goals: to succeed as a coach-manager in the NHL and to insure his position by being responsible to no one. Given the conditions in hockey at the time and the nature of the man, the target was obvious: the St. Patricks of Toronto, where amateur hockey continued to dominate public attention while the NHL was dominant wherever else it played.

Smythe was in Madison Square Garden for the Rangers' opening game against the Maroons. When Tex Rickard asked him if the new team could hold the champions down, Smythe said, "*Hold* them? You'll beat them." That accurate prediction reportedly brought an offer—or perhaps a facetious remark- —from Rickard for Smythe to be vice president in charge of hockey at the Garden. Smythe grandly indicated that he would never work for an outfit that had short-changed him $2,500 for his efforts. Rickard took him to Hammond's office and, when the details of the original agreement had been rehearsed, ordered Hammond to give him a check for $2,500.

The satisfaction of having his contract fulfilled neither brought Smythe back

Checking Back

into the Ranger fold nor endeared Colonel Hammond to him. Yet he maintained a partiality to the first professional team he had assembled. During the famous playoff game when Chabot had to be replaced in the Ranger goal, Conn Smythe was among the well-wishers in the dressing room. Frank Boucher remembers him waving his arms, shouting, marching around, and finally bellowing, "Hang the nets on me and I'll go in there." Boucher assumes he meant "pads" instead of "nets" and supposes that he was "moved up a couple of lengths." Presumably that was a natural high, since Smythe was a teetotaler.

That $2,500 settlement, however, was more significant as a beginning than as an end. It has been widely reported that Smythe bet the money on a hockey game in Montreal and then parleyed his winnings on a St. Patricks–Ottawa Senators game in Toronto. One writer, trying to corroborate the story, found no game in Toronto that suited the details and changed the opposition to the Rangers. It is not hard to see how these distortions came into wide currency, and it must be remembered that it was a time when sports and sportsmen and wagers were closely and commonly associated, a time before the hypocritical separation of betting and athletics, a time when the gambling action was openly and straightforwardly reported in the press.

The case was this. When he received his settlement from the Rangers, Smythe took a train to Montreal and bet all the money on a *football* game, backing the underdog University of Toronto team against the McGill Red team in the semifinals of the Intercollegiate Football Union championships. When Toronto won, 12–2, Smythe took his winnings and parleyed them two weeks later on Toronto against Ottawa for the Dominion football title. Toronto had shut out Queens for the intercollegiate championship, but they were still underdogs when they beat Ottawa, 10–7. Now, with almost $20,000, Smythe was in a position to deal. He formed a company that included broker Peter Campbell and mining millionaire J. P. Bickell, who already owned stock in the team, and they bought the St. Pats for $160,000. On February 14, 1927, Smythe took over the team, changed the name to Maple Leafs, and began the process that was to give Toronto an NHL winner. Meanwhile, Babe Dye, the player whose value Smythe and Hammond had disputed, was sidelined first with a bad back and later with a broken leg. He played only one more game in the NHL.

The first game Toronto played as the Maple Leafs was significant less for the fact that they beat the Amerks than for Smythe's first move: switching Hap Day to defense. It was the first of so many moves that Smythe came to be known as the "David Harum of hockey." While he had taken just a matter of weeks to put the Rangers together, he built carefully for the future in assembling his own Maple Leafs. He was determined to build a team better than the Rangers, he wanted to establish a dynasty, and he didn't mind taking five years to do it. But he also intended to build box-office appeal, and so he dealt for youth and speed and excitement. He wanted what he called "sportsman players" and not those like Babe Dye, whom he had called "more like a union man than a sportsman."

Toronto was last in the NHL in 1927. By 1932 they had won the Stanley Cup. Crucial to this development was Smythe's relationship with Frank Selke, who encouraged the concept of putting young skaters on the ice, particularly those developed by Selke's Marlboro Club. Joe Primeau was the first. Originally slated for the Rangers, he loyally refused to sign with them after Hammond fired Smythe. By the time the Leafs were rebuilt around the young centerman, only Day and Ace Bailey remained from the St. Pats.

The Leafs improved to 18–18–8 in 1928 but failed to make the playoffs. For the following season, Smythe took over as coach as well as manager. He hired Selke as his assistant in charge of scouting, publicity, and programs. That season they brought up Red Horner for the defense and signed center Andy Blair from St. John's College in Winnipeg. They bought Baldy Cotton from Pittsburgh, and they traded Roach and Keeling to the Ranger for Chabot and right wing Alex Gray. For a rebuilding year, it was a rewarding one. The Leafs broke the Bruins' thirteen-game unbeaten streak in Boston, then the Canadiens' seventeen-game unbeaten streak in Toronto. Bailey led the league in scoring, and the third-place finish put them in the playoffs for the first time under Smythe. After beating Detroit, they were eliminated by the Rangers, a bitter loss for Conn Smythe.

The 1930 season brought Busher Jackson and Charlie Conacher up from the Marlboros, but the Leafs were still weak on defense and missed the playoffs one more time. The building process, though not the wheeling and dealing, was completed the following year when Smythe bought Clancy from Ottawa. But for the purposes of this chapter and from the point of view of historical landmarks, a much more important building process took place in the years 1929–1931.

Smythe had an NHL team, and he made it attractive to the hockey fans of Toronto, but he had only the eight-thousand-seat Mutual Street Arena to put them in. He dreamed of a new capital building for hockey, and he even worked out an agreement for Foster Hewitt, whose play-by-play descriptions had brought a new dimension to Canadian hockey fandom, to broadcast from a building that hadn't been started. The Wall Street crash and subsequent depression could not stop Conn Smythe. Hewitt and Selke helped promote the project, along with businessmen Larkin Maloney, Alfred Rogers,

Checking Back

W. A. H. MacBrien, J. P. Bickell, and Ed Bickle. When J. J. Vaughan of T. Eaton and Company cleared the real estate deal with Bickle and also bought stock in the project, they were well under way.

The cost was to be $1,500,000, but for all the bandwagon effect the group came up $200,000 short. What made it possible to complete the actual construction was Selke's successful idea: persuade the Allied Building and Trades Council of Toronto to permit the workers (who would otherwise be unemployed) to take 20 percent of their pay in Maple Leaf Gardens stock. The economics made sense, even if Smythe was later to buy up most of these stocks for as little as twenty-five cents on the dollar as the Depression deepened for the hard-pressed laborers.

The backing of labor was won. The investment of Sir John Aird, President of the Canadian Bank of Commerce, led to other investing directors, and the Thomson Brothers construction firm went to work. On target in terms of schedule and the budget, Conn's Gardens opened for the start of the 1932 season. On November 12, 1931, the Maple Leafs entertained the Chicago Black Hawks before sixteen thousand well-dressed fans in a clean, well-lighted hockey palace with no smoking (Smythe abhorred the habit) and Foster Hewitt fifty-four feet above ice level in the broadcasting "gondola."

Throughout the Depression, Maple Leaf Gardens paid its bills and earned a modest profit. The team profited from the move, though not immediately. Chicago won that opening game, 3–1, and the Leafs lost the next five games as well. Under new coach Dick Irvin, however, they rounded into shape and started the second season in the Gardens in possession of the Stanley Cup, but that success story belongs in Chapter 12.

Perhaps Conn Smythe's most consistent success was at the game of feuding, and the most persistent of his feuds was the one with Art Ross. Selke describes them as natural antagonists in their great similarity: "Both were witty, sarcastic, and quick to anger; each had [great] courage; [and] both were extremely egotistical." They also had in common a fierce competitiveness and an uncommon capacity for doing whatever would get under each other's skin. Besides, they had the temperament to enjoy the feud and went out of their way to fuel it.

In Smythe's first year with the Leafs, the Bruins unloaded Sailor Herberts to them for eighteen thousand dollars, but Herberts had little future or value in the NHL. Conn had been conned and never forgot it. The Ross-Smythe feud flared up in angry words from time to time, and sometimes in practical jokes, but there were quite serious periods of deep contention. At one stretch, according to Leo Dandurand, they were silent for two years (twelve years according to more expansive legendmongers), which made league business difficult to transact at meetings of the board. One meeting was held shortly after one of Smythe's horses, Shoeless Joe, was found to be drugged after winning a race at Saratoga. Conn and his trainer were cleared in the investigation, but when Smythe sat down at the NHL governors' meeting, Art Ross said, "Mr. President, I insist that a saliva test of all those present be taken before proceeding any further with the business at hand."

Yet like most everything else in hockey, violence or the threat of violence was an overtone in the Ross-Smythe feud. Ross threw a punch at Smythe after a 3–3 tie in Boston and once planted a couple of longshoremen near Smythe's seat in Boston Garden. They played the role of thugs to the hilt, baiting the Leaf leader all through the game, but Conn guessed that Ross had staged the show and he never bit. In a similar incident in 1934, Selke happened to be sitting in the Boston Garden seat reserved for Smythe. An "elderly Italian" started slapping him with his program and then his big companion threw a punch. Selke fought back, got some help from companions, and welcomed the arrival of Boston's finest. He then learned that he had taken on Beano Breen, "the toughest gangster in New England," and his trigger man. When, years later, Breen was assassinated in Boston, Selke twitted Art Ross with the intriguing suggestion that the Leafs happened to have been in town that night.

The laughs and the enmity seemed to go hand in glove. Smythe took an ad in a Boston paper: "Attention Hockey Fans! If you're tired of seeing the kind of hockey the Boston Bruins are playing, come to the Garden tonight and see a real hockey club, the Toronto Maple Leafs." Instead of thanking Smythe for drawing the largest gate of the season, Ross tried to have the league fine him a thousand dollars. In response to Ross's unflattering remarks about Smythe's lack of class, Conn appeared at the Boston Garden for a game dressed in top hat and tails. He grandly presented a bouquet of roses to Clancey, who delivered them to Ross at the Bruin bench. Ross, recovering from rectal surgery, seemed pleased, though he could not translate the Latin inscription on the card. Equally grand, Art Ross presented the bouquet to a patrician lady in a box seat behind the bench. But she had enough classical training to get the message: "Here, take these roses and shove them."

11

To Habs and Hab-nots

One of the early nicknames of the Canadiens was "Habs" for *habitants,* indicating the basic idea of their conception—to have a French team promote rivalries in the league and in Montreal itself—and echoing the rallying cry, "Les Canadiens sont là." Many of the early stars of the team were indeed of French descent: Lalonde, Corbeau, Pitre, Berlinquette, Laviolette, Poulin, Vezina, Bill Boucher, Coutu, and Sylvio Mantha. Moreover, the team played with a style and a flair that seemed to typify the Gallic heritage: determined backchecking, sudden bursts of speed on attack, graceful and even acrobatic skating, and a fierce competitiveness that did not deteriorate or slow down into heavily physical play. Yet the one player who epitomized the great Canadien teams of 1930 and 1931 was the non-Frenchman, Howarth Morenz.

From the 1924 Stanley Cup winners, only Joliat and Mantha were on hand for the 1930 championship. Cecil Hart had taken over as coach, but Dandurand continued to manage. Dandurand had brought defenseman Mantha up in 1924 and five years later added his brother Leon-Georges to the roster. That was Morenz's rookie year, but a broken shoulder kept him out of the Cup playoffs. In the championship series with Ottawa, however, he had scored three of the Canadiens' five goals and assisted on a fourth. Joliat had come from Saskatoon in a trade for Lalonde (young Aurel beat veteran Newsy into the Hall of Fame by five years). Joliat and Mantha were still young, then, as they had to be to skate with the 1930 team regarded as one of the greatest of all. In the same era of fine Ranger, Bruin, Leaf, Maroon, and Black Hawk teams, the Canadiens won back-to-back Stanley Cup championships.

George Hainsworth was in goal and making some fans stop waxing nostalgic over Vezina. Hainsworth won the Vezina Trophy his first three seasons in the league, 1927–1929, recording 14, 13, and 22 shutouts in forty-four-game seasons. In eleven NHL seasons, his goals-against average was 2.02, with 0.98 in 1929. On defense Herb Gardiner, the great poke-checker who had won the Hart Trophy in 1927, was gone, but there were Sylvio Mantha, whose consistency led many to call him the league's best; Albert Battleship Leduc, who was famous for his body-checking and rink-long rushing; Marty Burke, whose solid play and stolid temperament made him a foil to his high-strung teammates; and a number of spares, including Gerald Carson, Albert McCaffrey, Art Lesieur, and Jean Baptiste Pusie. The latter was renowned as hockey's clown prince, but not much of a defenseman.

To consider briefly the performances that earned Pusie his reputation as a comedian is to gain some insight into the nature of the game and its players in the thirties. His first goal for the London Tecumsehs in the International League was on a hard shot that took the goalie's mitt into the net along with the puck. Pusie bowed to the goaltender and elaborately counted his fingers before restoring the glove. In his second home game he was awarded a penalty shot, stopped short of the line, skated in without his stick, shook hands with the goalie, returned to center ice, and scored on a mishit roller past the psyched-out goalie. Another time, alone on the blue line against a four-man rush, he dropped his stick, lifted his hands in surrender, and fell to his knees in supplication. The opponents scored anyway while the fans laughed, which is an apt summary of his career. He played few NHL games—for the Canadiens, Rangers, and Bruins—but left a legend for laughs with his clownish pantomimes and his one-liners delivered with a thick French-Canadian accent. He finished the thirties in the American Association, retired in 1942, and died of a heart attack in 1946 at forty-three.

The Canadien forwards, with one notable exception, were even more solidly French than the defensemen. They included the younger Mantha, Larochelle, Lepine, Mondou, and, starting in 1931, Jean Gagnon, skating on right wing on the line with Morenz centering for Joliat. That first line, of course, was the heart of the team that over seven seasons, 1925–1931, finished first or second in scoring five times. Rarely, however, did they have individual leaders, except for Morenz, who won the Hart Trophy and had most goals, assists, and points in 1928 and repeated with the Hart and most points in 1931. His career-high forty goals in 1930 put him three behind Boston's Cooney Weiland.

Morenz and Joliat ranked with the Cooks and Boucher among hockey's great checkerboard passers, and they complemented each other perfectly. Morenz was fast, flashy, and tireless. Joliat was quiet, unassuming, and workmanlike, yet at 135 pounds he skated with a baseball cap on and dared opponents to knock it off. The one was regarded as the scorer, the other as the playmaker, yet at the end of their careers each had scored 270 goals, and Morenz had 7 more assists than Joliat's 190, while Black Cat Gagnon, most of whose ten years were spent on the same line, had 120 goals and 141 assists.

King Clancy said that Morenz was the best ever, that he "could start on a dime and leave you a nickel change," but it was the long-striding, bounding, arm-pumping speed up and down the ice that most observers remember. He had been reluctant to come to Montreal, insecure about his ability to play in the NHL. In Stratford, Ontario, he was a local hero and had a good railroad job. Even after accepting Dandurand's and Hart's offer, he tried to return the check and not report to training camp. Blandishments, importunities, threats to blow the lid off amateur hockey in Ontario—which had paid him eight hundred dollars—and promises of the good life, however, brought him into camp. He was the Habs' centerman almost as soon as he stepped on the ice. Joe Malone said, "He moved past me so fast that I thought I was standing still. I knew right then I was ready for an easy chair."

Morenz was a legend off the ice as well as on. Odie Cleghorn found him a willing accomplice in practical jokes and a victim as well. On the train west to defend the Stanley Cup against the Victoria Cougars in 1925, Cleghorn convinced him to advance his clock one hour at every "main divisional point." Morenz was a full day ahead when they got to Vancouver, but he was also five hundred dollars ahead in poker winnings. The Canadiens lost the Cup on that trip but nevertheless held a monumental party on the train home, including a sojourn of several hours on a siding in Banff.

Morenz enjoyed company, parties, gambling, eating, and drinking (though he rarely went over his playing weight of 165 pounds), but he hated to lose a hockey game or even a face-off. After a 1–0 loss to Boston in 1929, he walked the streets all night, blaming himself that Weiland had won the draw from him and fired the winning shot past Hainsworth. But he never blamed an opponent for an injury, once testifying on Hec Kilrea's behalf before President Calder's hearing, though Kilrea had cut open his head by swinging his stick at him. Still, it was his speed that won him acclaim and such names as "The Stratford Streak," "The Mitchell Meteor," and "The Swift Swiss." The latter was a fiction, calculated to make this all-star skater of German descent ethnically acceptable to the Habs' fans.

Certain incidents are often rehearsed to demonstrate that speed. Once Morenz split the Boston defensemen, Shore and Hitchman, but was cut off by a checking wing and fired a shot from twenty-five feet. It missed the goal and caromed off the boards back to Shore at the blue line. Shore launched his rush as Morenz rounded the Bruin nets. Although Conn Smythe called the play "amazingly impossible," Morenz not only caught Shore but stole the puck from his stick and took it back toward the Boston goal. Another time, against Ottawa's Alex Smith, he gained twenty feet to foil a breakaway, poke-checked the puck into the corner, passed Smith going the other way, and passed to Joliat for a goal that tied the game, won in overtime by a Morenz goal.

The rink at the Forum in Montreal, completed in 1924, was 200 by 85 feet, as large as that of Maple Leaf Gardens, and second in length only to Detroit's

Olympia. It gave Morenz and the Flying Frenchmen room to roam. In the upset victory over the Bruins for the Stanley Cup in 1930, Morenz had scored only the last of the Canadiens' seven goals, but it won the second game. In 1931 he had gone scoreless through nine games, and the Cup series was tied, 2–2, with the Black Hawks. Gagnon scored on a pass from Joliat, and the Canadiens held that lead into the third period, when Morenz scored his "goal of goals" to retain the Cup. Here is Joliat's description of the play:

> Morenz had rushed away from us with the puck down centre and was checked at the Chicago defence. Some Chicago forward picked up the loose puck at the gallop but I check him at mid-ice.
> I had taken only two strides when I heard "Joliat!" screamed at me from right wing. It was incredible; even with the play going at top speed Morenz had raced back on my left wing, whirled around behind me and had again picked up full speed down right wing.
> To catch him before he went offside at the blueline I had to fire a shot rather than a pass. Howie picked up the puck as if he was using a lacrosse stick and without losing a stride.
> He was by the Chicago defence in a flash and in on goalie Chuck Gardiner before anybody really recognized the menace. His shot, fired with every last ounce from an exhausted body, hit an upper corner of the net. The Forum crowd gasped then raised the roof in one ear-splitting wave of cheering thunder. That had to be Howie's finest goal.

When Morenz began to lose speed, his effectiveness was severely curtailed. He could no longer launch himself at defenders with the power generated by the speed, nor could he feint and circle on offense nor check back on defense. His scoring fell off to eight goals in 1934. Dandurand traded him to the Black Hawks and his Number 7 was retired in Montreal. A year in Chicago was followed by a year in New York with the Rangers, but he was returned to Montreal for the 1937 season, reunited with Gagnon and Joliat, with Cecil Hart back behind the bench. They skated sparingly but with renewed vigor through the early part of the season, when Morenz went down in a crash with Chicago defenseman Earl Seibert. His leg was broken cleanly; his ankle was broken in three places. Despite the constant flow of well-wishers and gifts, he never recovered either his health or his spirits, and he died in the hospital less than six weeks after the accident, following a nervous breakdown and a heart attack. He was thirty-four.

Once again the NHL responded to tragedy with an all-star game, a benefit for the Morenz family. Howie had left a legend for a legacy but little in the way of security for his widow and children. And he joined company with Vezina as the two most cherished and lamented Habs, broken and dead in their thirties but with a glorious hockey career behind them.

Checking Back

The Canadiens' decline through the thirties was almost as spectacular as their success had been, and it persisted until 1944, when the Punch Line took them back to the top. They continued to skate outstanding individuals—Joliat won the Hart in 1934, Babe Siebert in 1937, and Toe Blake in 1939 (along with points leadership)—but the team efforts were unproductive. From 1932, the year of Morenz's last Hart Trophy, when they finished first in their division but lost three games to one to the Rangers in the championship series, they slid to last place in 1936, with the worst record in the league, the fewest goals, and the most against. The resurgence in 1937, when Hart returned to coach in place of Sylvio Mantha, was brief, ending with their elimination from the playoffs, three games to two, by the Red Wings en route to their second straight Stanley Cup.

But it was the Canadiens who had been the first team to win the Cup twice in a row after the consolidation of major league hockey in the NHL, and they did it the hard way. First, in 1930, they finished second in the International Division and had to take on the Chicago Black Hawks, second-place finishers in the American Division. It was two games, total goals to count. Montreal won the first, 1–0, but trailed, 2–1, at the end of regulation play in the second. That meant sudden-death overtime, and it was a grim 51 minutes 43 seconds before Morenz delivered the Habs into the second round.

The Rangers had come through against Ottawa and were well rested for another two-game total-goal series. The first game was another overtime affair, tied at 1–1 until more than sixty-eight extra minutes had been played. Then, in a scramble in front of the New York goal, Gus Rivers (Gustave Desrivieres) lifted the puck over the falling John Ross Roach. The Rangers didn't score again in the series. Hainsworth shut them out, 2–0, in the other game.

Hainsworth's next victims were the Bruins, who had taken three out of four in the playoff between first-place divisional finishers. The Canadiens won, 3–0, against a team whose 179 goals in a forty-four-game season stood as the record until broken in fifty games in 1943. While Weiland, Clapper, Shore, and company were shut out, Vezina-winner Thompson was beaten by Albert Leduc, Sylvio Mantha, and Lepine. In the second game, the Canadiens scored the first three goals (Bert McCaffrey, Nick Wasnie, and Mantha) before Shore broke Hainsworth's streak at 16:50 of the second period. But Morenz matched that one a minute later, and Boston goals by Galbraith and Clapper in the third merely shortened the winning margin, while the trophy was long gone.

As holders of the Stanley Cup, the Canadiens had their finest season the following year. They won the International Division by a comfortable 7 points over Toronto, led the division in scoring while second in the league to Boston, and in a season of spectacular goaltending had Hainsworth in fourth place for the Vezina with a 2.02 average. They discovered in the playoffs that no matter how hard it was to get to the top it was harder to stay there, especially since the Cup finals had been changed to best three of five games.

In the championship round, the Bruins extended them to the limit. Boston came from behind to tie the first game at 4–4 and then won in overtime on Weiland's goal at 18:56. Hainsworth dominated the second game, surviving even Art Ross's revolutionary ploy of pulling his goalie for an extra skater in the final minutes. Leon-Georges Mantha's goal, the only one in the game, evened the series at 1–1. Sylvio's younger brother was the hero of the next game, too, scoring the winning goal on a pass from Larochelle five minutes into overtime.

The Canadiens were held to one goal in the fourth game, while the Bruins scored three. The fifth game, fittingly, was another overtime affair. Nineteen minutes into the extra period, Larochelle scored on a pass from Burke to beat Thompson and the powerful Bruins, 3–2. Meanwhile, the Chicago Black Hawks had beaten the Maple Leafs and the Rangers to move into the Cup series. Chuck Gardiner, whose twelve shutouts had led the league, but whose 1.77 goals-against average had been second to Worters' 1.68, allowed Toronto three goals in their two-game series and then blanked New York twice.

Dick Irvin's Hawks had come a long way, and the series was no anticlimax even after the Montreal-Boston excitement. The first game was won in Chicago, 2–1, on another George Mantha goal from a Lepine pass, but the Hawks came back in the second. Tied at 1–1 through almost twenty-five minutes in overtime, the game went to Chicago on Johnny Gottselig's drive, and the teams moved to the Forum all even.

Overtime had become the rule, and the third game was no exception. The Hawks came from behind to tie it, 2–2, and then played two scoreless extra periods. Almost fourteen minutes into the next, Cy Wentworth scored to move Chicago in front. And in the fourth game, after one period, goals by Gottselig and Ernie Arbour had the Canadiens' grip on the Cup very shaky indeed. But Montreal had too much left and gave nothing to Chicago from that point on, not even risking another overtime. Gagnon scored in the second period and tied the game in the third. Then Lepine, on passes from Gagnon and Joliat, got the two goals that won the game and evened the series. The fifth game was all Montreal, a shutout for Hainsworth, the winning goal for Gagnon from Joliat, and the clincher for Morenz on the solo dash that produced his only goal of the playoffs (and Joliat's descriptive encomium above).

While the Canadiens had moved to the top, Pittsburgh had descended and disappeared. Winning only nine games in 1929, the Pirates had departed from the playoff picture, though Chicago won even fewer games. In 1930, however, while the Hawks began to climb, Pittsburgh sank lower, into the cellar with only five wins. The league rescued the Steel City by finding a new home for the franchise in Philadelphia. The new owner was Benny Leonard, one of the great battlers in boxing history, with more than 200 fights and undefeated as light-weight champion from 1917 to 1925.

The Philadelphia Quakers, as they were called without overt attempts at irony, produced Leonard's worst beating. They played as if among friends, without an enemy in the world, and won only four games, while allowing an astonishing 184 goals against. For the 1932 season, they were gone from the NHL. The Ottawa Senators, who couldn't get out of the International Division cellar all season, also took a sabbatical, leaving two four-team divisions in the league for the Leafs to conquer. The Quakers' swan song, however, was a big hit. They won their last game, in New York, beating the Americans in a game the home team needed. Big Bill Dwyer, the Amerks' owner, had bailed Leonard out in midseason and paid the Philadelphia bills until the final fold. The payoff was that his step-team had kept his real team out of the playoffs. "At least," he said, "the game was honest."

12

A King and a Kid Line

Conn Smythe's five-year plan was right on schedule. The Toronto Maple Leafs were undisputed champions of the hockey world in 1932. Of all the major's deals and moves, three in particular coalesced in that one season to bring the Stanley Cup to Toronto. They involved the forward line, the defense, and the coach.

The Kid Line typified Toronto's style of play, fast and flashy. At center was unselfish Joe Primeau, who three times led the league in assists. Selke's pride and joy, Primeau had come up at the beginning of Smythe's youth movement in 1927. On the right wing was Charlie Conacher, called by Foster Hewitt the "most feared forward in the game" and by Red Dutton the owner of "the fastest shot I've ever seen," who joined the team in 1929 when he was still a teenager. The two clicked together right away, with Baldy Cotton on the left wing, but it wasn't until Cotton was replaced by Busher Jackson that the proper chemistry was achieved. Jackson came up at the same time as Conacher and was even younger, by more than a year. His speed was outstanding and his shots always dangerous, but his unique skill was as a sure receiver of passes from Primeau and Conacher.

In their first full season together, the Kid Line finished second, fourth, and seventh in scoring in the league. As good as they were, they were always looking for new ideas for razzle-dazzle plays. Among their inventions was what Conacher called the "baseball play," in which Primeau would carry the puck, draw the defense, and—instead of passing to a teammate's stick—pass off to an open wing, where Conacher or Jackson would arrive in clear ice on time to receive the pass and get off a quick shot. The ultimate compliment to this line was paid by General John Reed Kilpatrick, who said to Lester Patrick, "Could you not have the Cooks and Boucher pattern their play after Toronto's Kid Line?" When Patrick objected, "Our line is better than theirs," the general replied, "That's not the point. When that blasted Kid Line attacks, they're lightning. And when I see those big bruisers rushing in on our goal like that, my heart stops beating!" Conacher weighed close to 200 pounds, Jackson about 185. The other bruiser, Primeau, was not so much as a legitimate welterweight.

Behind the Kid Line, Cotton worked well with Andy Blair, the young collegiate center, and Ace Bailey, who had led the league in goals and points in 1929. But behind the lines, the Leafs' chief weakness was defense. In 1929 they had led their division in goals against, and in 1928 and 1930 only the cellar-dwelling Amerks had allowed more goals. Red Horner's distinction was as a penalty-earner. For eight consecutive seasons, 1933–1940, he led the league in penalty minutes. In a memorable game in 1935 he spent seventeen minutes of the first period in the box. At the other point, veteran Happy Day was a steady performer, but not an effective complement to the flashy forwards without an attacking defenseman at his side.

The ideal solution was King Clancy, whom Smythe called "probably the best all-round man, as far as morale, ability and effort for his team is concerned, that ever was." And as Conn's luck would have it, Clancy became available in the fall of 1930, because Ottawa needed some money. Clancy, at twenty-seven just entering his prime, was already an established star of nine NHL seasons. As a rookie substitute with the Senators in 1923, he had played all six positions in the Cup finals against Edmonton, earning $750 in the playoffs after an $800 season. He became the mainstay of the Ottawa team, which led the league in 1926 and the Canadian Division in 1927, recapturing the Stanley Cup that year in a four-game series with Boston. His best year was 1930, when his seventeen goals and twenty-three assists set records for defensemen and placed him seventh in the league in scoring. But Ottawa had been slipping both in the standings and at the gate and had to make some moves.

Smythe's acceptable offer to the Senators for Clancy was Art Smith, Eric Pettinger, and $35,000, but it took a Rare Jewel to produce the purchase price for the King. Rare Jewel was the inappropriate name of a thoroughbred Smythe owned. Entered in the Coronation Stakes at Woodbine and going off at 100 to 1, he carried not only Conn's colors on his back but also $150 of his money on his nose. When his horse won, Smythe had won almost half the cash he needed for the Clancy deal and he carried it off forthwith. Since Clancy had a Customs Department job in Ottawa and lived at his family's home, he figured he needed a $10,000 salary just to break even. Smythe offered him $8,500 and promised him a $1,500 bonus if the Leafs had a good year. Clancy, who loved to play and appreciated the compliment implied in the deal, gladly accepted.

It is difficult to overstate Clancy's value to Toronto. Bill Chadwick, a Hall of Fame referee now TV commentator, called him the Babe Ruth of hockey, though most reserved that title for Shore. The analogy is appropriate in the sense that Clancy typified the wide-open offensive play that packed paying customers into Maple Leaf Gardens. In style of play and in competitive spirit, he was a perfect fit for the team that Smythe and Selke had assembled. As a measure of his worth, however, consider this remarkable statistic: in sixteen NHL seasons, 96 of his 137 goals—70 percent—were either the first, the tying, or the game-winning goal.

One of the first things Smythe wanted from Clancy was information. How did the Senators always manage to stop the Cooks and Boucher when they played the Rangers? What was the strategy? Clancy couldn't tell him—"I don't know," he answered with a shrug—but when the Leafs played the Rangers he showed him. Clancy played defense directly in front of the goal and intercepted either the direct shots or the close-in passes that the Ranger line tried.

One major move remained before the second-place but inconsistent Leafs of 1931 could become the second-place but Cup-winning champions of 1932. It was not, as might have been expected, in goal, where Lorne Chabot had been exceptionally erratic. He started the 1931 season with five consecutive shutouts, then lost, 2–1, to the Philadelphia Quakers—their first win in a record-breaking losing season. Then he averaged almost three goals against for the rest of the season. But Smythe stayed put with Chabot in goal. The change he made was behind the bench.

Art Duncan had ended his distinguished career as defenseman at Toronto, and Smythe had rewarded him with the Leafs' coaching job for the 1931 season. In Chicago, Dick Irvin had produced a winner with some stability for the Black Hawks and taken them to the Cup finals. But in a typical clash of temperaments, McLaughlin had fired Irvin. Now, as the 1932 season began and the Leafs graced their palatial new stadium by losing their first six games, Smythe hired Irvin to replace Duncan. In his debut his new team bowed to the Maroons, 8–2, but Irvin knew exactly what he had to do.

He had a potentially great team. The first two lines—Primeau, Conacher, and Jackson; Blair, Bailey, and Cotton—were unsurpassed. Behind them were Frankie Finnigan, an experienced penalty-killer who had come over from Ottawa in the dispersal of Senator players; Harold Darragh, who had been bought from Boston after some productive years in Pittsburgh; rookie Bob Gracie; and Earl Miller, whom Irvin acquired during the season from Chicago. At defense were the rushing Clancy, the steady Day, the policeman Horner, young Alex Levinsky—an all-around athlete from Syracuse—and spare Fred Robertson, an unlikely hockey product from Carlisle, England. But Irvin knew he also had a team of poorly conditioned athletes, and he set about making a change in that condition.

In that, Irvin and Smythe were completely at one. Smythe the martinet had revolutionized preseason training for hockey players with a vigorous conditioning schedule, only to lose sight of that aspect of the program under the easy-going Duncan while he himself was occupied with cultivation and completion of his Gardens. Irvin the martinet instituted an on-the-job training program, and in a matter of four weeks he not only whipped the Leafs into shape but led them from last to first place in the division. The key game in the streak was on Christmas Eve against the Canadiens, won on Busher Jackson's goal just as the gong was about to end the overtime period.

Irvin and Smythe had clashed on another matter of policy. The manager wanted the wings checked from the outside to clog the middle and frustrate offensive plays. The coach wanted the wings checked from the inside to break momentum and keep the ice open for transition from defense. They fought bitterly. Irvin insisted on having things done his way, and Smythe with grudging admiration yielded the point (to Selke's silent satisfaction). And now the Leafs were ready—in a league reduced to eight teams but with a schedule expanded to forty-eight games, with a wide-open style of play well suited to the recent dropping of forward-pass restrictions, with some weakness in goal but the ability to outscore anyone, with a palatial new home rink and the coach called by Andy O'Brien the shrewdest ever.

The season was a spectacular success. Conacher led the league in goals and was fourth in scoring, Primeau led in assists and was second in scoring (and won the Byng to interrupt Boucher's string), and Jackson led in scoring. The team scored 155 goals in all—13 more than their nearest competitor, 69 more than the Black Hawks who were second in the American Division. They finished in second place in the International Division, just four points behind the Cup-holding Canadiens, because an injury to Conacher brought on a late-season slump. But the Leafs were all fit for the playoffs.

While the Maroons were edging the Detroit Falcons in the series for third-place finishers and the Rangers were upsetting the Canadiens three games to one, Toronto took on the Black Hawks. Gardiner, the Vezina-winner, shut out the Leafs, 1–0, in the first game, but in the second Hap Day got the equalizer and the Kid Line went to work to produce a 6–1 rout that must have been sweet revenge for Irvin.

The two-game series with Montreal (with Charlie Conacher playing against his brother Lionel) was much harder. The first game was a 1–1 tie. The second was scoreless into the third period, when Hooley Smith scored. Again it was Hap Day who got the equalizer, and the game and series went into sudden-death overtime. The Maroons backchecked desperately and kept fighting off the Kid Line, while rookie Gracie told Irvin *he'd* get the winning goal. Irvin sent him out and he put one past Flat Walsh, only to have it waved off by an off-sides. The next time he was given a shift on the ice, Gracie told the official scorer to write him down for the winning goal. Thirty-two seconds later, Andy

Blair won a draw, passed to Gracie, and the rookie's shot glanced off Walsh's pads into the net.

The Rangers-Leafs match was a promoter's dream: the Kid Line against the Cooks and Boucher, Smythe's team against the team that he had organized only to be let go, the two fastest-skating, freest-styled teams in hockey. The first game was played in Madison Square Garden. In the first period Day scored on a pass from Cotton, and the Cooks got even, Bun from Bill. But in the second the Kids exploded, Jackson scoring three times and Conacher once, despite Muzz Murdoch's shadowing job. The final score was 6–4.

The second game was played in Boston, because the home-team Rangers had to yield the home ice to the circus. New York got the first two goals, but Jackson and Conacher got the Leafs even after two periods. The third period was all Toronto—four goals, two by Clancy and one apiece by Conacher and Cotton—and the Maple Leafs returned to their own Gardens prepared for their greatest triumph.

The issue was never really in doubt. Blair scored twice in the first period, Boucher matched Jackson in the second, and the Leafs moved ahead, 5–1, on goals by Finnigan and Bailey in the third. There were only three and a half minutes left when Bun Cook scored for New York, and the remaining goals (Gracie for Toronto, Boucher twice for New York) had no bearing on the result. It was Toronto in straight sets, 6–4, 6–2, 6–4, in what came to be known as the tennis series, the most decisive victory since the new playoff format had been instituted. They happened to be the identical scores of Jean Borotra's three winning sets against Ellsworth Vines in the decisive match of that year's Davis Cup play. The marvelous Basque thus extended France's hold on the Cup to a fifth year, though Henri Cochet lost to Vines after beating Wilmer Allison, who teamed with John van Ryn to beat Cochet and Jacques Brugnon in the doubles.

These Maple Leafs were more than a remarkably good hockey team; they were also remarkably good copy. Despite the martinet nature of the management, the fastidious models of no-drinking-no-smoking decorousness, they were renowned as hockey's Gashouse Gang. Clancy, Conacher, Cotton, and Day were especially rambunctious among a squad Selke called "a rare and unique combination of personalities." On the one hand, Conn Smythe insisted that the Leafs stay in the stodgiest possible lodgings, like the University Club in Boston. On the other hand, it was there that Hap Day, on a bet, swam in the pool with his clothes on.

Conacher's favorite stunt was to hold people by the heels outside hotel windows, while Cotton usually played the buffoon's role of butt for public and practical jokes. Clancy was as game off the ice as on, where he never won a fight and never dodged one. Typical of the heavyweight bravado in his ban-

Checking Back

tamweight body was the night he fought opposing defenseman Harold Starr, his former teammate at Ottawa. Starr gave him a thorough beating, but as he was being helped off Clancy shouted back, "You never saw the day you could lay a hand on me."

Clancy was better disposed toward another former teammate, center Cowboy Convey, who was being given a chance in New York. When the Amerks came to Toronto, Clancy knew that Convey was about to be farmed out, and he conspired with his teammates to help him. With a 4–0 lead, the Leafs gave Convey his opportunity. Conacher let him skate by with the puck, Clancy himself stumbled out of the way, and Chabot deliberately froze in the goal. The Cowboy's shot went high and wide into the stands. The Leafs gave him another chance. Conacher, playing the matador defense, waved him past. Clancy faked a missed bodycheck, and Chabot considered giving Convey an open net to shoot at. Too soon, he fired, and the puck caught the goalie in the neck. The Leafs gathered around the fallen Chabot, who said, when he could stop choking, "Cut the nonsense out or that guy'll kill me." Clancy turned to Conacher who settled the matter in two words: "Screw Convey!"

This Gang was not above losing a game to irritate Dick Irvin, as they did once in Chicago, according to legend. But they were embarrassed about it and determined to make up for it when the Hawks came to Toronto. They bombarded Charlie Gardiner, until he had to be carried off for fourteen stitches. The bombardment continued against his replacement until a Conacher shot knocked him cold. Gardiner came back. When the score soared to 10–1 a fan sailed a derby hat onto the ice. The Chicago goalie entered into the spirit by wearing the hat for the rest of the game.

The Cup victory in 1932 was not to be repeated for a decade. Yet the Toronto Maple Leafs were a dominant power throughout that period and probably the best team in the league, year in and year out, through the mid-thirties. They led their division in 1933, 1934, 1935, and 1938, and they didn't miss the playoffs until 1946. They led the league in team scoring five straight years and six out of seven in the decade. Conacher led in goals and points in 1934 and 1935, tied in goals in 1936 with teammate Bill Thoms; Primeau led in assists in 1934. In 1937 and 1938 new leaders appeared: Syl Apps, who led in assists in 1937, when he won the Calder Trophy (Rookie of the Year) and 1938; and Gordie Drillon, who led in goals and points in 1938, scoring mostly on clever deflections, and won the Byng as well.

But they seemed to be snake-bit in the playoffs. In 1933, after the memorable overtime win over Boston, they could not recover in time to handle the Rangers. In 1934 they lost to Detroit, 1–0, in the fifth game of the Championship Series. In 1935, after they beat Boston three games to one, the Maroons landed to eliminate them in three straight. In 1936, after surviving the first rounds against the Bruins and the Amerks, they fell to Detroit again. The Rangers knocked them out early in 1937, but in 1938 they again beat the Bruins in the Championship Series, only to lose the Cup finals to Chicago.

Smythe was never one to stand pat, and by the time the two-division setup was abandoned for the 1939 season, the Leafs of the golden years were no longer in evidence. Dick Irvin would last another year as coach before Hap Day, who had been released as a player in the 1937 season, took over for the 1941 season. Chabot had been traded for Hainsworth in 1933, but in 1936 Turk Broda won the job. Smythe had passed up the promising Earl Robertson to get Broda, again showing his shrewd judgment of talent. The night that Broda debuted marked the end of an era for another reason: the retirement of Joe Primeau. And in the same year, Clancy retired, Finnigan retired, and Jackson was sold to Boston. The last of the old gang was Conacher, who lasted until January 1938, despite kidney trouble, a smashed shoulder, and fractures of the wrist, hands, and collarbone. He finished the season on an enforced sabbatical and by the beginning of the following season—when kid brother Roy was breaking in with Boston—Charlie was skating as a Red Wing. The King was gone, the Kids were gone, the Leafs had fallen, but with new kids and old hands in control Toronto would rise again.

13

Endangered Species and Jingo Champions

The commercial success of the Toronto Maple Leafs and their Gardens throughout the Depression years was unfortunately not typical of the entire NHL, although attendance was close to two million for the 1934 season. From a heyday of two strong five-team divisions, the league shrank to a single seven-team circuit in 1939, and at least two of the remaining teams were in trouble. The passing of the Pittsburgh franchise to Philadelphia and then out of existence has already been noted; a similar process began in Ottawa.

Ottawa, home of the Silver Seven, had an illustrious hockey heritage that included Cup-winning teams in 1903, 1904, 1905, 1909, 1911, 1920, 1921, 1923, and 1927. The 1927 Senators, managed and coached by Dave Gill, are considered one of the greatest teams of all time. With Alex Connell in goal, they gave up only 69 goals in forty-four games, winning thirty and losing only ten. Jack Adams was in his last year, George Boucher near the end of his career, and Cy Denneny and Frank Nighbor in their last really productive year. But along with these experienced players were several in their youthful prime, including Frank Finnigan, Hooley and Alex Smith, and Hec Kilrea (a Bobby Hull look-alike). And there was the rookie, King Clancy. In the playoffs they didn't lose a game, tying the Canadiens, 1–1, after shutting them out, 4–0, and then taking Boston, 0–0, 3–1, 1–1, and 3–1 (each tie lasting through one full overtime period). In four hundred minutes of Stanley Cup play, Connell had yielded only four goals.

From this peak the Senators slipped steadily away. Connell was outstanding in 1928, though his 1.3 average wasn't good enough to beat Hainsworth for the Vezina. But his fifteen shutouts tied his 1926 record, and six of them came consecutively. On January 28, the Canadiens' Mantha scored against him at 14:21 of the second period. The next time the red light went on behind him was on February 22, at 18:30 of the second period, when Chicago's Duke Keats broke the charm. In between, the Leafs, the Maroons, the Rangers twice, the Pirates, and the Canadiens had gone scoreless, including almost 40 minutes of overtime play. The total was 463 minutes, 29 seconds of perfect goaltending. But the team finished third, and the Maroons knocked them out in the first playoff round.

In 1929 they were below .500, in fourth place, out of the playoffs, and in trouble at the gate. A slight recovery to third place in the division in 1930 didn't bring the fans back. The only leader they had, belying his name, was Joe Lamb in penalty minutes. The Rangers disposed of them in the first round of the playoffs, and the management continued to dispose of the valuable players. The abysmal last-place finish in 1931 brought a one-year halt in operations, but most of the dispersed players were restored for the 1933 season. Twice more the Senators labored in the cellar, with ever-diminishing crowds in the stands, and when the 1935 season started the NHL had flown from Ottawa for good.

Over the objections of the AHA Flyers, the Senators became the St. Louis Eagles. But they flew no higher. They finished last in the International Division, winning only eleven games and tying six out of forty-eight. The last profitable move they made was to sell their best player, Syd Howe, to Detroit. Thus shorn, the Eagles folded up, and in 1936 the league had two four-team divisions.

The next casualty came three seasons later, with the sudden, rather than lingering, decline and death of the Montreal Maroons. Selke called them "the pampered darlings of the Anglo-Saxon minority population of Canada's metropolis" and "the most cordially hated group of puck chasers in the game." They were characterized by big, battering players, especially the Big Three S Line of Nels Stewart, Hooley Smith, and Babe Siebert. In the five years they skated together, 1928–1932, the three forwards amassed 453 points, including Stewart's 55 in 1930 when he won his second Hart Trophy. Stewart, or Ole Poison as he was called, had won the scoring championship and the Hart in 1926, his first year in the NHL. By the time he retired, after fifteen seasons, he had scored 324 goals, which stood as a career record until Richard passed him over a decade later. These were the Maroons that scored three goals in twenty-four seconds against the Rangers in 1932.

At defense, they were led by Red Dutton, Dunc Munro, Cyclone Wentworth, and Archie Wilcox. Benny Benedict was in the Maroons' goal for almost six seasons, until replaced by Flat Walsh in 1930. Walsh shared the chores with Davey Kerr in 1931, Norm Smith in 1932, and Kerr again in 1933. Kerr played the entire 1934 season and then went to the Rangers, but it was only with Alex Connell in goal, having come out of retirement for the 1935 season, that the Maroons won the Stanley Cup for the second and last time. By that time most of their mainstays were gone, except for Smith and Wentworth, but playing coach Lionel Conacher, who had skated to the Stanley Cup as a Black Hawk the year before, put together a winning combination under Tom Gorman's management.

Gump Worsley remembers growing up in an English-speaking neighborhood of Montreal where the folks didn't care very much for the Canadiens at all. His father's favorite players were Baldy Northcott, Dave Trottier, and Jimmy Ward. No wonder—they were leading scorers on the Maroons throughout the mid-thirties, though the championship came largely on defense in 1935. Connell led the league with nine shutouts and allowed only 92 goals, a 1.92 average second only to Chabot in his one Black Hawk year. It was his best performance since 1929.

The entire corps of defensemen had been rebuilt. Wentworth came over from Chicago in 1933, Stewart Evans from Detroit during the 1934 season, Allan Shields from Ottawa and Conacher from Chicago just that year. Among the forwards, along with Smith, Trottier, Ward, and Northcott, the only other veterans were Earl Robinson, who had his best season and led the club with thirty-five points, and Bob Gracie, who came from the Amerks that season. Gus Marker was a third-year man just acquired from Detroit, Sam McManus was a spare in his only NHL season, and Bill Miller was a rookie spare. Two outstanding second-year players were center Russ (Beaver) Blinco, coming off his Rookie of the Year season, and Herb Cain, who led the team with twenty goals on Hooley's left wing. Toe Blake and Dutch Gainor also played briefly during the season.

With that unlikely squad, the Maroons finished second to the Leafs in the International Division. Toronto was the only team to win the season's series from them, taking five of six games. In the first round of the playoffs, Montreal took on the Hawks in a defensive classic. Chabot and Cornell recorded back-to-back shutouts, until Northcott scored the only goal in the series at 4:02 of overtime in the second game. Northcott and Smith teamed up on the decisive goal against Kerr and the Rangers in a 2–1 victory at New York. Then a 3–3 tie in Montreal put them in the finals against their nemesis in Toronto.

Again the Cup finals provided a reversal of the season's form. For the fifth time in the seven years of the current format, the Cup was not won by a divisional champion. Connell withstood Leaf pressure throughout the two games in Maple Leaf Gardens, while Hainsworth could not keep up with him. The first game packed four goals into the second period, Robinson and Wentworth matching Finnigan and Clancy. Blinco and Robinson assisted Trottier on the game-winner at 5:28 of overtime. Blinco got the game-winner in the second game, after Busher Jackson had matched Robinson's goal. Back home in Montreal, the Maroons completed a sweep. Ward's first-period goal was equaled by Thoms in the second, but it was all colored Maroon after that, as Northcott, Wentworth, and Marker scored.

As defending champions the Maroons led their division in 1936, but not with the same style or combination. They shot more, scored more, and allowed more shots and goals. And in the playoffs they were outdefended by Detroit, though attacking far more, and were eliminated in three straight games. They struggled to second place in 1937, again playing rather undisciplined hockey, and were eliminated in two shutout games by the Rangers. They plummeted to the cellar in 1938 with a 12–30–6 record, allowing 149 goals. King Clancy's brief coaching tenure was a disaster. Suddenly, in 1939, the Montreal Maroons were extinct, and the NHL was back to one division, with seven teams.

Detroit had survived, but with great difficulty at first, and not with their original identity. They started as the Cougars; in fact, they were largely staffed by remnants of the Western League's Victoria Cougars. After one year under Art Duncan and a last-place finish, they moved up a notch under Jack Adams. Frank Calder had recommended Adams to Charles Hughes, the president of the club, who wanted to put fresh spirit onto the new ice in Detroit's Olympia. A year later, they had a new identity as Falcons instead of Cougars and made the playoffs for the first time. Fourth-place finishes kept them out for two more years, and though they finished third in 1932, the Falcons didn't win a playoff game until their final season.

Finishing second in 1933 (actually tied with Boston in record, 25–15–8, but second by virtue of fewer goals scored), the Falcons beat the Maroons, 2–0 and 3–2, in the playoffs before losing to the Rangers, 2–0 and 4–3. Much of the improvement was due to the play of John Ross Roach, the all-star goalie, whom they had bought from the Rangers for eleven thousand dollars. Roach's replacement in New York, rookie Andy Aitkenhead, won the Stanley Cup, but his NHL career ended after just three seasons, in the same year that Roach retired after fourteen.

The Detroit franchise then changed hands and plumage. James D. Norris, Sr., was the new owner; he called his club the Red Wings and gave them a flying wheel insignia. More important, he gave them the kind of aggressive management that would assemble a winning team, retaining Jack Adams as manager and coach. He got Carl Voss during the season from the Rangers, the year's Calder Trophy winner. Within a couple of years he had also bought Hec Kilrea back from Toronto for $17,000 and acquired Syd Howe from St. Louis for $35,000.

Norris's attitude was infectious. The Wings on wheels rolled to a first-place finish in the American Division and then shocked the other division's champion Leafs in a five-game series. The Kid Line was bottled up throughout by Cooney Weiland, Larry Aurie, and Herb Wilson, and in the decisive game Wilf Cude shut out Toronto while Ebbie Goodfellow got one past Hainsworth. In the Cup series, however, Detroit's big line could get only one goal in each of the first two games, while Chicago managed two and four. Three third-period Wing goals won the third game, 5–2, but Gardiner shut them out to win the fourth and the Cup.

The Wings dipped from first to last place in 1935 and out of the playoffs, yet it was a productive year in terms of opening up their style of play and building for the future. They scored by far the most goals in their history and for the first time had skaters among the league-leading scorers. Herb Lewis, who had been a Cougar and a Falcon, was sixth in the league as a Red Wing: Aurie, who had been with Detroit since Olympia opened, was third: Syd Howe, who came from St. Louis in midseason, was second. Scotty Bowman, who also came from the Eagles in a fifty-thousand-dollar deal, became the first NHL player to score on a penalty shot, against Connell of the Maroons. But Roach, in his last season, was not the needed safety man behind the wide open play of the new Wings, and they were the only team in the division under .500.

A year later Detroit was clearly the best team in hockey. They didn't score quite as many goals (124 as opposed to 127), and they didn't allow that many fewer (103 compared to 114), but they won the most games in a well-balanced eight-team league and won the Stanley Cup with only a single loss in seven games. The most obvious difference was Norm Smith in his first full season as regular goaltender, rising or scrambling to the occasion in big games and against crucial shots. Perhaps as important was the change at center on the first line. Frank Patrick, then with the Bruins, and Jack Adams had swapped Cooney Weiland and Marty Barry, the proverbial deal that helped both teams. Barry trailed only the Amerks' Sweeney Schriner in points that year, centering for Aurie and Lewis, while Weiland fused the Bruins' Dynamite Trio between Clapper and Gainor.

The defending Cup-holders were the Maroons, who had come back to win the International Division, so that the championship series figured to be a classic. And it was. The first game ended regulation play without a goal. Five overtime periods later, and early the following morning, it was still scoreless. At 16:30 of the sixth overtime period, at 2:25 A.M., Mud Bruneteau's shot off a pass from Hec Kilrea beat Chabot. Smith had made more than ninety saves, and Bucko McDonald had used his greatest talent as a body checker to stymie Hooley Smith and to flatten no fewer than thirty-seven Maroons.

Detroit easily maintained their edge through the next game, scoring three times while Smith shut out the frustrated Maroons again. When Montreal's Gus Marker scored at 12:02 of the first period in the third game, Smith's record streak was ended at 248:32, but the Red Wings went on to win the game anyway, 2–1, and sweep the series.

Now Detroit waited for their opponent to emerge from the playoffs, while all Motown anticipated a sports sweep. The Tigers had won the World Series, the Lions were NFL champions, and the city was roaring for a grand slam. The Maple Leafs put away the Bruins and then edged the Amerks in a tough series. During the year they alone had played the Red Wings even, but their veterans were wearing down from the long season. Opening at Olympia, Detroit scored three goals in the first period and contained Toronto with just one goal thereafter.

The second game was different. Instead of playing cautious, checking hockey, both teams looked for breaks at every opportunity and often created them. As far as the Wings were concerned, that was the squad that gave them the reputation for versatility they maintained for two decades or more, and they earned it in this series. After four straight careful, low-scoring wins, they now exploded in a 9–4 victory. Walter Kilrea—Hec's younger brother, who had come over from the Maroons—scored first and had an assist later. Barry had a goal and two assists, Lewis a goal, Hec two assists, McDonald two goals, Bruneteau an assist, Howe an assist, Bowman an assist, Doug Young an assist, Gord Pettinger two goals, and Johnny Sorrell two goals and two assists. Only Goodfellow, Aurie, Art Giroux, Wilf Starr, and Pete Kelly failed to get into the scoring act.

Over in Toronto, Detroit let down after two more good periods. Goals by Bowman, Bruneteau, and Howe had them ahead, 3–0, with only seven minutes to play, but Primeau scored and Reg Kelly scored twice to send the game into overtime. Buzz Boll ended it quickly after thirty-one seconds. The Red Wings regrouped after Primeau gave Toronto a 1–0 lead in the second period. Goodfellow tied it on a pass from Sorrell, Lewis fed Barry to put them ahead, and then he assisted Kelly for the Cup-winner, with Thoms getting the last Leaf goal.

Detroit came back even stronger a year later. They won one more and tied two more to win the division by six points. They scored a bit more, with Barry third in points and Aurie fourth in points and first in goals. They allowed fewer goals as Smith won the Vezina. Barry won the Byng and was joined on the all-star team by Aurie, Goodfellow, and Smith. Never since these teams had been selected, beginning in 1931, had any one franchise had four players on the first squad, and Adams was selected coach as well.

With all that strength the Cup defense should have been easy, but injuries and emotion worked against them to make it most difficult. First Aurie broke his leg at the end of the season and missed all the playoffs. Then Norm Smith injured his elbow and needed relief from James Franks and Earl Robertson to complete the Canadiens series. Finally they had to deal with the incentive Montreal had from Morenz's death just weeks before.

The first two games were played at Olympia. Hec Kilrea skated with the first line and scored twice in a 4–0 shutout for Smith. In the second game Detroit bombed Cude again for a 5–1 win. But over in the Forum, amid chants of "Win it for Howie," the Canadiens came back with two 3–1 wins. Game 5 was a tense battle through almost two hours of play before Hec Kilrea got the 2–1 win at 11:49 of the third overtime.

Against the Rangers, Earl Robertson, who had never played a regular-season NHL game, had to go all the way in goal. In Madison Square Garden, against the new breed of Patrickmen—including the Colvilles, Shibicky, Phil Watson, Art Coulter, Babe Pratt, and Lynn Patrick—the shaky Robertson allowed five goals, as the veteran Boucher scored once and assisted twice. The Wings' best save came from the circus, which sent the rest of the series back to Olympia. And there Robertson, helped by defensemen Goodfellow and Scotty Bowman, stood firm, allowing only three Ranger goals in the remaining four games. Detroit won the second game, 4–2, the New York goals coming after the game was out of reach. The Rangers' last gasp was the third game, a 1–0 shutout for Davey Kerr on a Neil Colville goal, but they never scored through the remaining 159:37 of the series. Barry scored to give Robertson a 1–0 shutout in the fourth game, again to give the Wings a lead in the first period of the fifth, and again after a Sorrell goal to put the Cup safely out of Ranger reach, 3–0.

For the first time a team had won back-to-back division titles *and* back-to-back Stanley Cup series. Norris decided to stay put with his team, and a year later he knew he should have been dealing. They had slipped to last place in 1938 and he said, "After this flop, I'll never hesitate to bust up championship clubs." The point was that there was a genuine balance of power in the league, and to remain stagnant was to give way to any team that improved even slightly. It was the last year of the two-division arrangement and the prevailing playoff system. Appropriately, the setup ended as it had begun in 1930, with neither first-place team winning the Cup. Indeed, the best teams in the 1938 playoffs were the American Division third-place Black Hawks and the International Division second-place Americans.

The Amerks, too, were endangered species, though a few conservationists kept them alive for a while longer. Big Bill Dwyer's team were considered to be the playboys of the NHL, but because of Dwyer's association with the rackets, most people knew better than to play around with them. Dwyer installed his own goal judge during the 1932 season, and when Detroit came to town the Falcon goalie, Alex Connell, lost his temper and almost his head. Upset with the persistent bad calls, Connell charged the judge and landed a punch to the face. The goalie had unfortunately taken on a notorious gunsel. When some of his associates converged on the scene, only quick action by New York's finest kept Connell blood off the ice. The goalie was escorted by blue-uniformed defensemen from then until he safely boarded the train for Detroit.

The Americans were successful in attracting crowds for most of their games and attention for their exploits off the ice, but they never put together a championship team. There were outstanding individual Amerk players, including Billy Burch, the Byng winner in 1927 who ranked high in scoring in 1926 and 1927; Normie Himes, an unselfish center who had fifty points in 1930, Art Chapman, a consistent scorer in the mid- and late-thirties, and their burly defensemen, Leo Reise and Bullet Joe Simpson.

On offense, the memorable Amerk was Dave (Sweeney) Schriner, Rookie of the Year in 1935, all-star in 1936 and 1937 (and later, with Toronto). But by far the most illustrious American was the Shrimp, Roy Worters, a twelve-year NHL goaltender with a lifetime average of 2.37. He had spent three harrowing years in the Pittsburgh nets before coming to New York in 1929. Then with thirteen shutouts and a 1.21 average in thirty-eight games, though losing the Vezina to Hainsworth, he won the Hart Trophy and led the Amerks into their first playoff—their only playoff in their first ten years. Typical of the kind of frustration that Worters suffered, his team could not score in two games against the Rangers. He gave up no goals himself through 149:50 before Keeling beat him. Earlier in the year he had lost a game to Montreal without giving up a goal, when Simpson threw his stick at Howie Morenz. The automatic score was the only one in the game.

Worters won the Vezina in 1931 and was second-team all-star in 1932 and 1934, but he never surpassed the records or the frustrations of 1929. In 1936, the Amerks were back in the playoffs and got their first win when Worters shut out Chicago in the first game. In the second round, Toronto eliminated them two games to one, but as usual the one they won was a Worters shutout.

Only three more times, 1938–1940, did they make the playoffs, but only once did they look anything like champions. That was 1938, when they finished second in the International Division and squared off against the Rangers.

Despite injuries to captain Art Coulter and Babe Pratt, the Rangers were 3 to 1 favorites in this series, having gone 4–1–1 against the Amerks during the season. When Cecil Dillon scored less than two minutes into the game, the smart money looked good. But Earl Robertson was unbeatable thereafter. Red Beattie, a former Red Wing, tied the game in the second period on a play set up by Hooley Smith. Cautious defensive play kept the game even throughout regulation and the first overtime, until Johnny Sorell, picked up from Detroit just a month earlier, scored the winning goal at 1:25 of the second overtime.

Still, the Rangers were 7 to 5 favorites to win the second game and even-up to take the series when the metropolitan rivals faced off two nights later in the Garden. The odds-makers were justified by the Rangers' domination of play. In the first period, Bryan Hextall took a pass from Phil Watson, and with Ching Johnson screening his own goalie's vision, put his shot past Robertson. In the second period, the Colvilles teamed up on a power play to set up an easy shot by Clint Smith, and then Shibicky scored on a solo rush for a 3–0 Ranger lead.

The Amerks came back on a power-play goal by Tommy Anderson, and then in the third period Sorrell stole the puck from Pratt and put his own rebound past Kerr. But they never got even. A goal by Joe Jerwa was waved off by referee Clarence Campbell, and a Clint Smith backhand put the game out of reach, although Sorrell scored again with two minutes left.

Now with Pratt and Neil Colville added to the injury list, the Rangers were installed as 8 to 5 favorites to win the rubber match on Sunday night. On Monday morning, while the headlines dealt with Mussolini and Catalonia and American economic reprisals against Mexico, the front page of the *Times* also carried the story of the Amerks' upset win. At 1:25 A.M. forty seconds into the fourth overtime period, Lorne Carr beat Dave Kerr on sharp passes from Jerwa and Chapman, for a 3–2 comeback win. Second-period goals by Shibicky and Hextall had put the Rangers in front. But Carr scored early in the third, and then on passes from Eddie Wiseman and Johnny Gallagher, veteran Nels Stewart tied the score and sent the game into overtime. Kerr made fifty saves, but Robertson was even more brilliant, making sixty.

The American triumph was the high point in the history of the franchise and took them on to the second playoff round against the surprising, high-flying Black Hawks. In Chicago the endangeries species was not the franchise but the coaches and players that their eccentric owner Major McLaughlin rang in and ran out according to his whims. Like the Amerks, the Hawks' early image on the ice focused on sound goaltending and husky defensemen. But what set them apart was McLaughlin's determination not only to win, but to win with American-born hockey players.

The first Hawk coach, Muldoon, lasted a full season, which was better than average over the first decade of the franchise. Through 1930, he was followed by Barney Stanley, Hugh Lehman, Herb Gardiner, Tom Shaughnessy, and Bill Tobin, when Chicago made the playoffs for the first time since their maiden season. Still one of the lowest-scoring teams in the league, they had a splendid goalie in Chuck Gardiner, who kept them competitive throughout the season, until they were eliminated by the Canadiens (who went on to win the Cup) after almost fifty-two minutes of overtime in the second game.

Dick Irvin put together a winning lineup in front of Gardiner in 1931. Though losing the Vezina race to Worters, Gardiner led the league with twelve shutouts, had a 1.77 average, and was named first all-star. After Babe Dye's injury in 1928, the Hawks had no genuine star outside the nets except for left-winger Johnny Gottselig. Never really a high-scorer, he was a master at ragging the puck, and though he was not American-born it seemed to please the major that at least Gottselig had been born not in Canada but in Odessa, Russia.

Irvin's method was to skate fast, fresh lines in short shifts, and the system took them all the way to the Cup finals. In the second-place series, after tying the Leafs, 2–2 they tied them again, 1–1, Gardiner holding them off until Stewart Adams scored at 19:20 of overtime. Against the Rangers Gardiner was perfect, winning 2–0 and 1–0, to send the Hawks after the Canadiens and the Cup.

In Chicago Stadium, with seventeen thousand of the NHL's most vocal fans in attendance, Montreal won the first game, 2–1, but the Hawks came back to tie the series. Hainsworth and Gardiner matched saves through one overtime period. At 4:50 of the second, Gottselig got the unassisted winner. Then at the Forum, trailing after goals by Gagnon and Mantha, the Hawks rallied again. Third-period goals by Hal March and Adams sent the game into overtime. Gardiner matched Hainsworth again through two full periods. Then Marvin Wentworth won it at 13:50.

After one period of the fourth game and goals by Gottselig and Ernie Arbour, it seemed that all curses against Chicago were inoperative. But that was as close as they got. Montreal dominated the rest of the game and all of the next game. The Hawks couldn't score another goal, and McLaughlin was looking for another coach early the following season.

Under Bill Tobin, and with Gardiner getting his first Vezina, they finished second again, but Toronto blasted them out of the playoffs in the first round. In the 1933 season, the Hawks had three coaches. McLaughlin's first choice was Godfrey Matheson, a man who was Irvin's opposite, an amateur in hockey rather than a hardened pro and quite formal rather than rough-and-ready. Moreover, his system was the opposite: an iron-man concept where the "first team" was to stay on the ice, spelled by individual substitutes who were to fill in by imitating the play of the regulars. Matheson's favorite strategy was to have little Mush March carry the puck, split the defensemen, and drop the puck for big Taffy Abel to crash the nets. He also refused to use Gardiner in practice for fear of injuries.

McLaughlin loved those ideas, but the players thought them absurd. Manager Bill Tobin, when the fantastic reports of training sessions turned out to be true, managed to get Matheson's resignation. When the season opened,

Checking Back

American-born trainer Emil Iverson was the coach. In January, an experienced hockey hand, Tommy Gorman, took over the helm. It was too late to salvage the season—Chicago finished last in the American Division—but at least he put an end to some of the bizarre practices, such as using a scarecrow or dummy in the nets during workouts.

In 1934, despite McLaughlin, Gorman had a competitive team on the ice. They scored fewer goals than any other team in the league, but in Gottselig, March, Paul Thompson, and Doc Romnes they had capable, consistent forwards. And that time Gardiner had help at defense. Lionel Conacher had come over from the Canadiens and teamed with Abel to form one of the great pairs in the game, with Art Coulter and Roger Jenkins as the other pair. Bolstered by the back lines, Gardiner won the Vezina by a wide margin, and the Hawks finished second to the Wings in the division.

Against the Canadiens, Gottselig scored twice and Conacher once to win the first game, 3–2. In the second game, Montreal had the only goal, so that the series hinged on a sudden-death overtime. March won it after twelve minutes, but Chicago was not through with Montreal because the Maroons had beaten the Rangers in the third-place series. Gardiner won a 3–0 shutout and Chicago swept the series with a 3–2 win, to set the stage for the finals against Detroit.

Gardiner was the key to the Hawks' success, and there was reason to be concerned. Happy-go-lucky and extroverted, he was the exception to the rule of high-strung, temperamental goalies. But now close to a championship for the first time, he seemed alternately melancholic and choleric. In fact, he was ill. He had been hiding a chronic tonsil infection that had begun to spread and cause uremic convulsions. Obsessed with the Cup, he was playing with great physical pain, and the stress of the games plus that of concealing his condition was causing emotional problems as well.

Chicago hadn't won a game in Detroit's Olympia for over four years, yet now, playing for the Stanley Cup, they never trailed in either of the two games on Red Wing ice. Conacher put them in front in the first, only to have Herb Lewis tie it in the third period and send it into overtime. Just over a minute into the second extra period, Paul Thompson gave the Hawks a leg up on the Cup. In the second game it was Rosario Couture who put Chicago ahead, before Lewis tied it. But this time the Hawks powered in three-period goals—by Romnes, Art Coulter, and Gottselig—to send them home to Chicago ready to sweep the championship without a loss through seven games.

Gardiner, however, was on the verge of a breakdown, and Gorman and Conacher discussed making a change. Gardiner insisted on playing and held his own through two periods as Thompson and Gottselig matched goals by Pettinger and Aurie. Cude's nose was broken by Couture's stick in the second period, but it was Gardiner who weakened in the third. Goals by Doug Young, Weiland, and Aurie kept the Wings and the series alive, but Gardiner's reaction to the loss seemed so severe that it was unlikely he could play again. He was sent to Milwaukee for rest and isolation, but two days later he was back in Chicago Stadium, telling his teammates, "Just get me one goal."

Cude was snorting and wheezing through his bandaged nose. Gardiner was numbing his pain through a kind of autohypnosis. Both were superb. Through two scoreless periods the Hawks held on and seemed to be holding their breath, too, because they didn't think the grim Gardiner could hold out. But in the third period he was suddenly manic, shouting encouragement to his team. Again there was no score, and when the overtime began there was another sudden change. Gardiner was his old self, grinning and confidently waving his stick to the crowd. Through the first overtime and ten minutes of the second, there was no score. Cude had more than fifty saves and Gardiner more than forty. Then, at 10:05, on a power-play faceoff in the Wings' end, Romnes won the draw and March sent a forty-footer past Cude.

Roger Jenkins wheeled the triumphant Gardiner through the Loop in a wheelbarrow, as Chicago celebrated its first hockey championship. Two months later, the goalie was dead of a brain hemorrhage.

Chicago began the next season not only without Gardiner but without Gorman (fired), Abel (retired), and Conacher (traded). Clem Loughlin was the new coach, veteran Lorne Chabot was in goal, and Howie Morenz was on a forward line. Alex Levinsky and Art Wiebe were the new pair of top defensemen, and they helped Chabot to his best season in a long time; a 1.83 average and his only Vezina. Chicago also had its best winning record, finishing just a point behind the Bruins in the American Division, but were shut out by the Maroons for two games plus four minutes of overtime in the first round of the playoffs.

Nevertheless, Loughlin stayed on as coach, with a peculiar charge from the major: to win with American-born players. Thus Chabot was traded to make room for Mike Karakas from Aurora, Minnesota, who was rookie of the year, second in average to Boston's Tiny Thompson. Paul Thompson tied for second in scoring and Romnes won the Byng, but Chicago slumped to third in the division and were eliminated from the playoffs in the first round by the Amerks. In 1937 they were back in the cellar, and when they had been eliminated from a playoff spot, McLaughlin demanded that Loughlin put an all-American team on the ice.

Karakas, Levinsky (from Syracuse), Romnes (White Bear, Minnesota), and Lou Trudel qualified for this team, and the Major added five rookies: Ike Klingbeil (Hancock, Michigan); Butch Schaefer, Curly Brink, and Al Suomi (Eveleth, Minnesota); and Bun LaPrairie (Sault Ste. Marie, Michigan). In five

Checking Back

games, this chauvinistic crew managed one win against the Rangers, while Art Ross and others protested the "disgrace to hockey" that attempted experiments while other teams were fighting for playoff berths.

Coach Loughlin's tenure ended with the season, and referee and baseball umpire Bill Stewart (Fitchburg, Massachusetts) took over. The team struggled through the season winning only fourteen games but edging the Red Wings for third place. Rookie-of-the-Year Cully Dahlstrom was a fine addition and so were veterans defenseman Earl Seibert and center Carl Voss, but the Hawks hardly seemed viable Cup contenders—at least, not until they beat the Canadiens two out of three in the first round. Montreal won the first game, 6–4, only to have Karakas shut them out in the second. The decisive game was in the Forum, and the Canadiens led, 2–1, with a minute to play when Seibert tied the score. Less than twelve minutes into overtime, Wilf Cude was visited by an old Chicago nemesis as Paul Thompson deflected Lou Trudel's shot past him, setting the stage for that memorable second-round series with the Amerks.

Here was the best New York American team, fresh from beating the Rangers, going against a Chicago team with eight American-born players. Back in 1929, Myles Lane of the Bruins had been the first American-born skater to have his name inscribed on the Stanley Cup, but this was expecting too much. Schriner, Stewart, and Sorrell all beat Karakas in Madison Square Garden, and the Hawks had to come back again. Again Karakas turned in a shutout in Chicago, Levinsky blunting most of the Amerks' attacks, and Dahlstrom getting the overtime goal past Earl Robertson. Back in New York the Amerks went all-out in their last major attempt at a title. With the scored tied, 1–1, Levinsky's scoring shot failed to turn on the red light because New York fans had immobilzed the judge's hands. Chicago went on to win, 3–2, and then they had to face the Leafs in Toronto without the services of Mike Karakas.

The Chicago goalie had broken a toe in New York and couldn't get his boot on. Paul Goodman, the spare, had been sent home. Davey Kerr of the Rangers was available, but Conn Smythe wouldn't allow that substitution, suggesting instead Alfie Moore, a minor-league goalie at Pittsburgh, who lived in Toronto. Gottselig and Thompson were sent to recruit Moore and finally tracked him to a neighborhood bar. When he saw Gottselig he said, "Am I glad to see you. How about a couple of tickets to the game tonight?" The answer was, "You're going to get the best seat in the house."

If the news didn't sober Alfie up, or the coffee they poured into him, perhaps the shot that Gordy Drillon whistled by him in less than two minutes did. Moore allowed no more goals the rest of the night, while Gottselig got two and Thompson one for Chicago. Smythe had enough of Moore and demanded that Goodman be summoned for the next game. Drillon and Seibert matched first-period goals, but it was all Toronto after that. Jackson scored, Drillon scored again, and George Parsons scored twice for a 5–1 win that evened the series. Moreover, Red Horner broke Romnes's nose in six places and March was also knocked out of action.

Back in Chicago, Karakas was fitted with a special boot and Romnes with a football helmet and faceguard. The Hawks battered Horner around the ice. Karakas allowed but one goal in the first period, by Apps. Voss tied it in the second, and Romnes with poetic justice won it in the third. And then the Hawks won their second Stanley Cup by skating away with the next game. Drillon matched Dahlstrom's goal in the first period, but that was as close as Toronto could come. Carl Voss of Chelsea, Massachusetts, scored on passes from Gottselig and Roger Jenkins of Appleton, Wisconsin. Jack Shill scored unassisted. And Mush March scored with assists to Thompson and Romnes of White Bear, Minnesota.

Alfie Moore got three hundred dollars and a gold watch for his storybook part in the championship. He also got sweet revenge on Conn Smythe, who had exiled him to Pittsburgh. The jingoistic Major McLaughlin got the last laugh about American-born hockey players. And Fitchburg's Bill Stewart got to stay on as Chicago's coach through twenty-two games of the next season. The Hawks were in third place at the time, but an overtime loss to Les Canadiens was more than the major could bear, by jingo.

14

The Kraut Line and Mr. Zero

In Chicago, Major McLaughlin had the satisfaction of seeing his Hawks win the Stanley Cup in 1938 with eight American-born hockey players on his squad. The satisfaction was short-lived. A year later the Hawks were grounded in the cellar of the seven-team league and out of the playoffs.

A much more successful ethnic mix had been achieved in Boston, featuring three Germans from Kitchener and a rookie goalie from Eveleth, Minnesota. Art Ross called the 1939 Bruins "the greatest hockey team ever assembled," and a solid case can be offered for that claim in terms of both personnel and performance. Eddie Shore was in his last full season in Boston but was still effective enough to be named first-team all-star alongside his teammate Dit Clapper. Flash Hollett, John Crawford, and John Portland backed them up. They allowed only seventy-six goals against in forty-eight games, twenty-nine goals better than the second-best defense.

At forward they had probably the best pair of centers ever to skate as teammates. The masterful stickhandler Bill Cowley had Roy Conacher and Mel Hill on his wings, while ever-aggressive Milt Schmidt had Bobby Bauer and Woody Dumart on his. On a third line all the Bruins could put at center ice was Cooney Weiland, just another Hall-of-Famer, playing his last season. Other forwards on the team were Ray Getliffe, Gord Pettinger, Bob Hamill, and Charles Sands. The Bruins led the league in scoring with 156 goals, more than double what they allowed.

It was in goal that Ross had made his most decisive move. Tiny Thompson was a great favorite in Boston. He had won the Vezina in 1930, 1933, 1936, and 1938. At the beginning of the 1939 season, Thompson was nursing a bad eye and Frank Brimsek, who had made them forget Mike Karakas at Eveleth High School, played two games before returning to Providence. Tiny returned for five games until November 28 when, at thirty-three, he was sold to the Red Wings for fifteen thousand dollars. Brimsek was installed in the Boston nets and lasted nine full seasons, until he was thirty-three and sent west to finish his career in Chicago.

Under the pressure of replacing Thompson, Brimsek performed brilliantly. He lost, 2–0, to the Canadiens and then recorded three straight shutouts, his scoreless streak of 231:54 breaking Thompson's modern mark of 224:47. Then he came right back with another three consecutive shutouts in a scoreless streak of 220:24. He completed his first season as first-team all-star, winner of the Vezina and Calder Trophies, with ten shutouts, and he also won for himself the name of Mr. Zero.

The year before, the Bruins had led the league with a record of thirty wins and seven ties in forty-eight games, only to be eliminated from the playoffs in three straight one-goal decisions by the Leafs. Now they improved that record to thirty-six wins and two ties, sixteen points ahead of the second-place Rangers, and were determined to carry through to the Cup. Aside from Brimsek's goaltending, they boasted Conacher's league-leading twenty-six goals and Cowley's league-leading thirty-four assists, and they finished the season with an eight-game winning streak.

The revised playoff system called for a best-four-of-seven series between the first two finishers. Meanwhile, the third- and fourth-place teams and the fifth- and sixth-place teams played two out of three. They had played a forty-eight–game season to eliminate one team from the playoffs. Detroit (fifth) took two out of three from Montreal. Toronto (third) took two from the Amerks (fourth) and then two out of three from Detroit. Then they waited for the conclusion of the Rangers-Bruins battle.

The first game in this series was a classic. It was tied, 1–1, in overtime when Bill Cowley fed Mel Hill in the slot, only to have Davey Kerr kick the shot away. The situation was repeated near the end of the third overtime period, only this time Cowley's pass was a couple of inches off the ice. Hill shot it out of the air into the net. Two nights later Hill did it again—at 8:24 of overtime, to beat the Rangers, 3–2, and give the Bruins a two-game lead and their tenth straight win.

When the Bruins won, 4–1, in New York, most people counted the Rangers out, especially when injury prevented Kerr from continuing. But in the fourth game Muzz Patrick took on Shore in a spirited fight, broke his nose, blackened his eye, and turned things around for New York. They won the game, 2–1, and the next one by the same count as Byng-winning Clint Smith scored at 17:19 of overtime. When the Rangers took the sixth game, 3–1, it seemed that the Bruins might be denied their championship again.

In the decisive game, Ray Getliffe scored for Boston and Muzz Patrick for New York before it went into overtime. At one point Neil Colville broke in on Brimsek. Weiland, on the bench, ducked his head under the boards and never would believe that Cowley, of all people, was the only man backchecking. But the shot slithered across the goal mouth, and the game went on into a third overtime. Finally, after 108 minutes of play, Cowley dug the puck out behind the cage and centered it, and Mel Hill whipped it past Bert Gardiner to retain the name of Sudden Death Hill. Hill's heroic emergence was no accident. Patrick's strategy was to bottle up Cowley and Conacher. As soon as Ross had seen what the Rangers were doing, he instructed his team to feed Hill.

The Bruins had gone ten years in quest of their second Stanley Cup, and they weren't about to treat the Toronto series as an anticlimax. Dumart's goal in the first period stood up through half the third period until Red Horner beat Brimsek. Less than two minutes later, Bauer got the unassisted game-winner. They got into another overtime duel in the second game, and when Doc Romnes scored at 10:38 the series was all even. But that was as close as the Leafs would come.

At Maple Leaf Gardens, the Bruins bombarded Turk Broda for three third-period goals (Bauer, Conacher, and Crawford) before Gus Marker got a meaningless shot past Brimsek. Nothing got past Mr. Zero in the next game, as Conacher scored twice. Then, back in Boston, though Bingo Kampman matched Hill's first-period goal, the Bruins got the game-winner in the second, as Shore and Cowley fed Conacher and then put the Cup away safely when Hollett scored from Crawford and Schmidt in the third. It was a particularly satisfying goal for Flash, who had been dropped, farmed out, traded, and sold over a three-year period of failing to impress Conn Smythe.

The following season, the Bruins were nearly as good, winning 31 and tying 5 to lead the league for the third straight time. Brimsek lost the Vezina to Kerr, but in a remarkable display of firepower Schmidt, Dumart, and Bauer were 1–2–3 in scoring and Cowley was tied for fourth. In assists, Schmidt led with thirty, Cowley was second with twenty-seven, and Bauer, who also won the Byng Trophy, was third with twenty-six. Schmidt and Dumart had twenty-two goals each, second to Bryan Hextall's twenty-four. Schmidt and Clapper were first all-stars, Bauer and Dumart second.

Weiland had taken over the coaching chores from Ross, but there was little change in the Bruins' play. The Kraut line was at its peak, and there has been no greater testimony to the virtues of team play and togetherness than Milt Schmidt, Bobby Bauer, and Woody Dumart. They grew up together in Kitchener (Berlin) and played together on a champion junior team. Boston signed Bauer and Dumart, but it took their persistent urging to get the club to take on seventeen-year-old, 125-pound Schmidt who, they kept saying, was the best of them. Reunited at Providence, they were dubbed the Sauerkrauts by coach Battleship Leduc, and they brought the shortened form of the name with them to Boston in 1937.

As with all the great lines, the Krauts' individual skills were complementary. Dumart, called Porky almost as much as Woody, used his weight at left wing equally well behind a check and behind one of the heaviest shots in hockey. Bauer was smooth and deceptive, his shots and passes effective for being disguised. Schmidt was one of the all-time competitors of sport, always going at full speed and intensity, a Pete Rose or Jerry Sloan on the ice, and unique in his ability to make plays while moving at maximum acceleration.

Schmidt attributes their success to their total devotion to the game and to each other. They lived together and they lived hockey. Even as married men, they were as inseparable in couples as they had been as boyhood musketeers. And they were constantly working at their play, theorizing and experimenting, reviewing and anticipating. With confidence and communication born of mutual knowledge and trust, their performance as a unit surpassed anything yet seen on the ice, even the drilled intricacies of the USSR's passing game.

In 1940, when the Krauts scored 61 goals and totaled 138 points among them, the defending champion Bruins were undergoing some changes. Getliffe and Sands went to Montreal for Herb Cain, a consistent left wing. Rookie centers Patrick McReavy and Terrance Reardon made the squad, but it was Art Jackson, acquired from the Amerks, who took over Weiland's slot on the third line. Desmond Smith was brought over from Chicago to bolster the defense. The major change, however, involved the man who had been the franchise in Boston Garden since 1927, Eddie Shore.

Art Ross felt that the best thing he could do with Shore, regardless of his good season in the Cup year, was to deal him while he was still worth something on the market. The Amerks were interested at a $25,000 figure, but Shore was doing some dealing of his own. He bought the Springfield Indians for $42,000 and planned to play for his team while running it and on occasion help out the Bruins as well. Ross publicly poor-mouthed the Bruins' loss and privately pressured Shore to play. Shore played three games early in the season, scoring his last Bruin goal on December 5, but in the face of Ross's demands announced that his Springfield obligations came first. By the end of January, Ross had managed to get Eddie Wiseman and cash from the Amerks in exchange for Shore's occasional services, so Boston's four-time MVP, a seven-time first all-star, played his final few NHL games for the New York Americans.

The excellence of the Bruin teams in these years needs to be considered in the context of their competition. It was not a case of a champion on a bum-of-the-week campaign, giving clinics in exhibitions against outclassed opponents. The league was strong throughout, especially in the 1940 season, but the last three teams had trouble winning games. Montreal had hit bottom and were starting to rebuild under Alfred Lepine. The Amerks had not yet hit bottom. The improving Red Wings had not yet discovered a scoring punch. Fourth-place Chicago won better than half their games, though the Bentleys had not yet arrived on the scene. And challenging Boston throughout the season, genuine threats of course in the playoffs, were two of the outstanding teams of the era, the Leafs and the Rangers, both characterized by wide-open offense, though neither could match the goal production of the Bruins.

In Dick Irvin's last season behind the Toronto bench, he was getting inconsistent goaltending from Turk Broda and thinking of replacing him with Phil Stein. Bucko McDonald, brought from the Wings, anchored the defense along with Reg Hamilton, Bingo Kampman, young Jack Church, rookie Wally Stanowski, and veteran Red Horner. At forward, Busher Jackson and Doc Romnes had gone to the Amerks, but in return Sweeney Schriner was a Maple Leaf. Don Metz had come up to join brother Nick, and along with Gus Marker there were promising young forwards in Lex Chisholm, Red Heron, and Pete Langelle. The heart of the team was the DAD line: Gord Drillon, Syl Apps, and Bob Davidson.

Conn Smythe had said that no one with a name like Sylvanus Apps could possibly become a pro hockey player. He also said that he never wanted a Lady Byng Trophy winner. Smythe never changed his mind; he simply accepted Apps as the exception that proved the rule. Rookie of the Year in 1937, Apps led in assists with twenty-nine and was edged in scoring by Schriner. He repeated his assists total in 1938, but this time linemate Drillon won the scoring title, many of his twenty-six goals coming on deflections from Apps—a play they made Broda practice with them for hours at a time. Drillon won the Byng in 1938, four years before Apps won it (after Bauer got it twice), but the skillful Syl was never anything but a splendid sportsman, to the dismay of Smythe and Irvin. He had been an outstanding football player and in the 1936 Olympics had placed sixth in the pole vault. The most memorable description of him is that of Vincent Lunny, who called him "a Rembrandt on the ice, a Nijinsky at the goalmouth."

In 1940 the Leafs could do no better than third place, eight points behind the Rangers. Like the Bruins, New York was playing for a new coach, Frank Boucher, but unlike the Bruins' Weiland, Boucher was an innovative coach, not just trying to carry on Les Patrick's method. Patrick called the 1940 team the Rangers' "greatest of all time," and Boucher called it "the finest I ever saw" (with the 1939 Bruins as second best). Davey Kerr was in goal, and at defense were captain Art Coulter and Muzz Patrick, Babe Pratt and Ott Heller. The three lines got nearly equal time: Phil Watson, Bryan Hextall, and Lynn Patrick; the Colvilles and Shibicky; Clint Smith, Kilby MacDonald, and Alf Pike.

Early in the season they set a record unbeaten streak of nineteen games, Hextall and MacDonald getting forteen and ten goals respectively during that span, while Kerr was living up to Boucher's praise as "better than Brimsek." In the twentieth game, trailing Chicago by a goal near the end, Boucher pulled Kerr for an extra forward on the fly. But no one had told Les Patrick about the plan. His yells alerted both the Hawk bench and the referee, who mistakenly blew the play dead before everyone realized that the Ranger goalie was off the ice. New York failed to tie that game and went on to win five straight, so that the streak might have gone to twenty-five games if Boucher's ploy had worked.

His innovations also included the box defense when short-handed and, growing out of that (perhaps suggested by Neil Colville), the concept of attacking four against five. During the season, the Rangers outscored their opponents almost 2 to 1 when short-handed, usually with Coulter and the Colville line on the ice. Hextall and Neil Colville scored thirty-nine and thirty-eight points (sixth and seventh) in 1940. The following year Hextall and Lynn Patrick were in a five-way tie for second in scoring with forty-four points, with Colville only two behind. Hextall and Patrick were complemented by the colorful play of Watson, an excitable and exciting Frenchman who once responded to Gottselig's needling by calling him a *"been*-has." In 1940, Hextall began a three-year streak as first all-star right wing, MacDonald won the Calder Trophy as best rookie, and Kerr won the Vezina. The Rangers lost only eleven games in forty-eight. Yet they finished second, three points behind the Bruins, who had lost twelve but tied only five.

Toronto put away the Hawks and the Red Wings in two games apiece and waited to see who would emerge from the showdown between New York and Boston. This memorable series turned out to be Davey Kerr's. He shut out the mighty Bruin scoring machine in the first game, 4--0. Then, after Boston had taken the next two games and seemed about to reassert their dominance, Kerr took over again. Though the Rangers got only one shot past Brimsek in each of the next two games, that was enough, since Kerr was perfect. One Bruin goal in the sixth game was meaningless as New York got four, to reverse the previous year's result.

This time there had been no overtime games for Hill to win. But perhaps the major difference from one year to the next was in the policeman role. Eddie Shore was gone from the scene, and his apparent heir to the title of Mr. Pugnacious was on the other side: Phil Watson. New York still had both the Leafs and the circus to contend with. They scheduled back-to-back games at the Garden and won them both, 2–1 on Alfie Pike's overtime goal and 6–2 on a Hextall hat trick against a badly bothered Broda. Then they turned Gotham over to the Ringlings and went to Maple Leaf Gardens to finish the job, but not without a struggle. Toronto came back with two third-period goals to win the third game, 2–1. Then Broda blanked the Rangers to even the series.

Checking Back

The fifth game was decisive. It was tied, 1–1, in overtime, when Muzz Patrick scored the winner. And in the final game, after Apps from Davidson and Nick Metz from Schriner had given the Leafs new life, Neil Colville and Pike scored within a two-minute span of the third period to bring on another overtime. The Rangers got the winner after just two minutes, Hextall scoring with assists to Heller and Watson.

A winter storm that marooned the Rangers in Toronto failed to put a damper on their victory celebration. Lester Patrick planned a small party for thirty-five people (team, management, press) at the Royal York Hotel. Somehow a large dance in the hotel ballroom joined the Cup party. Sometime in the evening a Toronto fan was caught trying to get out with the Stanley Cup under his coat. And sometime the next morning Patrick received a bill for $3,700 for the affair.

A year later there was little for the Rangers to celebrate other than Hextall's league-leading 26 goals. New York's younger NHL franchise not only finished fourth but was eliminated by Detroit in the first playoff round. The senior franchise finished last and was just eliminated. Detroit also beat Chicago in two straight and waited for the winner of the Boston-Toronto series.

Toronto was an improved team in Hap Day's first year as coach, mainly because of Turk Broda's improvement. Smythe sold Phil Stein to New Haven and sharpened Turk's play with an offer of a one thousand dollar bonus for a Vezina. Day had him playing handball to sharpen reflexes and praticing without his stick to improve his style. Ed Fitkin wrote that he had his heart set on the Vezina: "He wasn't flopping. He was better on rebounds. His timing was sharper, and he had more confidence. . . . He was always 'on' the puck, barking instructions to defense mates or lagging forwards in his high-pitched voice."

Broda's competition came from Brimsek, of course, but also from Detroit's stocky rookie, Johnny Mowers. With two games to play, Broda had allowed ninety-eight goals, Brimsek ninety-nine, and Mowers only ninety-six. Broda held the Black Hawks to one goal, then shut them out in his final game to finish with ninety-nine against, while Mowers and Brimsek went head-to-head in a 2–2 game. Now, with Brimsek eliminated and the Leafs in the stands at Boston Garden, Mowers faced the Bruins again with a chance to win the Trophy. Just fifty seconds into the game, Jack Crawford got a puck past Mowers for the 99th time that season to take some of the pressure off. Then, in the third period, Cowley scored from Conacher and Wiseman, as Broda leapt from his seat to cheer his bonus-earning goal.

Boston won the game, 4–1, so that Mowers and Brimsek tied for second. "Turk won't be smiling very long," Art Ross said. "My boys won the Vezina for him, and now we'll win the Cup from him." The Bruins had finished with the best record for the fourth consecutive year, scored the most goals, and had the scoring leader (Cowley), the assists leader (Cowley), the MVP (Cowley), the Byng winner (Bauer), and a first all-star defenseman (Clapper). They had put together record unbeaten streaks of twenty-three games of fifteen on the road. But in the Leafs they were taking on the strongest possible challenge.

These teams had the greatest respect for each other, and over the years the Smythe-Ross feud had provided them with the inspiration of fierce rivalry. Another dimension of the spirit of this competition is provided in the confrontation that had taken place during the season between Syl Apps and Flash Hollett, players not made in the image of their managers. After a collision, Apps approached Hollett and said, "By hum, Flash, you knocked my tooth out."

"For gosh sakes, Syl, I'm sorry," he said. "I didn't mean to do it."

"By criminy, Flash, that was a bad thing to do to a fellow."

"Aw gee, Syl. My stick just bounced up off your stick and hit your face. You know how these things happen, doggone it."

At this point Dit Clapper, the Boston enforcer, who alone of those on the ice seemed to be able to control his laughter, skated up and said, "See here, fellows, cut out that bad language! It's terrible for the fans to hear. Shame on both of you. I MEAN IT!"

Apps was returning to play after an injury, but Cowley missed the first three games of the series with a wrenched knee. Brimsek got the Bruins the first game with a 3–0 shutout, but the Boston defense fell apart in the next two games and Toronto won them, 5–3 and 7–2. Cowley came back for the fourth game, and he and Herb Cain got Boston even in the series with a 2–1 win. The fifth game was the best-played of the series, a typically fiercely checking Stanley Cup game. It was tied 1–1 in overtime, when Conn Smythe offered a bonus of one hundred dollars to Pete Langelle if the flashy skater would pass up his passes for a change and take three shots on goal. Langelle obliged. Brimsek took care of the first two, but the third, on a pass from Red Heron at 17:31, put Toronto ahead in the series.

Boston came back on Toronto ice in another 2–1 game, as Cain scored the winner. The seventh game was yet another classic. Bucko McDonald put the Leafs ahead, only to see Flash Hollett tie it up. For the fourth straight time in this playoff, there was a 2–1 score. And the decisive goal was scored by none other than Sudden Death Hill. But this time he did it in regulation, while Brimsek and the Bruin defense held on against every Toronto attack.

After that spectacular series, the finals against Detroit were routine. Wiseman, Schmidt, and McReavy had Boston in front 3–0 in the first game before two third-period goals (Carl Liscombe and Syd Howe) made the score respectable. In the second game, also in Boston, Mowers matched Brimsek through

Checking Back

two scoreless periods. Mud Bruneteau gave Detroit a third-period lead for over ten minutes, but Reardon tied it and Conacher won it.

The best action came after the game. A heckler shouted at Ross, "Are you going to let this go to seven games the way you did against Toronto?" Ross went after the man and scored with a right to the eye.

When the Bruins returned to Boston, they had already won the championship. Schimdt scored twice including the winner in a 4–2 game at Olympia, then assisted first Hollett and then Bauer in the 3–1 game that completed the sweep—the first ever in a best-of-seven final series. It would be almost two decades before the Bruins failed to make the playoffs agin. Yet it would be nearly three decades before they again finished first or won the Stanley Cup. In the four seasons 1938–1941, including two Cup championships, they had won twenty-nine and thirty more games than two other outstanding teams, the Rangers and the Maple Leafs. But the changes brought on by the war and the shifting of balances of power in the league ended this brief period of dominance.

15

The Great Comeback and the Vanishing Americans

The world of prewar hockey came to an end in 1942 with both bangs and whimpers. The loudest cries and greatest anguish came from the vicinity of New York, where Red Dutton's team had become the Brooklyn Americans, a desperation move made in the hope that interborough rivalry would stimulate increased revenue to meet the climbing rental fees in the Garden. For Busher Jackson the shift to Brooklyn did not bring a satisfactory contract offer. He held out until January, when Dutton sold him to Boston for $7,500. Also gone were Charlie Conacher, who retired, and Lorne Carr, who was reunited in Toronto with his old Amerk linemate, Sweeney Schriner, after a trade which brought Heron, Marker, Nick Knott, and Johnny O'Flaherty to Brooklyn.

Defenseman Tommy Anderson, who won the Hart Trophy, was the only genuine star left for the Amerks, but neither he nor beleaguered goalie Chick Rayner could prevent Brooklyn from being the most scored-against team. They also scored the least themselves and finished last, with only sixteen wins and three ties. Thus one of the most colorful groups in hockey was disenfranchised. From the time of Billy Burch and Bullet Joe Simpson; from the barnstorming days when Tommy Gorman led them out to Portland, where periods ended with a gunshot and the Amerks scrambled for cover thinking Big Bill Dwyer's mob was in action; from the brief resurgences of aging stars like Lionel Conacher and Eddie Shore, the Amerks had played entertaining but losing hockey. But now the show had to be folded, and out of town at that.

Throughout the season, especially after Pearl Harbor had brought the war home to American-based Canadian hockey players, NHL rosters underwent changes to keep pace with enlistments. At the start of the season, another Toronto-Boston battle for the lead was anticipated. Halfway through it was just that. But by season's end the Rangers had come on to pass them both.

In Boston, Schmidt, Bauer, and Dumart, who had done everything else together most of their lives, flew off to join the Royal Canadian Air Force after three quarters of the season. They combined for eight points in their last game, beating the Canadiens, 8–1, and they were carried off the ice by both teams while the Boston Garden organ played "Auld Lang Syne." The Bruins missed them so sorely that when a heckler taunted Art Ross, "Where the hell's your power play?" he shouted, "In England, France, and Germany, you slacker!"

Important changes had taken place in Toronto, too. Conn Smythe was now Major Smythe, commanding officer of the Thirtieth Light Antiaircraft Battery, and Frank Selke was managing the team. Smythe had advised all his players to volunteer for training, and most of the club signed up with the Toronto Scottish Reserve. But they were still in Maple Leaf uniform and the team seemed actually improved, with Carr and Walt Stanowski and a number of fast, promising young players.

The Rangers were the leading goal-making team. Hextall led the league in scoring, Lynn Patrick was second and led in goals, Phil Watson was fourth and led in assists, Grant Warwick was rookie of the year, and rookie Sugar Jim Henry was showing steady improvement under fire in the nets. They finished strong to lead the league, but at the end of the season the hottest team was Detroit. Jack Adams had assembled an eager, battering team, led by the Don Grosso–Sid Abel–Eddie Wares line, and they finished the season in fifth place but with a streak of nine straight wins at home. This was a team that pioneered the contemporary style of dumping the puck into a corner and forechecking to pressure opponents into mistakes in their end.

Detroit won the opening playoff round from Montreal, as expected, and then upset Boston in two straight games. Meanwhile Toronto was battling its way into the Cup finals for the eight time in eleven years, though they hadn't won since 1932. Apps, Drillon, Davidson, Nick Metz, Schriner, and Gaye Stewart simply overpowered Henry in this series to win in six games, though Sugar Jim had a sweet shutout in the third game and a good 3–1 win in the fifth.

This set the stage for one of the most remarkable series of all, so rich in material for analysis that Stan Fischler could call it in one place "the most thrilling comeback win in hockey history" and in another the "classic choke of them all." The hard-checking Wings opened up with a 3–2 win in Maple Leaf Gardens that Hap Day called "hoodlumism." Leaf goals by John McCreedy and Schriner in the first period matched Wing goals by Grosso and Abel, but an unassisted score by Grosso in the second held up all the way. Smythe, about to ship out for Europe, told Selke that he was really worried about his team. He predicted it would be hard for Hap Day to straighten the team out. They seemed to be intimidated by the style of play typified by the way Jimmy Orlando had checked rookie Bob Goldham bloody to the bench.

The second game was more of the same. Grosso scored, assisted by Wares, and Bruneteau, assisted by Liscombe, in the first period. A second-period goal by Schriner got the Leafs close, but Wares fed Grosso again in the third and Gerry Brown added another before Stanowski scored a meaningless goal for Toronto. The Maple Leaf Gardens were stunned. Apps and Drillon had been shut out for two games, and Bucko McDonald seemed completely bewildered by Adams's strategy.

Things got worse before they got better. The third game was at Olympia, and Lorne Carr got the Leafs off in front with two first-period goals. But before the period ended, Brown and Joe Carveth got the Wings even, rookie Eddie Bush assisting on both goals within a thirty-eight–second burst. It was all Detroit after that, even though Sid Abel retired for the night with an injured cheek. Bush and Grosso assisted first Pat McCreavy and then Syd Howe on second-period goals. And in the third period, Bush completed a five-point game when he scored on a pass from Liscombe. Broda, McDonald, Drillon, and company were totally embarrassed. Day, in what seemed like deep despair or high dudgeon or plain panic, decided to make some changes.

In the fourth game, kid brother Don Metz replaced Drillon on the first line and raw rookie Ernie Dickens replaced McDonald at defense. After a scoreless first period, Mud Bruneteau put Detroit in front and Sid Abel scored with assists to both his wings. But Toronto would not quit. Almost fourteen minutes were gone in the period when Davidson beat Mowers to suggest that the Leafs were not yet ready to fall. A minute and a half later, Lorne Carr got them even. When Liscombe scored early in the third, Detroit thought they had the Cup, running over the hapless Leafs, who had become perennial bridesmaids. But Syl Apps broke out of his slump two minutes later to tie the game. Then, at 12:45, he and Don Metz fed brother Nick for the game-winner.

More than the game itself, which had been very evenly played, it was the immediate aftermath that proved the turning point in the series. Adams was disappointed at the loss, and enraged at referee Mel Harwood for penalties plus fines handed out to Wares and Grosso in the third period. As soon as the game ended, Adams went over the boards and charged Harwood, pummeling him until the linesmen and the police pulled him off. President Calder was not amused. He added fines to Wares and Grosso and suspended Adams indefinitely.

The fifth game was at Toronto. Day announced that he not only was going along with young Metz and Dickens, he also was bringing up teenager Gaye Stewart to replace Hank Goldup at left wing. For Detroit, veteran Eb Goodfellow took over behind the bench. The Red Wings did not respond well to the changes, but the Maple Leafs were charged up. In the first two periods, while keeping Detroit at bay, they shelled the shocked Mowers for seven goals, three by the Metzes (with three assists). Apps had a goal and two assists, and

Goldham and Stanowski had one and one each. Detroit managed three goals in the third period (three points for Howe), but Toronto was cruising home, Apps and Don Metz feeding each other to complete Metz's hat trick and make the final score 9–3.

Detroit went all-out from the start in the sixth game, their last chance to win at home. Grosso and Abel pressured Broda, but he saved and saved again. Goodfellow sent out rookies Gus Giesebrecht and Doug McCaig, but Broda turned back their shots, too. When Don Metz opened the second period with an unassisted goal at fourteen seconds, it seemed that the Red Wings had shot their load. Goldham and Taylor, both assisted by Schriner, scored within thirty-two seconds of each other in the third period. Broda got his shutout, and the series moved back to Maple Leaf Gardens with the games tied at three but the Leafs in clear control and the Wings in present danger of collapse.

To give credit to the Red Wings, they did not simply fold up in the seventh game. It was a game more typical of Stanley Cup play than much of the rest of the series had been, played with great intensity but conservative checking, before a record crowd of over 16,200. The first period was scoreless. In the second, Howe got an early goal with assists by Abel and Orlando, while Detroit continually stifled the Toronto offense. Mowers was brilliant, especially when the Leafs had a two-man advantage.

The power play turned the tide in the third period. With Orlando in the box, Sweeney Schriner scored on passes from Taylor and Carr to tie the score at 7:46. At 9:43 Langelle scored, from Goldham and McCreedy. At 16:13 Schriner scored again, with assists to the same linemates, and Toronto had the Cup. The final buzzer brought a tremendous ovation. Major Smythe received another when he accepted the trophy, and Hap Day got the largest of all when Goldham escorted him onto the ice.

There have been many explanations for the turnabout in that series, and most of them rightly focus not on the fourth game but on its aftermath. Detroit had played their head-banging, dump-the-puck-in game and had simply been outgamed by fresh, young Leafs. But with Jack Adams suspended, the Red Wing battle plan lacked something in execution for the remaining three games. It was as if, with the head bully gone, the rest of the gang didn't have the heart for the bullying.

Nevertheless, as a distinctive era came to an end, it was that Detroit team that gave a glimpse of things to come. That brief period, less than half a decade that ended with wartime changes, was dominated by three outstanding teams. The Boston Bruins, the New York Rangers, and the Toronto Maple Leafs, each featuring a pair of lines with superior speed, stick-handling, and playmaking ability, played an excellent brand of hockey that has not since been seen. Indeed, the 1938–1942 period may well be regarded, though it has not often been, with the kind of poignant nostalgia reserved for something splendid gone forever.

The war was the occasion, but not the cause, of the essential change. One rule that came with the war affected style of play inexorably; another affected attitudes on the ice and in the stands. Ultimately both those rule-changes coincided and cohered with a change of strategy, and together they produced a new brand of NHL hockey. Yet it was not brand-new. It did not spring full-grown from the head of Frank Boucher or anyone else.

In the techniques employed by Jack Adams's Red Wings at the end of the 1942 season could be found anticipations of the future. Detroit lost the Stanley Cup in the seventh game but found the key to later success. What was truly lost was a particular concept of the game that had been executed with maximum skill and high style by three teams. One line of development had reached full maturity in Boston, New York, and Toronto. Now another line would have to be played out.

PART *III*

The Closed Circuit

For twenty-five seasons, 1943–1967, the National Hockey League operated as an exclusive oligarchy, six and only six clubs atop a rigidly controlled hierarchy of all hockey. It was perhaps the most successful operation in the history of professional sports. The precise figures are not available, but a consensus of the estimates is that the league drew better than 90 percent of capacity for the entire period and that by 1963 the 210 league games drew 92 percent while the playoffs continued at 100 percent.

The teams played fifty-game seasons through 1945, sixty- through 1949, seventy- for the rest of the period. That was the only kind of expansion tolerated under the titular leadership of Clarence Campbell, who became president when Red Dutton retired in 1947 after less than four years as successor to Frank Calder. As long as Conn Smythe and James D. Norris, Sr., remained in firm positions of leadership on their teams and on the board, the concept of successful exclusivity was maintained. When a younger generation of executives eventually took over, Campbell shifted with the winds of change and the quarter-century era came to an end.

But until that time and during the period, the NHL's power over hockey solidified in a massive, pyramidal structure with the six clubs at the apex. Beneath them were three professional leagues—the Western, the Central, and the American—which served primarily to develop NHL players and where fewer and fewer veterans could be found. The major amateur leagues—the International and the Eastern—served the same purpose. But the NHL's hegemony reached beyond these levels to the Junior leagues, A or B, to college hockey and the Intermediate and Senior leagues, and even down through the age groups to Juvenile (under 18), Midget (under 16), Bantam (under 14), and Pee Wee (under 12) leagues. The hockey played there was paler and paler imitation or travesty of NHL hockey, and most of the outstanding boys were contractual property of NHL teams. Jean Ratelle, signed by the Rangers at sixteen, was not that exceptional, but Reggie Fleming, signed by the Canadiens at thirteen, was about as far (or as low) as the practice would go. The word *am-*

Checking Back

ateur was as much of a misnomer as it had always been in big-time hockey.

Given those conditions, and a power structure determined to maintain the status quo, it is not surprising that the period—unlike the earlier ones—produced dynasties. First there was a brief postwar Canadien dynasty, followed by a somewhat longer Maple Leaf dynasty and then an even longer Red Wing dynasty through the early fifties. Montreal, Toronto, and Detroit all returned to power in the late fifties or sixties. Throughout the twenty-five–year period, those three clubs accounted for all but one league championship and all but one Stanley Cup championship.

The Black Hawks were the exception in each case, but as a rule they battled the Rangers and the Bruins for the fourth playoff spot. Only in eight seasons during the quarter century did two of these teams make the playoffs, never all three together. Chicago was in the cellar nine times, New York eight, Boston six, Toronto and Detroit once each. Toronto, changing personnel more than any other club in the closed circuit, missed the playoffs four times, Detroit three times, and Montreal only once.

And yet, despite the constancy, the sense of eternal continuity, the nature and style of the game changed greatly. Stan Fischler, as usual, puts it most bluntly: "By 1960 the beautiful hockey of the twenties, thirties, and early forties was totally unrecognizable compared with the new game. Intricate pass patterns were forgotten as players milled around, cutting up the ice, hacking at the puck and each other." This is not to say that there was diminished skill in the era of Rocket Richard and Gordie Howe, only that the skills were less aesthetically satisfying.

The following chapters account for these changes while describing the principal events and individuals of the period. The factors include new rules, new styles of physical intimidation, new attitudes toward regular-season games, and new techniques for shooting and scoring. Perhaps most instrumental in changing the face of hockey were the innovative contributions of a goaltender called Jake the Snake.

16

Red Line Express

Looking down at center ice of the Capital Centre, Milt Schmidt pointed to the red line and said, "That's what ruined the game of hockey." That is no solitary sentiment but an idea held in common by many people whose background in hockey extends as far back as the thirties. In fact, Frank Boucher, who devised the new rule in 1943, called for its repeal as early as 1949. Yet the red line was read at the time as the innovation that saved the game, and there is today no indication that it will be erased.

The war produced, as Foster Hewitt put it, a "weird pattern to the game." For a time, it seemed that the NHL would suspend play for the duration, not only because of the mass enlistments of front-line players but also because of the notion around Ottawa that continuance was unpatriotic. On this issue the American Hockey League took over the leadership. Under its president, Maurice Podoloff, and executives like Lou Jacobs of Buffalo, they took the position that hockey was needed for morale on the home front.

Podoloff, Jacobs, and Chicago's Arthur Wirtz persuaded the distinguished attorney Charles Sawyer to argue the cause of the American-based NHL teams in Ottawa. Red Dutton, the new NHL president, also ably supported the continuation of play, and the Canadian government agreed, with the single stipulation that no player avoid military service just to play hockey. Official Canada saw clearly, at this time, that such a situation would be better than having service teams satisfy the public need for hockey by keeping NHL players at home to play in the uniform of their choice—a mockery of spirited war effort in which many players pursued dangerous duty.

Over-aged veterans and under-aged rookies, like Maurice Richard and the sixteen-year-old zoot-suiter, Bep Guidolin, helped to staff the teams. But wartime travel restrictions made it often a problem to meet game schedules. For this reason, pressure was put on officials to speed up play, and they responded by calling fewer penalties and virtually ignoring penalty shots. The latter development has persisted, at the expense of one of hockey's most exciting features. But the most severe casualty of the travel problem came with the abandonment of overtime. Again a significant feature of the game—particularly in terms of fan interest—was sacrificed to expediency. But long after the causes ceased to exist, the effects have been retained. The prevalence of ties in regular-season play is a measure of the careless conservatism of official hockey thinking, the commitment to maintain the status quo whatever and however it came to be.

The 1943 season was a scoring bonanza, despite the loss of overtime minutes. Only once in league history had anyone broken the seventy-point barrier—Weiland's seventy-three in 1930—and now three players did it: the Bentley brothers for Chicago (Doug seventy-three, Max seventy) and Cowley for Boston (seventy-two). Seven other players scored fifty-eight or more points, ordinarily good enough for a title (Lynn Patrick and Hextall for New York, Carr and Taylor for Toronto, and Blake, Lach, and O'Connor for Montreal). Porous defenses and nonprime goaltenders were the reasons. In fifty games (the six surviving clubs played each other ten times each), Johnny Mowers won the Vezina in the Detroit nets with 124 goals against, while the next best was Broda, with 159 for Toronto. The Rangers gave up over 5 goals a game, with a succession of inept performers in goal: Steve Buzinski, Lionel Bouvrette, Bill Beveridge, and Jimmy Franks.

Detroit scored fewer goals than anyone but the Rangers, but the Red Wings had both a slight personnel advantage over most teams, as well as the incentive of the embarrassing 1942 Stanley Cup collapse. They also had a full season to implement Jack Adams's aggressive forechecking strategy. At the end of the season, they led the league with sixty-one points to Boston's fifty-seven. Toronto was third with fifty-three, and Montreal edged Chicago for fourth, fifty to forty-nine. With only four teams in the playoffs, the league wanted as many Cup games as possible, so that the semifinals, matching first against third and second against fourth, were to be best four of seven as well as the finals. That arrangement persisted until the expansion of 1968. Throughout the season there had been thirty-two tie games, compared to twelve the year before.

Boston could still put a good starting team on the ice—Brimsek, Hollett, Clapper, Cowley, Cain, and Jackson—and they put Montreal out in five games, three of their four wins coming on overtime goals by Don Gallinger, Art Jackson, and Ab DeMarco. Meanwhile Detroit got a measure of revenge against Toronto, eliminating them in a six-game series. The line of Abel, Grosso, and Wares totaled six goals against Broda.

In the finals, Detroit got off winging at Olympia. Jack Stewart and Art Jackson matched first-period goals, but then the Wings scored five straight, including a hat trick for Mud Bruneteau, to win 6–2. In the second game they came from behind, with goals by Lester Douglas, Joe Carveth, Carl Liscombe, and Syd Howe, to beat Boston, 4–3, despite two more Jackson goals.

Moving to Boston, the Red Wings made sure there would be no repeat of their collapse last year. Mowers simply shut out the Bruins in two games. Grosso had a hat trick in a 4–0 win on April 7. The next day Carveth and Liscombe got the only scores unassisted. Detroit had come all the way back from the humiliating Toronto comeback.

The Rangers had suffered through a horrendous season, winning only eleven games and finishing nineteen points out of fifth place. But the hockey had degenerated throughout the league, due as much to the style of play as to the loss of personnel. Red Dutton, temporarily out of hockey because of the Amerks' folding, had taken over in February the acting presidency of the NHL when President Calder died of a heart attack. Dutton made the appropriate appointment of Frank Boucher, coach of the hapless Rangers, to rewrite the rule book. With help from CAHA president Cecil Duncan, Vern Thomas of the Eastern Amateur League, Hap Day, and Art Ross, he accomplished that summer job, and the league accepted every clause including the innovative (or abominative) red line.

The problem was this. In the new style of play, both defensemen moved up into the center zone, and forwards would throw the puck into the offensive zone and chase it. The Bruins had shown the way, with Shore carrying the puck to the blue line and dumping it in for the Krauts to follow. Adams's Red Wings had made this a strategy for a whole team throughout a whole game. Now, with a considerable lack of major-league talent on the ice, there was endless jamming in the corners and around the net because nobody could get the puck out. The solution was to permit forward passing up to the midpoint of the rink—the first and only forward passing between zones in the game.

The results were striking and dynamic. The logjams were broken; there was a new breakaway style with emphasis on speed and long passing. No greater emphasis was placed on stick-handling, but the opening of new passing lanes put a new facet of team play in hockey strategy. Traditionalists scoffed at "basketball on skates," but most fans responded with enthusiasm to the faster game with its increased scoring.

Scores soared. No team had ever scored 200 goals in a season, but in 1944 the Wings and the Leafs had 214, the Bruins 223, and the Canadiens 234. Twice as many players scored 70 points in that season as there had been in all 26 prior seasons: Doug Bentley had 38 goals and 77 points. Cain, Carr, and Liscombe each had 36 goals, with 82, 74, and 73 points respectively. Lach had 72 points, Snuffy Smith—who had gone from New York to Chicago—72, Cowley 71, and Chicago's Bill Mosienki 70. The wartime personnel was most obviously weak on defense, but under the new rule that weakness showed up in a positive way in the speed and explosiveness of the offense rather than negatively in the inept muddle of failing to clear. Later, when peacetime manpower was restored, the defenses would adapt. Until then, wartime morale was kept high with speed, if not skill.

Ironically, Boucher's Rangers went nowhere on the red line express. From bad they went to worse—from the cellar to record-setting ineptitude. Ken McAuley played all but one period of the fifty games and allowed 310 goals. New York won only six games, totaled only seventeen points, and finished twenty-six points behind fifth-place Boston—all records, and there were more. They had a twenty-five–game nonwinning streak which survived all challenges for more than thirty years. In a single game in Detroit, with Lester Patrick handling the team because Boucher had gone home for a brother's funeral, the Rangers gave up 15 goals (to none) and thirty-seven points, with 8 goals and twenty-two points in the third period alone. Bryan Hextall and Ott Heller, says Boucher, were the only real hockey players left on the Rangers. Bucko McDonald, overweight and over the hill at thirty-three, could do little on defense but brag about the players he'd bounced off his chest à la Taffy Abel. Raffles Boucher, at age forty-two, came out of retirement himself after five years behind the bench and played fifteen games. Scoring 4 goals and ten assists, he actually outscored *nineteen* other players who had played for him and the Rangers during that season. McAuley was probably not as bad as his record shows. He simply had no help. But he kept his average under five in forty-six games the following season before the return of major-league goalies brought his retirement. Certainly McAuley's heroics, for which Boucher would have him given the Croix de Guerre if not the Victoria Cross, failed to erase memories of Steve Buzinski's nine-game stint in the New York goal in 1943.

Lester Patrick insisted that the skinny, bow-legged, cocky little guy from Saskatchewan and the Swift Current intermediates would fill the gap left by Sugar Jim Henry's and Chuck Rayner's enlistments. Of the 55 goals scored against him in NHL play (a career average of 6.11), only one was a shot he caught in the air and then tossed into the net himself. But his most memorable play came in Maple Leaf Gardens. Buzinski was knocked flat on his back, popped up suddenly, and then just as quickly was supine again. Lynn Patrick skated over to the bench and gave this report as soon as he could stop laughing:

> We thought Steve had been knocked out. We were yelling for a penalty to Davidson for high-sticking. Davidson said, "Hell, I didn't belt him. It was the puck. He got hit on the head by the puck." That's when Steve, lying there cold as a mackerel, sat straight up and said to the referee, "That's a damn lie. He high-sticked me," and fell flat on his back again with his eyes closed.

Buzinski retired without a win, but his replacements fared little better, until the veterans came skating home again.

17

Punch Line to the Forum

The first dynasty in the closed circuit came to power in 1944, with the war still raging and the NHL player ranks still thin with the underaged and padded with the overaged. But in Montreal, manager Tommy Gorman and coach Dick Irvin put together a team that not only dominated the weakened league but continued to dominate through four straight first-place finishes, even after the return of the veterans to the hockey wars.

Two major elements contributed to this successful period for the Canadiens: the arrival of Bill Durnan to tend the nets and the assembling of the Punch Line. Montreal had been having problems in goal for some time. Since 1938 they had been last or next-to-last in goals-against. Wilf Cude, second-team all-star in 1936 and 1937, had been their last adequate goalie, and he had retired in 1941, as he said, "before they came for me with the butterfly net." Indeed, he was already a nervous wreck; his wife's accidental jiggling of the dinner table had triggered Wilf into heaving his catsup-covered steak against the wall. Durnan might have found in this a personal omen, or at least a sign of occupational hazard.

Durnan was the classic stand-up goalie, six feet tall and about 200 pounds, naturally ambidextrous and quicker with both hands than most goalies are with one. He was one of the best softball pitchers in Canada and felt that he had found his proper level in hockey at age twenty-eight as a senior amateur for the Montreal Royals. But Gorman, who among many others calls him the greatest goalie in history, thought otherwise and signed him for the Canadiens just ten minutes before his first game in 1943, a 2–2 tie against the Bruins. In this era of porous defenses and increased scoring power with the red line, Durnan allowed only 109 goals to win the Vezina in his rookie year. It had been a decade since a Canadien goalie had allowed fewer goals. By way of comparison, in 1944 the second-best defense in the league, Detroit's, had given up 3.5 goals a game to Durnan's 2.18.

The creation of the Punch Line should be credited to the coaching genius of Dick Irvin. In the modern era, as Gordie Howe says, "less attention is given to individual lines than used to be given in the past," and he then rates only his own line with Ted Lindsay and Abel and the Punch Line on the same level as the Kid Line, and Kraut Line, the Barry-Lewis-Aurie line, and the Cooks and Boucher.

Toe Blake was a Montreal veteran who had come up with the Maroons in 1935 and played for the Canadiens since 1936, winning the Hart in 1939 when he led the league with forty-seven points. Elmer Lach had joined the team for the 1941 season and established himself immediately as an outstanding play-making center with a quick left-handed shot.

Richard came up for the 1943 season as a left winger, skating on a line with Lach and Tony Demers. They scored in their first thirty-six seconds together, against the Bruins. Richard got his first goal in his second game, unassisted, against the Rangers and Steve Buzinski. In his sixteenth game, with five goals and six assists to his credit, he tried his patented buttonhook move around Boston's Johnny Crawford, was checked heavily into the boards, and snapped his right ankle. When he returned for the following season, Joseph Benoit, Demers, and Drillon were all gone from right wing. Richard, with his power-ful backhand shot and the buttonhook, was moved to the position he never left, and Irvin had assembled the ingredients for a unique all-southpaw line.

The Punch Line devastated the league. Blake (26 goals and thirty-three assists), Lach (24 and forty-eight), and Richard (32 and twenty-two) scored nearly as many goals as whole opposing teams. The Canadiens had other talented shooters: Murph Chamberlain, Phil Watson, Ray Getliffe, Buddy O'Connor, Bob Fillion, Fernand Majeau, and Gerald Heffernan. At defense they had all-star Butch Bouchard, Glen Harmon, Leo Lamoureux, and Mike McMahon, and as a team they scored a record 234 goals. They glided through the season with only five losses and beat second-place Detroit by twenty-five points in the standings. The Wings were upset by the Black Hawks in five games, Doug Bentley scoring seven goals assisted mostly by Clint Smith and Bill Mosienko, while Montreal took on the Maple Leafs.

Toronto recorded a 3–1 upset in the first game, but that was the last Montreal loss of the season. In the second game, goalie Paul Bibeault was the victim of some Punch records. The score was 5–1, Richard scored five goals, and Blake was credited with five assists. When the three stars of the game were announced, the loudspeaker at the Forum roared, "Richard, Richard, and Richard." In Toronto, Durnan turned back the Leafs 2–1 and 4–1 in the next two games. Then the Canadiens closed out the series with a record-breaking 11–0 win in Montreal, scoring four times within two and a half minutes.

In the Chicago series, Irvin used the Punch Line to shut down the Hawk high-scorers—Bentley, Smith, and Mosienko. In the first game the strategy worked to perfection as each team's first line scored once, and the Canadiens'

Watson-Getliffe-Chamberlain line got four in the 5–1 win. The next two games in Chicago were well-played. The Rocket's hat trick beat Mike Karakas, 3–1, and third-period goals by McMahon and Watson gave Montreal a 3–2 come-from-behind win.

Irvin was not happy with the narrow margin. He locked the press out of the dressing room and dressed down his players for their "dangerous complacency." But then Gorman burst in, shouting congratulations. Irvin angrily kicked at a bucket, missed, and his pratfall signaled the beginning of a celebration. The Canadiens were relaxed and jubilant on the twenty-three–hour train ride back to Montreal. When Murph Chamberlain staggered drunkenly into the dining car, Tommy Gorman said, "Look at that crazy Chamberlain! He thinks this series was three games out of five!"

Irvin may have had a point, but few cared to listen. Always a fine coach, he was never very popular. But when a critic threatened to burn down the Forum unless he was replaced, the Canadiens all skated onto the ice wearing Texaco fire chief hats. Yet Irvin failed to motivate them for that fourth game. Defenseman George Allen scored his fifth goal of the playoffs on a pass from Cully Dahlstrom, but Blake fed Lach to get Montreal even in the first period. Then Dahlstrom and Allen assisted John Harms, and Bentley scored twice on passes from Smith. The Canadiens left the ice after two periods, trailing 4–1, and they came back for the third to chants of "Fake! Fake! Fake!"

The performance had been worse than dangerous complacency to the Forum fans, who evidently felt that Montreal was trying to stretch out the series. But the Punch Line took over. Blake fed Lach at 10:02 and then Richard at 16:05. At 17:20 both Blake and Bouchard assisted Rocket on the tying goal, and then Bouchard assisted Blake for the Cup-winner at 9:12 of overtime. The Canadiens were first to win the Cup with eight straight victories. In the nine games, the Punch Line had produced twenty-one of their thirty-nine goals. No wonder Frank Selke calls them the best ever.

In 1945, Lach, Richard, and Blake were 1-2-3 in scoring in the league. Lach, who was one of "three little peanuts" (along with Doug Bentley and Harvey Barnes) who failed to pass muster for Conn Smythe in a 1938 Leaf tryout, had a record fifty-four assists in his eighty points and won the Hart Trophy. He had learned from Earl Seibert to skate with his head up and he usually saw Richard open. The Rocket had a record fifty goals. Durnan won the Vezina by a wide margin, and Bouchard was the fifth Canadien on the first all-star team. Montreal, losing only eight games, beat second-place Detroit by thirteen points in the standings.

Toronto had a surprise in store for the playoffs. Bob Davidson was assigned by Hap Day to shadow Richard. Not only did Davidson and his linemates Lorne Carr and Teeder Kennedy shut out the Punch Line in the first game, but the high-scoring Habs were shut out by Frank McCool for a 1–0 win. Selke had wheeled and dealed to put that Leaf squad together for the last wartime season, but it took the nervous goalie, who had been discharged from service with stomach ulcers, to steady them through this opener. Davidson continued to shut down Richard as Toronto won the second game, 3–2, and Montreal the third, 4–1.

The pivotal game was the fourth, when the Rocket finally burst free for a single goal. But at 12:36 of overtime, Gus Bodnar gave Toronto a 4–3 win and a 3–1 lead in the series. Montreal exploded for a 10–3 win in Game 5, but McCool settled down and with the stalwart assistance of 6'3", 215-pound Babe Pratt beat the Canadiens, 3–2, to gain the finals against the Red Wings, who were beating Boston in a seven-game series.

Sweeney Schriner had the only goal in the first game as McCool shut out Detroit at Olympia. McCool did it again two nights later as third-period goals by Kennedy and Elwyn Morris put the Leafs up by two games. Back home at the Gardens, McCool recorded a third-straight shutout, Bodnar getting the only shot past Harry Lumley. In the fourth game, with the flags in Toronto flying at half-staff in memory of FDR, when veteran Flash Hollett scored for Detroit at 8:35 of the first period, McCool's scoreless playoff streak was stopped at 193:09. Three third-period goals won the game for Detroit, and they headed back toward Olympia with hopes of reversing the 1942 débâcle.

Lumley's shutout and goals by Hollett and Joe Carveth kept the hopes alive in the fifth game, and in the sixth Lumley was perfect again until Ed Bruneteau (younger brother of Mud) evened the series at 14:15 of overtime. The seventh game was a dramatic masterpiece. Mel Hill put Toronto in front in the first period on a feed from Kennedy, and that held up until Murray Armstrong tied it, assisted by Hollett, at 8:16 of the third period. McCool then suffered an attack of ulcers or perhaps nervous prostration, and play was held up for ten minutes while he was treated in the dressing room. It couldn't have worked better if it had been deliberate. McCool recovered and so did the Leafs. Pratt, perhaps the finest two-way defenseman of his day, scored the Cup-winner just a couple of minutes after play resumed.

But the Canadiens' dominance continued despite the loss of the Cup and the return of stars and strength to the other clubs. Even the Rangers, who would not get out of the cellar for another season, at least returned to respectability with rookie of the year Edgar Laprade, Tony Leswick, and demobbed Muzz Patrick, Lynn Patrick, and goalie Chuck Rayner. The Leafs had a bad year, despite Jim Stewart's league-leading thirty-seven goals. McCool failed to last the season, and Kennedy was badly hurt. With Toronto out of the playoffs, Selke took upon himself the role of scapegoat and resigned.

Detroit's point production fell off, and they finished a disappointing fourth, three points behind Chicago. The Hawks' two hundred goals led the league, with Hart-winner Max Bentley first, Clint Smith tied for third, Mosienko tied for fifth, Killer Kaleta ninth, and Pete Horeck tied for tenth in scoring. The Krauts and Brimsek were back in Boston and adjusted their game to the red-line innovation under coach Dit Clapper well enough to finish second. In first place, though only by a margin of five points, were the Canadiens, led by Blake (Byng winner, tied for third in scoring), Richard (tied for fifth), Lach (tied for seventh, first in assists), and Durnan (third straight Vezina).

In the playoffs, Montreal pounded Chicago in four straight, hounding Karakas into retirement with scores of 6–2, 5–1, 8–2, 7–2. In the other semis, Lumley's shutout in the second game gave Detroit its only win over Boston, Don Gallinger getting the winning overtime goal in the fifth game after the Krauts had scored six times in the third and fourth games. But Boston was overmatched against Montreal. What Art Ross labeled "strictly a wartime club" was even better than the 1944–1945 squad with the addition of Frank Eddols, Kenny Reardon, Billy Reay, Jim Peters, Dutch Hiller, and Ken Mosdell.

The Bruins played them tough, though, especially spurred on by the sibling rivalry of Terry and Ken Reardon. After Bouchard and Fillion had put the Canadiens in front quickly, Boston came back with a goal by Guidolin and one by the Krauts and went ahead on a Jack Crawford goal in the third period. But Richard fed Chamberlain to send it into overtime and then won it on a pass from Bouchard. In the second game it was Bouchard's score that tied it and Peters's that won it in overtime. In the third game, Montreal never trailed, winning 4–2. In the fourth, though, they not only trailed but lost in overtime, after Richard had twice tied the score, on a Terry Reardon shot.

Milt Schmidt's second-period goal tied the fifth game in Montreal, but that's as close as the Bruins ever got. In the third period it was Blake from Lach, Chamberlain unassisted, and Hiller from Lach, as the Canadiens had their sixth Cup, their second in the three-year-old Durnan era.

The dynasty extended through one more season and perhaps one game of the Stanley Cup finals. In the expanded sixty-game schedule, Montreal again came home first, six points ahead of Toronto. The Punch Line was outscored by Chicago's Pony Line (the Bentleys and Mosienko) and by the Krauts, who had regained their scoring touch. Indeed, Montreal was outscored by every team in the league except the Rangers. But Durnan reigned supreme, winning his fourth straight Vezina, beating second-place Broda by thirty-four goals.

The expanded schedule was not the only change in the league. The new president, Clarence Campbell, was a former official, as well as a lawyer and Rhodes scholar. The 1946 experiment of one referee and two linesmen was deemed successful and made permanent. Among the new faces was that of Gordie Howe, though Howard Meeker of Toronto won the Calder Trophy.

Montreal took Boston out of the playoffs in five games. Lach was out of action with a fractured skull, but the Canadiens got overtime goals from Ken Mosdell and spare John Quilty. In the other series, also five games, the revamped Maple Leafs got superb goaltending from Broda in all of their wins. The Turk bunched all his poor play in the one loss, 9–1.

The first game of the finals saw Durnan at his best. While he stopped cold the fast young Leafs team that had scored 209 goals during the season, the Canadiens poured it on at the other end. O'Connor scored from Roger Leger; Reay scored from Harmon; Richard shook off Bill Ezinicki's shadow and scored from O'Connor; George Allen scored from Bouchard; Reay from Allen and Bouchard; and Chamberlain from Quilty and Peters. It was 6–0 Montreal, but just as suddenly it was all over for Montreal. Before they returned to the Forum for the fifth game, one dynasty had ended, and the heir apparent had taken over for a short and not uninterrupted reign.

18

Leafs in Bloom

Conn Smythe was a dynamic man who seemed to operate on the assumption that change was valuable in itself. Even if specific changes did not improve the team's play, they might have positive effects at the box office. Smythe never lost sight of pro hockey's profit motive, for all the competitive instinct and fanaticism in his leadership, and it was he who responded to the warnings about increasing violence in the game with the line, "If we don't put a stop to it, we'll have to start printing more tickets."

One change he objected to was the deal that had brought Teeder Kennedy to Toronto. Even though Kennedy had led the Leafs to the 1945 Cup, the deal had been completed against Smythe's wishes and before he could countermand the orders. So when Toronto finished fifth and out of the playoffs in 1946, the onus was laid on Frank Selke, who had acquired Kennedy. Selke resigned and then replaced retiring Tom Gorman as manager at Montreal.

Other changes were to come. From 1942 to 1951, when Toronto won the Stanley Cup six times, no one player was on all six teams. Ironically, the only player on the 1945 Cup-winning squad whose name appears on the Cup for 1951 is Theodore S. Kennedy. Smythe fancied the multiple trade that would give fans plenty to talk about. Thus the 1945 squad featured Sweeney Schriner, for whom he had sent Armstrong, James Fowler, Boll, Jackson, and Romnes to the Amerks, and Lorne Carr, who had also come from the Amerks for O'Flaherty, Knott, Heron, and Marker. Now, in 1947, both had retired in the wake of Smythe's youth movement.

Syl Apps, Nick and Don Metz, and Turk Broda, all in their early thirties, were the old men of the team. There were five rookies—Bill Barilko, Garth Boesch, Joe Klukay, Gus Mortson, and Calder-winner Howie Meeker—plus Jim Thomson, who had only five games' experience the year before. Walt Stanowski was the only other man on the squad over twenty-three, though Harry Watson at twenty-three, Gaye Stewart at twenty-three, Bud Poile at twenty-three, Vic Lynn at twenty-two, Bill Ezinicki at twenty-three, Gus

Checking Back

Bodnar at twenty-one, and especially Teeder at twenty-one, all had at least a couple of years' experience under their belts.

After the 6–0 loss to Montreal in the first game of the Cup finals, the young Leafs and their old goalie settled down to make Durnan regret what he had said following the game: "How did that team even get to the finals?" Hap Day gave Ezinicki, a tough brawler from Winnipeg, the job of shadowing Richard, who exploded after a collision jammed his knee. He started swinging his stick, slashing Lynn's eye shut and opening a gash on Ezinicki's head. Richard got a game misconduct penalty, Toronto won, 4–0, on goals by Teeder, Lynn, Stewart, and Watson and Broda's shutout, and returned to their Gardens with the series tied, the momentum in their favor, and Richard suspended for the next game by Clarence Campbell.

Without the Rocket to worry about, the Leafs flashed their free-skating speed in the third game. They built up a three-goal lead (Mortson, Poile, and Lynn) before Gravelle and O'Connor scored for Montreal. But the third period was scoreless until Teeder iced the game for Toronto with less than a minute to play. In the fourth game, after Harmon and Watson traded early first-period goals, both teams played close-checking defensive hockey. Overtime seemed inevitable until, at 16:36 of the third, Syl Apps took a pass from Watson while heading behind the Canadien net, whirled back in the opposite direction, and slipped the puck in behind Durnan.

Back at the Forum and trailing 3–1 now, Montreal came back to life. Richard scored twice and Gravelle once while Durnan masterfully defended the nets. Poile's third-period goal had no effect on the outcome, but the Canadien win did not shake the Leafs' confidence. In Toronto, on the first-period face-off, Buddy O'Connor beat Kennedy—to the surprise of the Leaf defensemen, who had both rushed forward in anticipation of an opening rush. O'Connor followed the puck in alone and then beat Broda to it twenty-five feet from the net, sliding it home with ease at twenty-five seconds. It looked as if Montreal might extend their reign after all, but that was the last Canadien goal of the season. Kennedy and Meeker fed Lynn to tie the game in the second period. It was the first time the two teams had met in the championship series, and this last game was a classic. The young Leafs, youngest team ever to win the Cup, kept up the pressure on Durnan, who made ten saves in the third period to Broda's five. But the eleventh shot was the one that toppled one crown and raised another. And it was Teeder Kennedy, acquired by Selke for Smythe who didn't want him, taking a pass from Meeker to score at 14:39 and win the championship for Smythe against Selke's new team.

Smythe did not rest easy with the crown on the young team. Early in the following season he closed a major deal. He sent his entire "Flying Forts" line—Gaye Stewart, Bud Poile, and Gus Bodnar—along with two part-time

142

spares, Bob Goldham and Ernie Dickens, to Chicago for Max Bentley and a rookie, Cy Thomas, who did not last the season. The Black Hawks had to be in serious trouble to break up their only big-league unit—the Pony Line of Mosienko and the Bentleys—and they were. Dead last in 1947, they were simply outmanned by every team in the league. So they traded their one all-star for the chance of filling out an adequate squad. Smythe got the other center he wanted because Chicago needed the manpower he could afford.

Toronto's three lines showed great balance. Kennedy centered for Meeker and Lynn. Called the "Second Kid Line," they totaled forty-one goals through the 1948 schedule. Syl Apps had been conned out of retirement for one more season and, with Watson and Ezinicki on his wings, his line scored forty-two goals. Bentley centered for Nick Metz and Joe Klukay; their line had forty-five scores. Depth and balance were two of the keys for that Leaf team, as time and again they came from behind to win in the third period. No player towered above others. In the five seasons from 1947 to 1951, they had only two first all-stars; Broda in 1948—called by Smythe the greatest playoff player in hockey—and Gus Mortson in the non-Cup-winning year of 1950. Teeder, twice, and Jim Thomson once were second all-stars, but clearly Smythe's was not a star system.

Yet just as clearly the addition of Max Bentley was what had cemented the whole squad. One of five brothers from Delisle, Saskatchewan, he learned hockey by playing on a frozen river so narrow that he had to be good and clever to get past his brothers with or without the puck. Gordie Howe calls him "one of the great stick-handlers of the modern era." Nick Metz remembered playing baseball against a team with all five Bentleys; he couldn't tell them apart. One would get a hit, all five would huddle at the base, and then another would bat. The trouble was that it always seemed to be Max batting. Aside from centering the most productive Leaf line, Bentley played right point on the power play. Facing off in the offensive zone, Toronto's brawlers always seemed to manage to get the puck back to Max, who would never shoot long but stick-handled close in for a high-percentage shot.

Though Bentley fit Hap Day's plans perfectly, in one way he did not fit in with the major's ideas. Smythe often said he wanted no Lady Byngers on his team, and Max had won the Byng Trophy in 1943. Smythe wanted retaliation for every hit, and he wanted hard, aggressive play to begin with. He never objected to his men taking penalties as long as they didn't take a check or a punch without a countercheck or counterpunch. And he would lead the way himself, on occasion taking on fans in the stands who belabored his Leafs. As a result of this attitude and an offense-minded squad, Day's burden was to stress defense. Mortson and Thomson, known as the Gold Dust Twins, played well in tandem, and Barilko and Boesch pioneered the tandem knee-drop to stop shots. Equally important was the effective penalty-killing play of Nick Metz and Joe Klukay. In the five-year period they were never worse than third in goals against, second overall to Durnan's Canadiens.

Bentley took no part in the fighting, nor did gentlemanly Syl Apps, who had earlier won the Byng. But no opponent got away with taking advantage of the two classy pacifist centers, particularly with Wild Bill Ezinicki on the ice. Retaliation could have been his middle name. He was, as Stan Fischler says, "a very passionate hockey player" who loved the contact as much as the skating and lifted weights daily to build himself up for bigger opponents. Even Broda got into the act, taking part in a no-decision wrestling match with Lumley early in the 1948 season.

For the first time since 1942, the Rangers were bound for the playoffs, edging past the low-scoring Canadiens into fourth place. They had finished last four straight years, through 1946 and through many changes, including the retirements of Shibicky and the younger Patricks and the resignation of Lester Patrick as general manager. But there were promising signs for the future, as Boucher became manager: the arrival of Calder-winner Edgar Laprade, the pattern of alternating goalies with Henry and Rayner, and the start of the buildup of their farm system.

Boucher had problems with Lester Patrick's always looking over his shoulder from his new vantage as a vice president of the Madison Square Garden Corporation. After a fifth-place finish in 1947, Boucher arranged to deal three young players to Frank Selke for two experienced hands: Hal Laycoe, Joe Bell, and George Robertson for Frankie Eddolls and Buddy O'Connor. Patrick advised General Kilpatrick to veto the trade, but Boucher laid his job on the line and it was approved. And so, with Henry in goal while Rayner struggled in the New Haven Eagles' nets (reversing the 1947 arrangement), and with O'Connor doubling for the Byng and Hart Trophies, New York struggled back into the playoffs to face the vastly improved Red Wings.

Detroit fought Toronto down to the wire in the league race. With only a home-and-home series remaining, Toronto was just one point ahead in the standings, and in the race for the Vezina Broda and Lumley were dead even. The Leafs won the first game, 5–3, at home in their Gardens, with two goals for Teeder, and then insured their stay at the summit in Olympia by beating the Wings, 5–2. Syl Apps concluded his regular-season NHL play with a hat trick that brought his career total to 201 goals.

Surprisingly, Detroit had trouble with New York in the semifinals. With the series tied two games apiece, it took rookie Red Kelly (who lost out in the Calder Trophy selections to teammate James McFadden) to spark them to 3–1 and 4–2 victories. Toronto meanwhile took out Boston in five games, losing only the fourth game, 3–2. The finals failed to reproduce the drama of the pennant race. Detroit led in only one game, the first, when McFadden scored in the first period. The lead lasted sixty-one seconds until Watson tied it, and forty-two seconds later Klukay put Toronto in front to stay.

The first game ended 5–3, the second 4–2, with Bentley scoring twice and with Broda and Lumley taking some swings at each other again. In Detroit, goals by Watson and Lynn and formidable backchecking gave Broda help in a 2–0 shutout. To complete the sweep, the Leafs won the fourth game, 7–2, Kennedy and Watson getting two goals each. The Production Line had been held to one goal in four games, and Smythe hailed his team as the "greatest hockey club in history."

Yet it was not the same club the following year. Apps retired and so did Nick Metz. Walt Stanowski went to the Rangers for center Calvin Pearly Gardner and defenseman Bill Juzda, and Day also had rookie centers Bob Dawes, Fleming Mackell, and Ray Timgren to put to work. The team floundered throughout the season, finishing fourth, losing more games than they won, and scoring fewer goals than were scored against them. Their only league leader was Ezinicki in penalty minutes.

In the playoffs, the Leafs in general and Broda in particular turned things around. They beat the favored Bruins in the first two games, then dropped the third to an overtime goal by Dumart. At this point, Sid Smith, who had played with them for much of the previous season, was brought back up from Pittsburgh; he scored twice in a 3–1 win in the fourth game. Back at Boston Garden, King Clancy was the referee and the target for Beantown bottle-throwers, and Max Bentley scored the decisive goal in the 3–2 series-ender.

Meanwhile Detroit was struggling against Montreal, having to go into a seventh game before winning on Gordie Howe's seventh and eighth goals of the series. For the first time, the Wings would be favored over the Leafs, having beaten them seven times and tied them twice in twelve games during the season. Detroit had led the league in scoring, Abel was the MVP, and Abel and Lindsay tied for third in scoring, while for Toronto only Watson was in the top ten. But now the Red Wings folded once more. Toronto slowed the Production Line and swept through again.

The first game went into overtime, and Klukay won it, 3–2, at 17:31. Smith's hat trick won the second game, 3–1, leaving Detroit in a state of shock and Gordie Howe wondering, "Who's Sid Smith?" The two games in Toronto followed an identical pattern. Detroit scored first and then Toronto scored three times to win 3–1, 3–1, six different Leafs accounting for the goals. Toronto became the first NHL team to win three straight Cups, the first to sweep consecutive four-game championship series, and the first fourth-place team to win the Cup.

The dynasty was not yet over, but it seemed to be toppling of its own weight early in the 1950 season. The Leafs were in first place by November 1, but the month ended with a six-game non-winning streak. The major then announced that his troops were out of shape and would have to make specified weights, particularly Turk Broda, who was replaced in goal until he could trim his bulk to 190 pounds. Smythe ordered a weigh-in before the Ranger game the following Saturday, and one by one the sheepish Leafs got in under their limit—Boesch, Lynn, Meeker, Smith, and Watson, who had missed Friday's practice because he felt too weak from the weight loss.

Broda himself barely made his limit and then went out to shut out the Rangers, going on to one of his better seasons. But the Toronto offense kept sputtering and they did well to finish third. In the playoffs, the Red Wings put them out in a rough, exciting seven-game series on their way to the championship that broke the Leafs' streak. Yet when the obituaries were still being written for the Toronto reign of the late forties, the Leafs came back in 1951 to finish second to Detroit in the standings; second in goals scored, with Bentley, Kennedy, Tod Sloan, Smith, and Gardner all in the top eleven; and first in goals-against average, with Al Rollins winning the Vezina with a 1.75 average in forty games (though Detroit's Terry Sawchuk, at 1.98, with eleven shutouts, won the Calder), while Broda had a 2.19 average in thirty-one games.

The 1951 Leafs were essentially the same as the 1949 champions, with Barilko, Bentley, Broda, Gardner, Juzda, Kennedy, Klukay, Mackell, Meeker, Mortson, Sloan, Smith, Thomson, Timgren, and Watson. Boesch and Don Metz had retired, Bob Dawes had been dealt to the Canadiens, Harry Taylor would not make it back to the big league until 1952 with Chicago. Rookie Dan Lewicki had made the team and scored 34 points, while Hugh Bolton and Chief Armstrong got some playing time during the season. A major change was the acquisition of defenseman Fernie Flaman from Boston for Ezinicki and Lynn. Al Rollins, who had come from Cleveland during the weight-watching week at a cost of five players plus cash, was justifying his price by alternating brilliantly with Broda in goal. Indeed, he was so good that he got to play in four Stanley Cup games (with a 1.85 average) in place of Broda, the great money goalie who turned in two shutouts in eight games and a 1.16 average in his final Cup-winning playoffs. One other change should be noted, though it made little difference either on the ice or in actual leadership: Hap Day was kicked upstairs to be assistant manager, and Joe Primeau took over as coach. Smythe, of course, still ran the club.

Toronto struggled past Boston in the semifinals. With Jack Gelineau in goal, the Bruins shut out the Leafs, 2–0, and then tied them, 1–1, in a game called after one overtime because of the curfew law. Toronto won the next two, 3–0 and 3–1, and then—with Gordon Henry in the Bruin nets—blasted their way into the finals with 4–1 and 6–0 victories. Meanwhile, the renascent Canadiens were eliminating the heavily-favored Red Wings in six games, setting up the second-ever championship series between the two senior clubs in the league.

It was a memorable series, every game going into overtime. The first game belonged to Sid Smith. He scored the first goal, matched by Richard, and then at 5:51 of sudden death whipped a backhand shot past Gerry McNeil. He scored again in the second game, but it was the Rocket's turn in overtime. Richard drew Broda out of the nets after taking a pass from Doug Harvey and sent the series back to Montreal, deadlocked, after 2:55 of overtime.

Smythe and Primeau decided that Broda had had it, that Richard had his number. They decided to go the rest of the way with Rollins, who hadn't seen action since the opener with Boston, when Pete Horeck had sent him to the hospital with torn ligaments in his knee. Just two minutes into the game, the move looked like a mistake, as Richard put Montreal in front, but Rollins was perfect thereafter. Smith got Toronto even in the second period. As the third consecutive game went into overtime, Montreal's offense went into high gear, but Rollins made three quick saves within four minutes. Finally, Kennedy cleared the puck and as the action moved into the other end, Tod Sloan dug it out and set up Teeder with the winning pass at 4:47. Toronto never trailed again in the series.

The fourth game was almost a replica of the first. Smith scored first assisted by Kennedy, and Richard tied it up. Toronto went ahead (Meeker from Watson), and again Montreal tied it (Lach from Richard and Bouchard). In overtime, at 5:15, Harry Watson came onto the ice, took a quick pass from Bentley—who had just intercepted a pass—poked the puck past Doug Harvey, beat him to it, and then shot it past McNeil's kicking left leg. Back in their own Gardens for a Saturday night game, Toronto hoped to clinch the series without overtime. They wanted to take no more chances against Richard in sudden death, and they would also be facing the threat of a curfew to stop a deadlocked game.

Rocket beat Jim Thomson and Rollins to score first, but Tod Sloan matched that three minutes later. Paul Meger scored on a rebound of Harvey's shot early in the third period, and McNeil kept repulsing the Leaf attacks. With a minute and a half remaining, Primeau pulled Rollins and set up a power play in the Montreal end, with Bentley and Mortson at the points and Kennedy, Smith, Sloan, and Watson in a line across the slot.

Irvin put his best defenders on the ice—Ken Mosdell, Ed Mazur, Floyd Curry, Tom Johnson, Butch Bouchard—and they forced another face-off. Mosdell narrowly missed an open-net goal, but Watson flashed back to cut it off. Rollins came back for a face-off in the neutral zone, but Toronto forced the play and again pulled the goalie. Now Irvin sent out the Lach-Richard-Olmstead line, hoping to win the draw and control the puck for the last thirty seconds. Frank Selke cringed in his seat in the stands, anticipating the event. Teeder won the draw, sent the puck back to Bentley. Max skated in and shot. The puck bounced loose in a jam in front of the goal. Smith got a stick on it and shot, but it hit the goal post. This time Sloan got the carom and sent it home at 19:23.

It was the fifth straight overtime game, but it was the shortest of the five. After a little over two minutes, Watson took the puck up ice and, before Richard could cut him off, dumped it into the Montreal zone. Howie Meeker raced to it behind the net, wheeled around, and shot, but McNeil kicked it away. Watson rebounded and shot; McNeil went down to stop it, but it bounced all the way to the point. Bill Barilko picked it up in full stride, lurched toward the goal, and sent a slapshot between Richard and Bouchard over McNeil's shoulder for the Cup.

The Leafs' triumph brought great rejoicing to the Queen City, but it was the end of an era. If Bentley and Kennedy were the heart and soul of the team, Barilko—who made the hip-check famous, according to Brad Park—was the guts. The first two were past their prime seasons, and the latter had played his last game. Less than four months after his goal brought Toronto the championship, he was lost in the presumed crash of a small plane over northern Ontario. The Leafs would not make another Cup final for eight years, would not qualify for the playoffs in three of those years, would not win the Cup again for eleven years, and would not lead the league for twelve years, until the time of a flowering of another Toronto dynasty.

19

Howe High the Wings

If ever there was a case of overlapping dynasties it was in those five years when the Leafs won four Stanley Cup series. During those five seasons the Red Wings actually won ten more games than the Leafs and led the league three times on their way to a precedent-shattering seven straight pennants. But by the time this sequence was well underway, the Canadiens had already begun *their* new dynasty. Taking the decade and a half as a whole, one might perceive that there was a troika in power.

Jack Adams had learned a valuable lesson, not from Conn Smythe but the hard way, from the collapse of the 1938 Wings. After two straight championships the same team plunged to the cellar. It was the last time he would stand pat. From the 1943 Cup-winners only two players remained on the large 1950 squad that led the league for the second straight year, finishing with a record eighty-eight points and scoring 229 goals. One was veteran Sid Abel, the captain, center of the mighty Production Line, leading goal-scorer, MVP, and first all-star center in 1949. Always a feisty competitor, with a keen sense of team play, Abel was equally comfortable shooting, passing, or scrapping with the opposition. Ironically, he reached his peak as the least aggressive member of the unit that terrorized the league in 1950, finishing 1–2–3 in scoring. The other holdover was defenseman Jack Stewart, after four consecutive all-star seasons, playing his last year as a Red Wing.

Adams had even made a coaching change, replacing himself behind the bench with Tommy Ivan in 1948. But the philosophy of play in Detroit did not change. The Red Wings played tough, bullying, intimidating physical hockey. Like Smythe, Adams wanted no Lady Byng winners. He had had only one, Marty Barry in 1937, and when all-star defenseman Bill Quackenbush won that sportsmanship award in 1949 Adams promptly traded him away.

The whole corps of defensemen was in a state of flux. Albert Dewsbury and Lee Fogolin were both in their second year when the Cup was won in 1950, and both were gone to Chicago for the next season. George Martin had come over from Boston but in two years he was a Hawk. Marcel Pronovost arrived in time to get his name inscribed on the Cup, but he was still technically a rookie in 1951. Along with Stewart, the stalwarts on defense were Leo Charles Reise, Jr., a second generation NHL defenseman, acquired from Chicago in 1947 and sent to the Rangers in 1953; and Red Kelly, the one product of Detroit's farm system among the group, who came up in 1948 to begin his long, distinguished career.

The forwards were a comparatively stable crew, but not by much. In support of the Production Line were veterans G. J. W. A. Couture and Joe Carveth, who was back in Detroit for a second tour, and a host of recent arrivals: rookies Steve Black and the Wilson brothers, John and Larry; Jim Peters, just acquired from Boston for two seasons before going to Chicago; Pete Babando, also from Boston, who would play as a Red Wing just this year en route to Chicago; George Gee, who had come from Chicago in 1949, only to return in 1952; and three remaining rookies from 1948: Jim McFadden, the Calder winner that year, the pride of Belfast, Ireland, who was traded to Chicago in 1952; Max McNab, who lasted less than four seasons in the league before surfacing over two decades later as general manager of the Washington Capitals; and Marty Pavelich, who managed to survive for a decade on Adams's team.

The size of the squad is significant. The Wings survived an arduous playoff series, after a seventy-game season, and they needed everyone of these players, along with spares Gordon Haidy and Doug McKay, to make it. Also significant was the play in goal of Harry Lumley, the apple-cheeked one from Owen Sound. Lumley had come to Detroit by way of the Rangers in 1944, the year after Mowers won the Vezina, and he got better every year. His first full season he averaged 3.22 and improved steadily down to 2.35 in 1950. That was also his best playoff season, 2.0 with three shutouts, and the end of his tenure at Olympia. Adams traded him to Chicago, where he had two poor years, but at Toronto for four seasons he was twice under 2 goals per game, twice the first all-star goalie, and finally won the Vezina in 1954. Lumley played three years in Boston, finally retiring in 1960, a full decade after he got his name on the Stanley Cup in Detroit.

Throughout this Red Wing dynasty, the team was carried primarily on the strength of the Production Line. Abel—the last discovery of the same Goldie Smith, postmaster of Melville, Saskatchewan, who had scouted Eddie Shore among many others—was the hub of the unit. It was his intelligent grasp, along with coach Ivan's perceptions, that made productive use of the great skill of his wings. But he was a genuine star in his own right, as a skater and stick-handler and shooter, and he anticipated the age of curved blades by rounding off the heel of his stick to make his shots curve or drop.

When Ted Lindsay, the youngest child of the former Renfrew Millionaires goalie, came up to the Red Wings in 1945, he could still make the welterweight limit. And when he retired after his brief comeback in 1965, he was still a natural middleweight. Yet throughout his career he took on all the heavyweights. He was a strutting gamecock policing rinks full of heavier fowl. Lindsay fought everyone and everything, and when there was no action he was constantly taunting his opposition. He also was constantly egging on his teammates, so that when Abel retired in 1952 Adams's natural choice for team captain was Lindsay.

Year after year Lindsay was among the league leaders in penalty minutes (over eighteen hundred for his career), but that never curtailed his point production. He won the Ross Trophy in 1950, led in goals scored in 1948 and in assists in 1950 and 1957, and six times was among the top four scorers in the league. Eight times Ted Lindsay was chosen as the first all-star left wing, and he is the usual choice at that position on all-time squads (though Bobby Hull has been winning supporters in recent years). He was one of the leaders in forming a players' union in 1957, "to promote and protect the best interests of the players," but that kind of independent thinking had already led to a spanking by the paternalistic Adams, who had stripped Lindsay of his captaincy and accused him, of all people, of complacency. This time Lindsay was stripped of his Red Wings and traded to Chicago in the off-season. Jim Thomson, another organizer and twelve years a Maple Leaf, was branded "a traitor and a Quisling" by Conn Smythe, farmed out to Rochester, and then sold to Chicago.

Lindsay played three years as a Hawk, retired, kept in shape, and almost five years later, at the age of thirty-nine, he returned for one last season as a Wing under his former linemate Sid Abel. It was vintage Lindsay in 1965, Terrible Ted racking up 173 penalty minutes and taunting the Wings to their first first-place finish since he had left. He even scored three goals in their losing playoff series against Chicago. A year later he was voted into the Hall of Fame and continued his contentious way by refusing to take part in the ceremonies because wives and children were not welcome at the official luncheon. Then he continued to serve the game well as an outspoken commentator on NHL telecasts.

The arrival of Gordie Howe in 1946 completed the Production Line, and when he hit his superlative stride a couple of years later the Wings could not be kept down. Their aggressiveness, speed, and strength backed up their splendid shooting and passing. But they also had precision plays and finesse, Abel passing to either wing off the side or end boards, and Howe able to bank a pass to Lindsay in the opposite corner by hitting the same spot every time. In 1950 the team led the league for the third straight year, and Lindsay, Abel, and Howe led in scoring with seventy-eight, sixty-nine, and sixty-eight points, putting them in the exclusive company of the 1945 Punch Line and the 1940 Kraut Line. And this time they broke their playoff jinx against Toronto, but it took an exceptional effort.

Detroit hadn't won a playoff game from Toronto since March 29, 1947, had been beaten by them eleven consecutive times. The streak was extended to twelve in the first game of the semis as Broda shut them out. Worse, Howe was lost for the season in a third-period injury. He had gone after Teeder Kennedy and ended up against the boards with a fractured skull, cheekbone, and nose, and a scratched eyeball. After surgery he remained critical for several days, while his teammates sought revenge.

Bitter and frustrated, Detroit management fired up the fans, the press, and the players by accusing Kennedy of deliberately butt-ending Howe. President Campbell's investigation exonerated Kennedy (virtually all testimony supported referee George Gravel's report that it was an accidental injury), but not before bloody reprisals were exacted on the ice, led by Lindsay, naturally. That was the kind of play that best suited the Red Wings, and they tied the series, only to fall behind on a second Broda shutout in the third game.

Game 4 went over twenty minutes into overtime before Leo Reise, better known as a clubhouse lawyer than a scorer, tied the series up for Detroit. Once more the Turk, the great money player, blanked the Wings, but Detroit was not to be denied. Lumley took over, shut out Toronto, 4–0, in the sixth game, and remained impregnable throughout the seventh. Again it was Reise, on a lucky deflection off Barilko, who won the game and the series at 8:39 of overtime.

The Rangers, who had upset Montreal in five games, had given up home ice to the circus, but the Wings were without both Howe and Lindsay, who had injured his back. Detroit won the opener at home, lost the second game at Toronto despite Lindsay's return, and got a shutout from Lumley in the third to bring a 2–1 lead back to Olympia, where the series would be concluded. At that point, everyone conceded the Cup to Detroit—everyone but the Rangers. New York battled on into overtime and got the winning goal from Bones Raleigh. Then they, and Raleigh, repeated the act in the fifth game, and the Red Wings found themselves in danger of extinction.

Down 3–1 in the second period, Detroit rallied on goals by the Production Line (Carveth replacing Howe) and Couture (from Babando and Gee). New York went ahead on a Tony Leswick goal in the third, but Lindsay produced a tie on a pass from Abel and then captain Abel scored the winner. In the seventh game, New York led, 2–0 and 3–2, only to have Detroit pressure pay off in tying rallies. The third period was scoreless, and Rayner outsaved Lumley throughout a full overtime period. Eight and a half minutes into the second overtime, Gee beat Buddy O'Connor on a face-off in the Ranger end, got the puck to Babando, where he had placed him before the draw, and Pete's backhander, screened by Gee and Allen Stanley, caught the net before Rayner saw it. It was the first time the Stanley Cup had been won in overtime of the seventh game.

Jack Adams celebrated the championship by trading Stewart, Babando, Lumley, Dewsbury, and Don Morrison to Chicago for Bob Goldham, Gaye Stewart, Metro Prystai, and Sugar Jim Henry. For the fourth straight year Detroit led the league, scoring a record forty-four wins and 101 points. They led in scoring with 236 goals. The Production Line was first (Howe), fourth (Abel), and seventh (Lindsay) in points; and they allowed only 139 goals. Their season ended in the first playoff round, a case of too much Richard, but with a few more adjustments Adams and Ivan had what has been called the perfect team for the 1952 season.

In goal was Terry Sawchuk whose developing skills had persuaded Adams he could part with Lumley. As a rookie in 1951, Sawchuk won the Calder Trophy, led the league with eleven shutouts, and was named first all-star (though losing the Vezina to Al Rollins, who played less than forty games in the Toronto nets). The Boy Wonder had been rookie of the year with Omaha in the USHL in 1949 and with Indianapolis in the AHL in 1950, so his Calder was no upset. His crouching style was a trend-setter, and he had benefited from good coaching through the Detroit system. Mud Bruneteau in Omaha had taught him the angles, Ott Heller at Indianapolis had broken his habit of premature flopping, and Tommy Ivan worked with him on clearing straight-in shots. In his first five years, Ukey won the Vezina three times, led in shutouts three times (totaling fifty-six during that period plus nine in the playoffs), and never averaged over two goals against.

Detroit had lost nothing by trading away veteran stars, not so much because of the players gained that way but rather because Adams's extensive farm system kept providing young stars. Indeed, the produce of the Wings' farms kept the Black Hawks stocked as well. In 1952, youngsters who had not been on the ice for the 1950 championship included Alex Delvecchio, Glen Skov, Vic Stasiuk, Benedict Woit, and Larry Zeidel. Through the season, Detroit won forty-four games again, led the league again with one hundred points, led in scoring again with 215 goals, and led in goals-against average for the first time since Mowers' Vezina in 1943. Gordie Howe led the league with forty-seven goals and eighty-six points, winning the second of his six Ross trophies and the first of his six Hart trophies. As in 1951, he was joined on the first all-star team by Sawchuk, Red Kelly, and Lindsay, who was second in scoring. Abel was only tied for seventh in scoring.

And this time there was no letdown in the playoffs. The healthy Wings established dominance in the first game against Toronto and never looked back.

Checking Back

They needled the Leafs into a record-breaking, rough game and outfought them. Bill Chadwick whistled twenty-nine penalties for more than a hundred minutes, but in that style of play Detroit was at its best. Sawchuk shut out Toronto, and the Wings put three shots past Al Rollins. Smythe sent Broda out to defend the goal in the second game. He was brilliant, allowing only one goal by the defense-minded line of Delvecchio, Prystai, and Johnny Wilson, on a rebound. But Sawchuk was perfect again. Then back home in Maple Leaf Gardens, Broda was overwhelmed 6–2 in the third game, evoking a *Globe and Mail* headline: LET'S FACE FACTS! TOO MUCH CLASS. Rollins came back for the fourth game, but was beaten, 3–1, for a Detroit sweep.

The Red Wings had more than a week off while Montreal had to go seven games to beat the Bruins, and they arrived at the Forum fresh and fit. After a scoreless first period, Leswick scored on a pass from Pavelich, and again Detroit never looked back. Their second lines, one of the fastest in hockey, scored again when Skov fed Leswick, and Lindsay got the clincher from Abel in the 3–1 win. In Game 2, Gerry McNeil was a little better but Sawchuk was just as good as ever. The scooter line put Detroit in front, but Lach tied the game before the end of the first period. It was Montreal's last goal of the season. Lindsay's solo dash early in the second period won the 2–1 game.

In Detroit for the third game, Howe took over. He scored from Stasiuk in the first period, fed Lindsay in the second, and scored from Pavelich in the third. In the final game, while the Production Line concentrated on shutting down Richard and company, it was Prystai who supplied the offense, scoring twice, with assists by Delvecchio and Wilson, and feeding Skov on a power play: Detroit 3–0, Detroit in eight straight, thirteen goals to three against Toronto, eleven goals to two against Montreal. Never before had a team so dominated play from the first game of the season through to the Stanley Cup, and not since has such domination been matched.

"It's Sid Abel who makes us go," Adams said during the playoffs. Then he packed his thirty-four-year-old captain off to Chicago, where he played forty games as player-coach. The production of Howe and Lindsay did not decline. Again they were 1–2 in scoring, with Delvecchio tied for fourth, Prystai seventh, and Kelley eighth. For the fifth straight year they led the league, but this time the resurgent Bruins knocked them out of the playoffs in six games, Sawchuk having his worst series after shutting out Boston in the first game.

Adams's youth movement continued. His squad for 1954 averaged just over twenty-four years of age. Rookie Dutch Reibel was the best new wing, finishing seventh in the league in scoring, right behind Kelly, while Howe and Lindsay were first and third. Defenseman Bingo Allen and forward Bill Dineen were other rookies, while veteran Jim Peters had been brought back from Chicago. Sawchuk continued his remarkable play, though he was edged out for the Vezina, first all-star, and shutouts by his predecessor, Harry Lumley, who sparked the low-scoring Leafs. In the playoffs, however, Lumley was no match for his young former teammates. Sawchuk shut out Toronto in the first game, lost the second, 3–1, and then won three straight. The series ended with a Lindsay goal at 21:01 of overtime, setting up the anticipated finals against the Canadiens, who had swept four from Boston.

That Montreal team had outscored Detroit during the season, placed Harvey and Mosdell on the first all-star team, and boasted such other stars as Richard, Jean Beliveau, Boom Boom Geoffrion, Dickie Moore, and Olmstead. Young Jacques Plante had taken over in goal when McNeil was injured late in the season and allowed Boston only four goals in the playoff series. But he was beaten, 3–1, on goals by Lindsay, Reibel, and Kelly in the first game in Detroit. In the second game, the Habs scored three times within fifty-six seconds—Moore, assisted by Geoffrion and Beliveau, and then twice assisting the Rocket—to even the series. In the Forum, five different Wings scored in a 5–2 win, and then Sawchuk shut out the Canadiens for a 3–1 lead. Dick Irvin brought McNeil back to inspire Montreal in the fifth game, and he did. He matched Sawchuk's shutout throughout regulation time and held on until Mosdell beat Ukey at 5:45 of overtime. In the sixth game, Curry scored twice to lead a 4–1 win and send the series into a seventh game in Detroit. And just as they had four years earlier, the Wings won the Cup in overtime, this time on a lucky shot by Leswick that bounced off Harvey's glove over McNeil's shoulder at 4:29.

Back came Detroit in 1955, not quite the same old Wings, but the same old Adams putting young champions on the ice. They had a new coach in Jim Skinner. Marcel Bonin, Larry Hillman, and Red-Eye Jim Hay were fresh names to be inscribed on the Cup. Prystai was in temporary exile in Chicago, and Peters had retired. Injuries to Lindsay and Howe slowed the Wings in the early season, but they won their last nine games, including the riotous forfeit over Montreal, to edge past the Canadiens for their seventh straight pennant.

Again they were outscored by Montreal, but this time Sawchuk edged Lumley for the Vezina by three one thousandths of a point. The playoff matchups were the same, Detroit sweeping Toronto in four and Montreal eliminating Boston in five. The rematch in the finals, with the Wings near the end of their dynasty and the Canadiens on the threshold of a new one, was an exciting affair. In the first two games at Olympia, Detroit scored eleven times, including five by Lindsay, to extend their winning streak to a record fifteen games.

The streak was broken in the Forum on the strength of a Geoffrion hat trick, and then the series was tied when five different Habs scored in the fourth game. Back in Detroit, Beliveau scored first for Montreal, but after Skov tied it up Howe registered a hat trick and the Wings were up again. Montreal got even with a furious six-goal attack in the sixth game, but the seventh game belonged to Detroit once more, as the home team won every game in the series. Delvecchio scored first, Howe got the game-winner, and Delvecchio added an insurance goal. When Curry scored at 14:35 of the third period for Montreal, it marked the first time in his NHL career that Sawchuk did not get a shutout in a playoff series.

That must have been a signal for Adams. He dealt Sawchuk to Boston and installed Glenn Hall in goal. He also brought up Norm Ullman and Johnny Bucyk and brought Lorne Ferguson over from Boston. Bonin was sent to Boston along with Stasiuk, and Leswick, Wilson, Skov, and Woit were sent to Chicago. Of the nine players picked up in the two big deals with Boston and Chicago, none remained or became a star. Hall won the Calder and joined Kelly and Howe among the second all-stars; Lindsay was the only Red Wing first all-star. The end was in view. For the first time in eight years Detroit finished out of first, barely edging New York for second. And though they eliminated Toronto in five games they could not stay with Montreal this time and were badly beaten in five games.

The Wings rose again for one more flight into first place in 1957, but it was their swan song. Hall was beaten for the Vezina by Plante, but he was first all-star along with Kelly, Howe, and Lindsay. The latter were back in their accustomed places as 1–2 scorers in the league, and Normie Ullman was tenth. The dynasty was toppled in the semifinal round by the Bruins, whose playoff mastery over the Wings extended back to 1944. Except for a 7–2 outburst in the second game, Detroit was convincingly beaten, 3–1, 4–3, 2–0, and 4–3. Goldham had retired; now Pavelich retired. Lindsay was dealt to Chicago. In the years since, only once has Detroit led the league again, in 1965 on the strength of big years by veterans Howe, Ullman, and Delvecchio. Three times they have been Cup finalists—1961, 1963, and 1964—but only that last time did they extend the winners to a seventh game. Adams brought Abel back to coach in 1958, but the perpetual youth movement had petered out, and without Lindsay the fight seemed to have gone out of the Wings.

Throughout the years of the dynasty, Red Kelly had been the bulwark of the defense. It is the mark of his greatness that after more than twelve years as Detroit's premier defenseman, he skated more than seven years as a center at Toronto. Six times he was first all-star, twice second, on his way to the Hall of Fame. Four times he won the Lady Byng Trophy, extraordinary for a defenseman and shocking for anyone in a Red Wing uniform. And when the Norris Trophy was initiated in 1954 for the outstanding defenseman, Leonard Patrick Kelly was its first winner.

Only in the 1959 season of his twenty years as an active player in the NHL was Kelly's team out of the playoffs, and that was the year he played most of his games on a broken ankle—because Adams asked him to. It was also his last full season on Adams's team, his lowest point production over an eighteen-year span, and his second-highest total of penalty minutes. Kelly was the complete two-way player. No defenseman in the history of the game has ever been so thorough in all aspects of defensive play while at the same time contributing so much to a potent offense, and he was as good at killing penalties as he was on the power play. Like every great defenseman he never backed away from trouble, but unlike most he never provoked any. It is quite likely that he could have been regarded by many as the greatest player of all, except that for over twelve years he played on the same team with and in the shadow of Gordie Howe.

Only superlatives are admissible in describing Howe, despite paradoxes and contradictions in perception. Derek Sanderson, for example, called him the dirtiest player in the league, Phil Esposito said he had the greatest elbow, and King Clancy rated him with Ray Getliffe as the worst troublemakers. But while many call him the greatest hockey player of all time, Bill Gadsby called him the greatest professional athlete of the century (Gadsby had reference only to Howe's hockey, but as a novice Howe outdrove PGA champion Chick Harbert on the golf course, and he has hit major-league pitching out of the park without any practice).

A chronicle of Howe's records would fill a chapter by itself. In his twenty-five NHL seasons he played 1,687 games and scored 1,809 points on 786 goals and 1,023 assists, and then he came back to play in the WHA with Houston. Six times he led the league in scoring. He won the MVP six times. Twelve times he was first all-star, nine times second—and he played the same position as Geoffrion, Andy Bathgate, and Richard. Richard himself admits that Howe was the better all-around player, and Beliveau says he was the best he ever saw.

Whatever qualities are listed for hockey skills, Howe had them in abundance: speed, quickness, size, strength, agility, stick-handling, checking, shooting. He could play hurt, and he healed fast. He could not be intimidated, and he did a lot of intimidating. He backchecked as well as he forechecked. He had great vision (in spite of the aftermath of a concussion that left him with a nervous tic—teammates called him Blinky), great perception of the whole rink, and great instinctive sense of patterns of movement.

He was opportunistic, as he had to be to score as much as he did, but best of all he was a complete team player. He was where he should have been on defense, doing what had to be done. And on offense, despite the uncanny ability to shoot from either side and with either hand low on the stick, he never failed to set up a teammate with a higher percentage shot. Howe gave more goals away to others—both with passes and with reports to goal judges—than any other player.

He could do so many things on the ice that in his early years he was called a showboat, making opposing forwards look bad and rubbing it in, seemingly stick-handling around defensemen two or three times on a single rush. Yet most observers said that if you didn't know hockey and didn't watch very closely you'd miss many of the brilliant but unspectacular things he did. Howe's competitiveness is legendary, though he didn't let it extend outside the rink as his linemate Lindsay did. And he could be gallant in defeat, as in Maple Leaf Gardens in 1963 when the Wings had lost the Cup and he tossed his gloves one by one to a youngster in the stands. He was the roughest smooth player ever, and maybe even the dirtiest clean player (he logged 1,643 penalty minutes), but by all standards he has the best claim to being the best.

20

Rocket Man and Masked Marvel

For a decade, once their crown had slipped in the 1947 Cup series, the Montreal Canadiens were the Avis of the NHL: second in the standings in 1950, 1952–1955, and 1957; Stanley Cup runners-up in 1951, 1952, 1954, and 1955; second in goals scored in 1952; second in goals against in 1953; with Richard or Lach trailing Production Line members in scoring in 1950–1954. On all-star teams they had Richard five times, Reardon and Olmstead twice, and Harmon, McNeil, Mosdell, Geoffrion, Johnson, and Plante as *second*-team selections. Yet no team, management or players, could be said to have tried harder.

And there were triumphs to be hailed for the Habs. They did lead the league in 1956; they won the Stanley Cup in 1953 and 1956; they led in goals scored in 1954–1957; they had fewest goals against in 1949, 1950, 1956, and 1957, Lach led all scorers in 1948, Geoffrion in 1955, Beliveau in 1956, Lach scored the most goals in 1948; Richard in 1950, 1954, and 1955 (tied with Geoffrion); and Beliveau in 1956, Harvey was first all-star six times, Richard five, Beliveau three, Durnan and Lach twice, and Reardon, Mosdell, and Plante once each. Beliveau won the Hart in 1956, Durnan the Vezina in 1949 and 1950, Plante the Vezina in 1956 and 1957, Geoffrion the Calder in 1952, and Harvey the Norris in 1955, 1956, and 1957. For any other club, these would have made for a glorious decade; for the Canadiens it was a time of un-fulfilled aspirations. There was too much of finishing second.

The Cup finals defeat in 1947 was followed by a resounding collapse to fifth place and out of the playoffs in 1948. Durnan had his worst season and Blake, in his last year, suffered with injuries and diminished production for himself and Richard as well. With Blake's retirement, the punch seemed to go out of Montreal's attack, but Durnan's return to form put them in third place the following season, and they extended Detroit to seven games in the semis before Howe's seventh and eighth goals of the series eliminated them.

In 1950, despite a strong second-place finish, the Canadiens appeared to be weakening for the future. Kenny Reardon, a first all-star defenseman, decided to retire "while he is still in one piece," according to Selke. The manager himself had not recovered from trading Buddy O'Connor and Frank Eddolls to the Rangers for three players who never matured as major-leaguers. The hardest blow to the future was the retirement of Durnan. At thirty-five, in his seventh season and headed toward his sixth Vezina, the peerless goalie announced that this would be his last season. And then he didn't quite finish it. In the first round of the playoffs, the Rangers beat him three straight times, scoring ten goals in all. "My nerves are shot," he said. "I can't go on." Gerry McNeil replaced him for the last two games.

McNeil was the regular Canadien goalie for the next four seasons. His average very nearly matched Durnan's 2.35 for his career, and his 2.06 playoff average was even better than Durnan's. But he was a nervous type and something of a hypochondriac. "I'm retiring while I still have my health," he said, perhaps haunted by the ghosts of Vezina and Gardiner if not by more recent memories: Brimsek's nervous collapse, McCool's ulcers, and the lingering presence in the Forum of his predecessor who, just a little over a year before he had to quit, was unscored on through 309:21.

During most of the McNeil era, the Canadiens suffered from greatly reduced point production. But their concentration on defense improved, thanks largely to Doug Harvey's development into a star. On a team whose success was based on exciting individual players, flashy skating and shotmaking, and brilliant goaltending, Harvey was an anomaly as an exceptional team player. An outstanding all-around athlete, he was subtle while his teammates were showmen, cool while his teammates were volatile, and unobtrusively unselfish and steady while his teammates sought points and spotlights and headlines. Never a favorite with the Forum fans, Harvey nevertheless won over the professional observers of the game. He was first all-star ten of eleven years (1951–1961), and won the Norris Trophy four straight times (1955–1958), and three more times (1960–1962), the last as a Ranger.

More to the liking of the Canadiens' crowds was Bernie Geoffrion, who arrived in time to score fourteen points in eighteen games in 1951, just few enough to preserve his rookie status and the Calder Trophy for the 1952 season. Boom-Boom played right wing behind Rocket, and he made his line as exciting as the first. He lacked Richard's skating speed and style, but he equaled his total commitment to winning that made him want to carry the team on his broad shoulders whenever he was on the ice. As ebullient as Richard was moody, Geoffrion could lift the spirits of the team both on and off the ice.

Geoffrion's greatest asset was his shot, the hardest yet to be seen in the NHL, made by slapping at the puck with a stick raised off the ice. The sounds of stick hitting puck and then puck slamming off the boards earned him his nickname. His scoring won him the Ross Trophy in 1955 and 1961, the Hart in 1961, second all-star selections in 1955 and 1960, and first team in 1961—no mean feats when right wingers named Howe, Richard, and Bathgate were in the league. His career total of 393 goals and 822 points placed him in the top five on the all-time list when he retired, and for the nine seasons 1952–1960, he outscored Richard five times, and totaled 25 points more and only 6 goals less. In 1961, the year after Rocket's retirement, the Boomer had 50 goals; he was the first to match Richard's 1945 feat. Perhaps his greatest trophy as a Canadien was winning the hand of Howie Morenz's daughter. And now *their* daughter is married to Hartland Monahan, a hard-shooting wing with the Washington Capitals.

Throughout McNeil's tenure, however, the Canadiens were still the team of Richard and Montreal was still the Rocket's town. Selke called him his greatest player ever, and there are many hockey fans who rate him in a class by himself. He scored 544 NHL goals, and yet he never led the league in scoring—for several reasons. The practice of awarding cheap assists to playmakers, begun in the 1940s, is one, but more significant is the fact that Rocket disdained passing when there was a chance that he could get a shot on goal. Another reason is that in only one third of his seasons did he not miss games because of injuries (169 games in all, with injuries including three leg fractures, a depressed fracture of a facial bone, a left wrist fracture, surgery for bone chips in the right elbow, a nearly severed Achilles tendon, not to mention the groin injuries, the teeth knocked out, the cuts requiring hundreds of stitches, and all the sprains and bruises a hockey player's flesh is heir to). His single-directed pattern of play took a heavy toll, and so did his temperamental attitude. Feuds with other players, with officials, and even with the league president made him a marked man, and he lost many hours of playing time because of major penalties, fights, match penalties, and suspensions. With all of his skills, there is no doubt that he could have had an even more productive career than he had.

Yet no one player has ever been able to carry a team as Richard did. Aroused, he could, in Andy O'Brien's words, "literally and consistently beat whole NHL teams single-handed." In Stanley Cup competition he scored eighteen game-winning goals. He could score under the most adverse conditions, like the time in 1945 when his skates were dragging with the weight of Earl Seibert on his back after ducking the defenseman's check; he still faked Lumley out of the net to score against the Wings. Detroit often aroused the Rocket. In the 1951 playoffs, he won the first two games at Olympia on overtime goals against Sawchuk. The Wings tied the series by winning the next two games, but Richard got the game-winners in the following two to put Montreal into the finals. The Canadiens won only one of five overtime games against the Maple Leafs in that series, but it was Richard who scored the winning goal on his way to a record thirteen points (which he broke with fourteen in 1956 and again with fifteen in 1958).

Most of his playoff records have since been broken in extended series with diluted opposition, but some remain: eighty-two playoff goals, five in one game against Toronto in 1944, and three times scoring a hat trick in a single period (against Toronto, 1944; Toronto, 1945; and Boston, 1957). Richard's performance in the 1951 playoffs came after a late-season slump that saw Howe overtake him in goals scored, 43–42. Maurice had attacked referee Hugh McLean in a hotel lobby the day after suffering, unjustly he thought, from McLean's officiating. Clarence Campbell's five-hundred-dollar fine sent the moody Richard into a prolonged sulk, but when the Canadiens struggled into the playoffs, Rocket took off again.

With McNeil a little more at home in 1952, and the Habs rejuvenated by Geoffrion and another bright rookie prospect—the speedy Dickie Moore who was to win the Ross in 1958 and 1959—Montreal moved up to second place in the standings. Richard had a subpar year, missing twenty-two games during the season, but in the semis against Boston he took over again. He scored twice in the first game in a 5–1 win; Geoffrion's hat trick won the second. The Bruins proceeded to win the next three games and led the sixth with only nine minutes to go when the Rocket took the puck away from Milt Schmidt and tied the game with a thirty-footer. Montreal won in overtime when rookie Paul Masnick rebounded a Harvey shot and scored.

The seventh game was a classic, and it was vintage Richard. Both teams scored in the first period; the only score in the second was not a goal but a knockout by Leo Labine, with a stick to the head and knees to the stomach of the Rocket who had tripped on a headlong rush toward the Boston goal. With six stitches closing the gash over his left eye and still groggy, Richard returned to the bench in the third period. With less than four minutes left, he was on the ice again, though his head and vision were swimming and his ears thudding. Butch Bouchard pokechecked the puck away from Woody Dumart and fed a pass to Richard. He deked past Dumart, sped away from the other forwards, and headed toward Quackenbush, controlling the puck on his stick with his forceful skating style. Quackenbush tried a bodycheck but only detoured Rocket, who pushed off toward the right board, then veered left to buttonhook around Bob Armstrong who had hurried over to help. The left-handed shot caught the far left corner of the goal, the only angle that Sugar Jim Henry could not cut off.

The ovation that exploded in the Forum lasted a full four minutes. Richard barely knew what had happened. Billy Reay added an open-net goal in the final minutes to clinch the series that Rocket had won. In the finals, the weakened Richard was shut out. The tired Canadiens had only two goals in all as the Red Wings swept to the Stanley Cup.

Montreal was back in second place a year later, but Richard got a measure of revenge against Howe and Detroit. In the last game of the season, Irvin switched Rocket to left wing so that he could stop Howe from getting a fiftieth goal to match Richard's record. When Irvin saw Richard charge Howe at the first opportunity, he switched assignments, but Bert Olmstead and Goose McCormack did the job of blanking Howe. Montreal and the happy Rocket then received a surprise gift from Detroit as the Bruins eliminated the champions in the first round, Dumart doing a job on Howe while Jim Henry stopped scores of Wing shots. Meanwhile, the Canadiens struggled past Chicago in seven games, with Geoffrion leading the way. Trailing three games to two, Montreal had to replace McNeil with young Jacques Plante in goal when Gerry's nerves made him ask for help. Plante allowed only one goal in the last two games.

Physical disabilities played a major role in the Cup series. Milt Schmidt missed the first game, and Montreal won, 4–2. Schmidt's return lifted the Bruins to a 4–1 win in the second game, but Sugar Jim Henry hurt an ankle. Game 3 had a new pair of goalies, inexperienced Red Henry for Boston and overexperienced Gerry McNeil for Montreal. The Bruins took the attack to the Canadiens throughout the game, but McNeil defended perfectly on thirty-four shots on goal. Montreal scored once in each period, Henry making only fifteen saves in the game. Montreal rocked Boston Garden in the fourth game with seven goals, including a hat trick for the Rocket. Two days later in the Forum, Sugar Jim limped onto the ice to try to hold off the Canadiens.

Henry held them off for sixty minutes, but McNeil was equally stalwart at the other end. A little over a minute into overtime, Richard returned to the ice after a rushed patch-job on his bloodied face and swept up ice on Lach's wing. Lach had been shut out throughout the playoffs, though he had contributed six assists. Henry anticipated a pass to the Rocket but blocked Lach's shot with his stick. The angle sent the rebound right at Richard, who had six goals but no assists in the playoffs. He passed to Lach, who flicked an instant liner into the net before Henry or anyone else could react to the surprise, and the Canadiens had the Stanley Cup for the seventh time.

Frank Selke was an unusually patient and adaptable man in the hockey community. At Toronto he had implemented the Conn Smythe no-star system with a youth movement that brought eager, fast, tough Leafs to early maturity, without regard for long-range planning. In Montreal, however, a different philosophy obtained. The Canadiens were to thrive on durable stars, and Selke believed that when he had enough of them he would have a relatively enduring dynasty. And gradually the pieces fell into place to complete

Checking Back

his design, the four keys fitting in during a three-year period: Jean Beliveau signing on in 1954, Plante taking over in goal in 1955, Toe Blake returning to coach for 1956, and a second Richard beating the kid-brother jinx in 1956. The result of the patient planning was perhaps the greatest hockey team in history and an unprecedented five consecutive Stanley Cups. Of the eighteen players whose names were inscribed on the Cup in 1956, twelve were still on hand in 1960.

Before this dynasty assumed solitary hegemony, it contended with the still-mighty Red Wings, whose dominance spanned the early and mid-fifties. The Canadiens' Cup in 1953 was considered merely a brief interregnum, and Detroit returned to lead the league and take the Cup in both 1954 and 1955. But in each case they were carried to the wire by Montreal in close pennant races and seven-game Cup series. During the first of those seasons, Geoffrion demonstrated that his anger was as quick and explosive as the Rocket's red glare, earning a fine for charging a referee and an eight-game suspension for fracturing Ranger Ron Murphy's jaw with his stick. The Boomer finished fourth in scoring, just ahead of Olmstead, while Richard beat Lindsay for second behind Howe. Montreal led the league in scoring, four goals ahead of Detroit, but finished seven points behind them in the standings.

During the season Plante played seventeen games, his 1.59 goals-against average leading Lumley and Sawchuk by a wide margin. But McNeil was still the regular until he was hurt in February, with a 2.45 in fifty-three games. Plante started the playoffs, shutting out Boston twice as Montreal swept four straight. Detroit beat Toronto in five games, setting up another head-to-head battle between the two powers. They split 3–1 games at Olympia, Dickie Moore scoring once and feeding Richard twice in the second game. But at the Forum, Detroit won convicingly, 5–2 and 2–0.

Irvin sent McNeil back into the nets for the fifth game, and Gerry responded with a shutout. Sawchuk was also perfect through three periods, but at 5:45 of overtime veteran Ken Mosdell, who had broken in with the Brooklyn Americans, scored unassisted to prolong the series. McNeil was brilliant again in Game 6 as the Canadiens jumped on Sawchuk for three first-period goals. Floyd Curry scored twice in the 4–1 win, and Elmer Lach got the last two of his 687 NHL points in his next-to-last game. The final game, won 2–1 for Detroit by Leswick's shot deflected off Harvey's glove in overtime, was all that McNeil could take. Three years later he would return for nine games and thirty-two goals against, but his retirement at that time seemed the only reasonable relief for his nerves. And Plante was ready.

Jean Beliveau was not a factor in this series. Indeed, the most publicized signing in years of the most heralded rookie in decades had led to anticlimax and disappointment. Beliveau did not assert himself in style or attitude, and he was a marked man for the intimidation of head-hunters and reputation-seekers. He missed twenty-six games because of injuries, and though he scored thirty-four points in the forty-four he played, the Calder went to Camille Henry of the Rangers with thirty-nine in sixty-six games. In three years with the Quebec Aces, Beliveau had reached heights of achievement never matched in Canadian "amateur" hockey, not simply in scoring goals and dominating games, but in terms of salary earned and of fans attracted through the gates. To settle the conflict between the forces that strove to keep "Le Gros Bill" in Quebec City and those that strove to get him to Montreal, the Canadiens purchased the whole Quebec Senior League and the pro rights to all its players. At one time it had seemed that Beliveau couldn't afford to move to the NHL, but now he couldn't afford not to.

As a center, he was unusually big and strong—6' 3" and more than 200 pounds—yet his powerful, smooth skating style was deceptive, in that he didn't seem to be making an effort but was faster than most. Every hockey skill seemed easy and natural to him, stick-handling and quick release of shots no less than instinctive rink-sense. He revolutionized offensive center play by backing into the slot for shots while wings forechecked, a style adopted by Stan Mikita and Phil Esposito after him. By the end of his second NHL season, when he had reluctantly learned to retaliate against those who tried to intimidate him or slow him down with roughness, Beliveau was the premier center in the league. He was first all-star in 1955 and five of the six following years; he won the Hart twice (1956, 1964), the Ross in 1956, and the first Conn Smythe Trophy for playoff MVP in 1965. When he retired in 1971, with 507 goals and 712 assists, he was the highest-scoring center of all time. Perhaps the greatest tribute to his dominance was paid by Punch Imlach's Leafs in 1960, when they dealt for Detroit all-star defenseman Red Kelly for the primary purpose of playing center on a line against Beliveau, who had been beating Toronto for six years.

The disappointments of 1954 were repeated in 1955, with mounting frustrations at the foot of Mount Royal. Montreal led the league for most of the season, outscoring everyone by far, with Richard, Geoffrion, and Beliveau racing along at 1-2-3 in goals and points. Olmstead, who led the league in assists, was seventh in points and Mosdell tied for eighth. Plante, getting occasional relief from Charlie Hodge in goal, was showing signs of becoming a new Durnan, though Lumley and Sawchuk were having better seasons. During the season, one very questionable deal was made, Selke selling to Chicago for $15,000 rookie Eddie Litzenberger, who went on to score fifty-one points en route to the Calder Trophy. It wasn't that Montreal was overstocked with all-star centers; it was a matter of trying vainly to forestall the movement toward a draft system. The prolonged dominance of three clubs over the other three was perceived as a product of their extensive control over minor-league prospects throughout Canada, and the league was developing the concept of a draft system to achieve balance. The days of empire-building at the grass roots of hockey were numbered.

Late in the season, Detroit went on a seven-game winning streak, to move within one point of Montreal with four games left including two with the leaders. Feeling the pressure, the Canadiens got into a rough game at Boston that kept getting rougher. Irvin urged his men to come out fighting in the third period. Richard, who needed little prodding anyway, was dumped by defenseman Hal Laycoe and, bloodied, boiled over. He went after his former teammate but was intercepted by linesman Cliff Thompson, among others. The ensuing scuffle resulted in a match penalty for Rocket and, worse, a review by Clarence Campbell. Always the focus of attention by officials, Richard had also come under President Campbell's selective scrutiny. This time a stern verdict was handed down: suspension for Richard for the rest of the season and the playoffs.

On St. Patrick's Day, Campbell defied threats of violence and attended the Red Wings–Canadiens game in the Forum. Detroit was already ahead of the Rocket-less Habs when Campbell arrived, but then the center of attention moved from the ice to the presidential box. Fans tried to get at him, garbage was heaved at him, and one man got close enough to squash a tomato on his head. Detroit moved ahead, 4–1, which heightened the anti-Campbell feelings. He was saved not by the inadequate police protection but by a potentially disastrous distraction. A tear-gas bomb was exploded in the rink, and the crowd of 14,000 thronged through the exits to join a riotous crowd outside. Campbell was hit by one punch but managed an orderly withdrawal out through the first aid room. The whole city was incensed, and though there were no major casualties, the riots continued well into the morning, resulting in over $100,000 worth of damage. The game was forfeited to Detroit. To prevent further disturbances Richard went on the radio next day, saying in French, "I will take my punishment and come back next year to help the club and the younger players to win the Stanley Cup." The Rocket's brother would help make him a prophet.

Montreal came back to beat New York and went into the final game tied with Detroit. Meanwhile, Richard's hopes for his first scoring championship were threatened by his teammates who were still trying to win the pennant. For Canadiens fans, the worst happened in Olympia. Montreal lost, but Geoffrion overtook Richard. In playoffs, Detroit swept Toronto in four and Montreal whipped Boston in five, setting up a rematch. The power of the league wavered in the balance, a great Red Wing team seeking to extend their reign, the heir apparent seeking to ascend the throne. Even without Richard, Montreal was nearly equal to the task.

Floyd Curry, assisted twice by Calum MacKay and Mosdell, had Montreal in front in the first game until less than seven minutes remained. Stasiuk, assisted by Howe and Lindsay, tied it up, Pavelich gave Detroit the lead, and Lindsay from Howe put it out of reach. The game had been held up for ten minutes when Dickie Moore incited a brawl in which he took on Detroit fans as well as players from both teams. The second game was no contest. Pronovost, Lindsay, Delvecchio, and Howe pounded shots past Hodge in the first period, and Lindsay scored three times against Plante in the second. The 7–1 game was Detroit's fifteenth straight win.

The streak was broken in Montreal on the strength of a Geoffrion hat trick, and the Canadiens tied up the series with a 5–3 win in the fourth game, Tom Johnson scoring the winning goal. Back at Olympia, Gordie Howe took over, his hat trick against Plante dominating the 5–1 game. Montreal got even again at the Forum as Geoffrion, Beliveau, and Harvey had three points each in a 6–3 game. But Detroit was unbeatable at home, winning the deciding game 3–1 on two goals by Delvecchio and the Cup-winner by Howe.

Selke was faced with a difficult decision. His long-time associate Dick Irvin had apparently lost his effectiveness. He seemed more interested in winning battles for intimidation than games, he didn't automatically command the respect of the younger players, and he didn't seem to be a positive influence on Richard, who in turn was setting a negative example for Geoffrion, Moore, and others. So after twenty-five seasons behind the bench at Chicago, Toronto, and Montreal, Irvin was offered a front-office job by Selke. He declined and returned to Chicago to replace Frank Eddolls after his one dismal season behind the Black Hawk bench. The subtle personality changes in Irvin, perhaps the greatest coach in hockey history, may have been caused by the bone cancer that was to take his life within two years of this final move.

The new coach in Montreal was Toe Blake, a popular figure in Quebec hockey for twenty years, liked and respected by the players, and firmly in control from the first day in training camp. With Selke's help, Blake set out to create a cohesive squad out of the Canadiens' star-studded roster, and the focal point would be the Rocket. To curb his temper without having him sulk and lose his competitive drive was crucial. They were assisted immeasurably toward that goal by the emergence of Henri Richard, the Pocket Rocket. Small as he was—only nineteen when he came to camp and clearly inexperienced—he was still too good to farm out for seasoning. He was the other center the team needed, one who could control play whenever he was on the ice. He seemed to be everywhere, darting and cutting with his unique skating style, aptly described by Fischler as "his lilting hop-steps."

Blake put Henri on a line between Rocket and Moore, forming an equally mighty second unit of Beliveau centering for Geoffrion and Olmstead. Mosdell and Curry were on a third line with rookie Claude Provost, Don Marshall, or

Checking Back

Jackie LeClair. At defense, Harvey had some fresh help in rookies Jean-Guy Talbot and Bob Turner, along with veterans Dollard St. Laurent, Tom Johnson, and the captain, playing his last season, Butch Bouchard. In goal there would be no alternating. Blake let Plante know he was there to stay.

This team responded to Blake's leadership and fulfilled Rocket's prediction. They were awesome, winning a record forty-five games and beating Detroit by a full twenty-four points for the pennant. Their 222 goals were the league's best production, with Beliveau first, Rocket third, Olmstead fourth (first in assists again), and Geoffrion seventh in scoring. Beliveau won the Hart as well as the Ross and was joined on the first all-star team by Rocket, Norris-winning Harvey, and Vezina-winning Plante. Johnson and Olmstead were second-team all-stars. Henri Richard failed to win the Calder because Detroit, for the third time in a little over a decade, had come up with an exceptional young goalie, Glenn Hall.

For a few games during the season, Rocket neglected his own vendettas to rush to the Pocket Rocket's aid whenever Henri scuffled with an opponent. But the little brother was not only fearless, he was also very successful in fights. Maurice soon learned to enjoy watching, and Henri gratified him often. Fischler claims that in a single fight in Boston he won KOs over Leo Labine and Jack Bionda and a decision over Fern Flaman. That would have been in 1958, the year the Pocket Rocket was first all-star center, and he later earned second-team selection behind Beliveau in 1959 and 1961, Mikita in 1963.

The most devastating part of Montreal's attack was the power play. Olmstead joined Rocket and Beliveau up front with Harvey and Geoffrion at the points. One out of every four Canadien goals that season came from that line-up, and when the season was over a new rule was adopted. It has always seemed hypocritical to some that a team which is being penalized for breaking the rules of the game should be given the special privilege of icing the puck without restriction whenever possible. But now a special dispensation was granted to protect a penalized team from the cruel and unusual punishment of the Habs' power play. A minor penalty would be terminated as soon as a goal was scored against the short-handed team.

As potent as the offense was, the real improvement in the team was on defense, and perhaps this was what brought them together as a unit. They fought less, except for the newly combative Beliveau, but checked better. They scored almost as much but without neglecting positional defense. The fast young defensemen worked well with the clever veterans, and they all benefited from Harvey's presence. Most of all, they benefited from the coming of age of Jake the Snake.

Plante had always been flamboyant and cocky; now he was confident. No goalie in the modern era, maybe ever, has had as much influence on the game.

Plante revolutionized goaltending style in two ways. First, he was a rover, actually performing some of the functions of that position from seven-man hockey, coming far out of the crease to break up attacks and going behind the net to cover or clear loose pucks. In 1959 the league passed an anti-Plante rule, instituting a minor penalty when a goalie freezes the puck behind the goal. Actually it was Sawchuk who, imitating Plante by going after the puck but lacking Jake's passing ability, developed the habit. Plante's other stylistic innovation was the mask, introduced during the 1960 season when an Andy Bathgate slapshot opened a gash in his face that required seven stitches to close. He was ridiculed for the mask just as he was for his wandering ways, but in time every goalie in the league had adopted them.

Plante's best season was 1956, when he had a 1.86 average, but he won the Vezina the next four years as well and again in 1962, though in three of those years he lost the first all-star selection to Glenn Hall. In 1969, at forty, he shared the Vezina with Hall, at thirty-seven, and after a three-year retirement, in goal for the St. Louis Blues. Two years later he was in the Toronto nets for more than thirty-eight games and a 1.88 average (his best since 1956). He finished his NHL career as a forty-four-year-old Bruin in 1973. The practice of alternating goalies, in which he was prominent at its inception in the fifties and at its full implementation in the expansion era, was something he had long advocated. Whether it was because he was a hypochondriac or a prima donna, as his detractors argued, or asthmatic or high-strung, as his admirers urged, his way has proven to be the most effective under the rigors of changing styles of play and longer schedules. Plante's hobby of knitting *toques* may have helped him last as long as he did, particularly since his roving and comparatively erect style made him vulnerable to hard low shots, and the alternation certainly helped in the later years. But in the five years of the dynasty, Plante missed few regular season games and none in the playoffs.

For the third year in a row, Montreal faced Detroit in the finals, but this time with home ice advantage and confidence in a cohesive, record-breaking squad. After two periods of the first game, down 4–2, they had begun to wonder where all that strength had gone, but Blake shook them up with a tongue-lashing in the dressing room, and they came on to win on goals by LeClair, Geoffrion, Beliveau, and Provost. Game 2 was all Montreal, five goals to one, but over in Detroit the Production Line managed a 3–1 win in Game 3. The fourth game broke the home-ice streak as Plante got the shutout and Beliveau two goals in the 3–0 win, and Le Gros Bill wrapped it up by scoring first and then feeding both Rocket and Geoffrion in the 3–1 finale.

Despite their domination that year, the new dynasty seemed shaky in 1957. Montreal finished second to Detroit and barely edged Boston. Beliveau dipped to third in scoring and Rocket sixth, with Moore eighth and Henri ninth, only Beliveau and Harvey repeating as first all-stars. Injuries hurt the season's record as most stars missed several games, including Geoffrion's twenty-nine (making fifty-seven games without Boom Boom in two years). LeClair didn't finish the season, Mosdell had gone to Chicago, and Bouchard had retired, but rookies Phil Goyette, Andre Pronovost, and Connie Broden picked up the slack.

By playoff time they were at full strength. They beat New York in five games, losing only an overtime game to Andy Hebenton's goal and winning the fifth in overtime on a Rocket goal. Boston, having eliminated Detroit in five games and having beaten Montreal in their season's series, 7–4, with three ties, should have had some momentum. But after Mackell put the Bruins in front in the first game, Maurice Richard blazed four rockets past Don Simmons, the Canadiens won, 5–1, Harvey assisting Richard twice (as did brother Henri) and Geoffrion on the other goal.

Simmons was brilliant in the second game, but Plante was perfect, and Beliveau's third-period backhander won the game, 1–0. In game 3 Geoffrion scored twice, including the winner of a 4–2 game, and in game four the Bruins won on Simmons' shutout and two goals by Mackell, who had four of Boston's six goals in the whole series. Back in Montreal for the fifth game, the Canadiens and Bruins reverted to earlier form, staging fight after fight, with ten penalties in the first period alone. But the game was no contest, Montreal retaining the Cup with a 5–1 win.

The following season could have been disastrous. The change at the top—Senator Donat Raymond selling out his controlling interest in the Forum and the Canadiens to Senator Hartland Molson for about two million dollars—didn't seem to bother anyone on the ice. But again the team was riddled with injuries, the most serious to Geoffrion, Rocket, and Moore. Marcel Bonin was brought up to help, along with rookies Junior Langlois and Ab McDonald. But the balance throughout the rest of the league left Montreal in clear control. They won by a comfortable nineteen points, scoring a record 250 goals, with Plante an easy Vezina winner. Moore, wrist in a cast through the late season, led in scoring, with Pocket Rocket second. They joined Harvey as first all-stars.

In playoffs they swept Detroit in four games, while Boston struggled past New York in six to set up a rematch. Power-play goals by Geoffrion and Moore beat Simmons, 2–1, though he outsaved Plante, 42–28. Bronco Horvath scored twice in Boston's 5–2 second-game win and the teams moved to Boston all even. They came back the same way. After the Richards scored all three goals and Plante got a shutout, the Bruins won, 3–1, with Don McKenney scoring twice. In a rare change of policy, Milt Schmidt had counseled Boston to avoid penalties in that game, and the lack of power-play opportunities took the punch out of Montreal.

The punch returned in overtime of the fifth game. Rocket scored at 5:45 in the 3–2 win. Then Montreal tied Toronto's record of nine Stanley Cups with a 5–3 win in the sixth game, Geoffrion's second goal the game-winner.

The draft took Bert Olmstead to Toronto and Dollard St. Laurent to Chicago, but Selke had rookies Bill Hicke and Calder-winner Ralph Backstrom waiting in the wings and brought Ken Mosdell back. Montreal cruised home first again by a comfortable margin and broke their own scoring record with 258 goals. Moore repeated for the Ross, and Plante, despite openly feuding with Blake, won the Vezina by a wide margin. This time the injury plague hit during the playoffs. Beliveau missed eight games and Rocket seven, but there was no stopping the flying Frenchmen, led by Bonin, Provost, Geoffrion, and Backstrom. They beat Chicago in six games, Toronto in five.

Selke and Blake had the same team on the ice in 1960 and they seemed stronger than ever. They led the league by thirteen points, scored 255 goals (35 more than Boston), allowed only 178 goals (Plante edging Hall for the Vezina, though not for first all-star selection. Of those teams he played on, Henri Richard called this the best because it was best-balanced, particularly as the scoring was divided among three lines. They came through the season in good health and through the playoffs without a loss. Chicago was shut out twice by Plante, in the last two games of the semis, and Toronto once, in the final game. Beliveau had 5 goals and seven points in the eight games, Geoffrion 2 and twelve, Moore 6 and ten, Henri 3 and twelve.

Eleven Stanley Cups, five in a row. Then suddenly it was over. Montreal won the pennant the next two seasons and continued to dominate the scoring, but there was something missing in the playoffs. Two obvious factors were Rocket's retirement after eighteen seasons and Plante's growing disaffection. There was also the resurgence of the Maple Leafs as a dominant power in the league. But the main factor was the natural one: with comparatively little turnover, the mighty Montreal machine had simply run down. When they returned to the championship in 1966, only Backstrom, Beliveau, Provost, Henri Richard, and Talbot remained from the glorious years of unmatched dynastic control.

21

Turning Over New Leafs

While Detroit and Montreal were trading dynasties, the third member of the power troika, Toronto, was suffering through bad times. The Maple Leafs continued the Smythe tradition of trading and dealing and changing lineups. The team was barely recognizeable from one season to the next, and when they regained the Stanley Cup in 1962 not a single player remained from their last champions of 1951, they had gone through four coaching changes, and even the management had changed hands.

Turk Broda's brilliant performance in the 1951 playoffs was considered a swan song. After giving Al Rollins one full season in goal Smythe sent him, along with Mortson and Cal Gardner, to Chicago for Lumley. Chicago then made the playoffs for the first time in seven years, while Toronto was out of them for the first time in seven years. But it wasn't Lumley's fault. In his four years in the Leaf goal, 1953–1956, Apple Cheeks led the league twice in shut-outs, was twice first all-star, and won the Vezina in 1954, though his team was never better than third. Ed Chadwick was installed for the 1957 season and in his two years as regular Toronto was fifth and sixth. The resurgence began when John Bower took over in 1959.

Throughout most of the fifties, the Maple Leafs looked like a caricature of Smythe's no-star system. From 1952 through 1959, Lumley (twice) and Sid Smith (once) were their only first all-stars. Besides Smith, only Jim Thomson (1952), Tim Horton (1954), Teeder Kennedy (1954), and Tod Sloan (1956) cracked the second-team selections. Aside from Smith, only Sloan in 1956 made the top five in scoring. Teeder won the Hart Trophy in 1955, a senti-mental gesture to a veteran star playing his last full season, and Smith the Byng twice, but the award significant to the resurgence was the Calder to Frank Mahovlich in 1958.

The whole club seemed to reflect the lack of cohesive organization at the top. Conn Smythe was determined to pass control of his little empire on to his son Stafford, but only when he was good and ready. Stafford was early put into a position of power but then stymied when he felt ready to take over. Conn had given up the job as manager but still ran the show as president. Hap Day, who had been replaced by Joe Primeau as coach, became manager, but to all intents and purposes was still Conn's assistant. King Clancy coached the team through three seasons, 1954–1956, two third places, and a fourth, then became yet another assistant manager. Howie Meeker was given the dual charge of coaching and managing in 1957, but the fifth-place finish cost him both jobs.

At this point Conn Smythe was thinking like King Lear. He sort of divided his kingdom by appointing a hockey committee, with Stafford as chairman, to run the club. Billy Reay was named coach, but there was no manager. Reay's authority was undermined when Stafford Smythe appointed Punch Imlach as assistant general manager, and it didn't help that Reay's team finished last in 1958 and showed little signs of improvement at the start of the 1959 season. The committee chose this juncture to make Imlach manager, and Imlach promptly went over the committee's heads to Conn Smythe and persuaded him of the rightness of his next move: Imlach fired Reay and took on the coaching job himself. Stafford Smythe and the committee had no choice but to yield operational command to Imlach. Stafford encouraged the Napoleonic ego of Imlach, though he resented his father's undermining of his own ambitions for control. Eventually, Stafford—along with Harold Ballard and John Bassett—bought out his father's interests in 1961. It was several years until he could fire Imlach and install his own man, though, because until 1969 Imlach's teams, despite an abundance of problems and personality clashes, were successful in living up to the brightest Maple Leaf traditions.

The team that Imlach took over in November 1958 was in last place, but the personnel was better than that. There was nobody left from the 1951 champions. In fact, of the eighteen names inscribed on the Cup in that year, only five remained on NHL rosters: Flaman and Mackell for Boston, Sloan and Danny Lewicki for Chicago, and Mortson for Detroit, with the latter two playing their last year. Sloan had good years left, but he'd been sold in reaction to his activities in organizing a players' association. The new Leafs were Chadwick and Bower in goal; at defense Bobby Baun in his third season, rookies Carl Brewer and Noel Price, Marc Reaume, veteran Tim Horton, and dependable Allan Stanley, who had come over from Boston; at forward Brian and Barry Cullen, George Armstrong, Bert Olmstead (drafted from Montreal), Dave Creighton, Rudy Migay, Dick Duff, Bill Harris, Ron Stewart, Bob Pulford, and Frank Mahovlich. Most of those players had come up through Toronto's farm system, and twelve of them were still around when Leaf names were again inscribed on the Cup in 1962. This was the squad that established Imlach's leadership with their great finish in 1959, but it was the changes he made that brought the championship back to Toronto three years later.

Punch was like a crude version of the young Conn Smythe. He drove his men hard, criticizing them bitterly when they made mistakes, always egging them on and cheering them on. Most of the team responded well to that abrasive leadership. Chief Armstrong, whom Reay had appointed captain, kept up his aggressive play. Pulford, who had greeted Imlach's announcement that he was taking over as coach with a classic line ("Whose side are you on, players or management?"), had the right kind of toughness, and he was Imlach's leading scorer that season. Bert Olmstead, a seasoned professional, always did his job. In the long run perhaps Frank Mahovlich, the big sensitive youngster with a world of hockey talent, reacted worst to the imbalance between praise and condemnation, and to the gap in communication between coach and players that widened over the years. His temperament never adjusted to Punch's foul-mouthed presence or the fact that the coach never pronounced his star player's name other than "Mahallovitch." And for a squad that was never among the younger teams in the league, the unusually arduous workouts under Imlach were a growing burden.

Imlach picked up Larry Regan on waivers from Boston and put him on a line with Duff and Armstrong. Then he traded minor-leaguer Willie Marshall to Hershey for Gerry Ehman and put him with Harris and Mahovlich. Pulford centered for Olmstead and Stewart on the other line. In early December the team had a six-game unbeaten streak but hadn't struggled out of last place. They were playing good defense and beginning to score better, but as late as March 9 they were still sixth. They passed the low-scoring, slumping Red Wings but were still seven points behind the Rangers for the last playoff spot when New York came to town on March 14. Toronto won at home, then beat the Rangers in New York and were three points back with three games to play. New York split their next two games, but the Leafs won two and trailed by a single point going into the season's finale. When the final score from New York—4–2 for Montreal—reached Detroit, the Wings were leading, 2–0. Toronto rallied to win 6–4.

There was a natural letdown against Boston in the playoffs as the Bruins won the first two games easily. But Imlach, who now had a team seemingly at one with him in spirit, rallied them to three straight wins. They went on to win in the seventh game before losing the Cup to the great Canadien team in five. Still, the late-season drive had turned things around for them; the resurgence was well underway.

One change for the 1960 season was the assembling of a fourth line, called the Rocks, with Duke Edmundson at center between Gerry James and Johnny Wilson. Their forte was knocking the opposition down whenever possible, and they became a great favorite in Maple Leaf Gardens. They never scored many goals, but they turned many games around by upsetting the patterns and rhythms of other teams. The major change occurred in February, with the

Leafs involved in a close battle for second place with the Wings. Jack Adams had become disenchanted with Red Kelly (salary demands after a last-place finish are difficult for management to tolerate) and traded him and Billy Mc-Neill to New York for Bill Gadsby and Eddie Shack. Kelly and McNeill said they'd refuse to report, and the deal was killed. Imlach moved in, ever-faithful King Clancy came to terms with Kelly, and Marc Reaume was traded even-up to Detroit for the eight-time all-star defenseman.

Imlach's idea was to put Kelly at center, and the goal was to stop Beliveau and the Canadiens. Incidentally, the presence of the veteran redhead at forward sparked the Leafs to pull comfortably ahead into second place. The aggressive play of Brewer and Pulford, not to mention the Rocks, was paying off in intimidation value, and solid play from Stanley and Bower was making up for Mahovlich's reduced production. Big Frank, however, scored the winner in the key third game of the playoff series against Detroit, at forty-three minutes of overtime, and it was a very satisfying six-game win for Kelly at Olympia. Still it was too soon to topple the Habs, and Toronto meekly left the Stanley Cup in Montreal after four games, only one of them close.

A year later the Leafs were on a par with the Canadiens. Montreal had slipped a little with the end of the Rocket Era, but they were still the class of the league. Only now they had Toronto for company at the top. Larry Hillman had come over from Boston to be fifth defenseman behind Baun, Brewer, Horton, and Stanley, and there were two prominent rookies at forward, Bob Nevin and Dave Keon. Nevin, on Kelly's wing opposite Mahovlich, got off to a fast start and finished with fifty-eight points. Keon, off to a slow start before catching on, had only forty-five points but won the Calder Trophy. Another addition was Eddie Shack, who had disappointed the Ranger fans and brass for not living up to his performances as a junior against Mahovlich and Hull. Imlach gave up Johnny Wilson and Pat Hannigan and got a bargain in Shack, who provided some of the police work the team needed.

Throughout the season the Leafs duelled the Canadiens for first place. When it was over, Montreal had won by just two points, but there was a gap of fifteen down to third-place Chicago. Toronto had been outscored only by Montreal, and Mahovlich's forty-eight goals were second only to Geoffrion's fifty, prompting Beliveau to say, "You're playing for the wrong team, Frank." Bower had beaten Hall and Plante for the Vezina, and Imlach bragged he had the best team in hockey. But the expected showdown for the Stanley Cup did not take place. Both teams were upset in the semis, Toronto in five games by Detroit, Montreal in six by Chicago. There is no playoff for a bronze medal in the NHL, and so the series that both teams and most fans had been looking forward to all season to decide the supremacy of the league was never played. Nor was it to be played the following year, when a similar duel took place.

Checking Back

In December, Conn Smythe completed the agonizing process of relinquishing the reins. In January, Toronto picked up Eddie Litzenberger on waivers from Detroit. Young John MacMillan and veteran Al Arbour were new faces among the spares. Later that month Toronto gained first place, then yielded it to Montreal. The Canadiens lengthened their lead through the end of the season, while the Leafs, plagued with injuries, easily beat Chicago by ten points for second place. Instead of going all out in pursuit of first place, Imlach's idea was to rest up and get healthy for the playoffs and his first Cup. It was not a banner year for the Leafs, though Brewer, Keon, and Mahovlich were second all-stars, and Keon succeeded Kelly as the Byng-winner. Bower played hurt and also missed eleven games, with Don Simmons brought up from Rochester to take over when needed (except for two games for young Gerry Cheevers). And at the end of March, Punch had them all up and ready.

The Cup-holding Black Hawks surprised Montreal again, spotting them two games and then taking them out in the next four in a row. Meanwhile Toronto took on the Rangers. A short-handed goal by Tim Horton was the game-winner in the first game, but after a 2–1 win in the second game the Leafs dropped two straight in New York. Injuries were getting to them again: Olmstead out with a broken shoulder, Brewer out with a bruised leg, Armstrong playing with a bad leg, Bower playing with a bruised hand, Pulford playing with torn shoulder ligaments, Ron Stewart playing with cracked ribs. And their big line with Kelly and Mahovlich had been in a slump since Shack replaced Nevin at right wing, scoreless in their last eight games.

That slump ended in the fifth game in Toronto. In the second overtime period, Mahovlich's heavy shot went off Worsley's shoulder. Gump fell to the ice but didn't cover the puck, and Kelly, who had assisted on both earlier Toronto goals, found it near the goalie's head and poked it in. Worsley had made fifty-six saves to Bower's thirty-nine, but the Leafs had taken command of the series and blasted New York out of Madison Square Garden, 7–1, to move to the finals. They won two from the hard-hitting Hawks in Toronto, but Glenn Hall shut them out in the third game as Chicago pushed them around the Stadium ice and incidentally pushed the puck past Bower three times. Early in the fourth game, Bower did a split to make a save against Hull, and he felt something snap in his leg. He played on for several minutes, during which Hull scored, but had to leave the ice.

Don Simmons came out of the stands to finish the game and the series, but as rusty as he was he couldn't stop the Hawks that night. They evened the series with a 4–1 win. Back in Toronto, Olmstead was back in uniform, feeding Pulford for a goal in just seventeen seconds as the two damaged shoulders put the Leafs in front. Pulford scored again, but Chicago scored three times in just five minutes of play to take the lead. Then Toronto took over with a furious offensive assault. Mahovlich and Horton assisted both Harris and Keon to put the Leafs in front. Big M scored himself, Armstrong scored, and Mahovlich again. After Turner's goal for Chicago, Pulford completed his hat trick for an 8–4 win.

When they got back to Chicago, the Leafs played a game Black Hawk style, making crunching bodychecks all over the ice. It was a model of modern-day Stanley Cup play, defensive and physical. It was scoreless into the third period, before Hull broke the ice for Chicago. Nevin tied it for Toronto. Duff won it at 14:14 after Horton had controlled a play the length of the ice, passing to Armstrong and then to Duff. Imlach had his first Cup, and fifty thousand Torontonians welcomed the team on their triumphal ride up Bay Street, as Eddie Shack, who hadn't had much exercise lately, did the twist on a seat of one of the open cars.

Imlach decided to stand pat for the 1963 season, almost. In order to protect some of his minor league prospects in the draft he left Olmstead unprotected, and the Rangers grabbed him quickly. Olmstead had been steadfast in performing his services for Imlach, and many felt that his return to the lineup after Chicago had tied the series was what sparked the Leafs to the Stanley Cup. At thirty-six he decided to quit rather than make the move to New York, and his parting shot at "that s.o.b. Imlach" put him in the large company of Punch-haters. Indeed, there was a prevailing climate of opinion summed up by columnist Dick Beddoes in his remark that Punch Imlach "reached puberty but forgot to touch second base."

During the league's preseason meetings, a major deal was reported: Mahovlich was sold to Chicago for a million dollars. Questions remain about how serious the people involved were about the deal. Toronto officials were unhappy about their problems in trying to sign Big M. Jim Norris, who made the offer in a mood of festive bravado, had the temperament and the cash to have followed through if his hand had been called. Tommy Ivan, the Hawks' manager, was simply going along with his boss. Harold Ballard, who accepted the offer on behalf of the Leafs' Hockey Committee, was apparently serious and urged approval on the basis of a cash windfall. When Stafford Smythe arrived on the scene, he apparently did not take it seriously, saying, "Well, I guess we knock the World Series off the front page today." Imlach, for one, was not amused. He had to approve any deal involving personnel, and he gave a flat no to this one, saying he'd have to be fired first. But for a week the story—and the negotiations—went on. Scott Young reported the deal as "hokum, bunkum, nonsense, guile, delusion, gullery, bluff, hanky-panky, sham, make-believe, spoof, hoax, bamboozle, gerrymandering and humbug." John Bassett, another member of the committee, responded by having Young taken off the Hockey Night in Canada team of broadcasters. The official rejection of the offer did

177

little to refute Young's version, but Imlach (in his autobiography, ghosted by Scott Young) insists that "it wasn't really a phony publicity stunt." Imlach, of course, would not have recognized or been let in on the joke-hoax in the first place.

Mahovlich would have been sorely missed. He led the Leafs in scoring, was second in goals in the league only to Gordie Howe, and was first all-star along with Brewer. Horton was second-team, Keon won the Byng again, and Kent Douglas the Calder. Toronto's total goal production was down from the previous year, but only four behind league-leading Montreal, and their defense was just as good, giving up only two more total goals than Chicago, the league's best. Bower played only forty-two games. Simmons played the other twenty-eight and actually was a fraction better than Bower in goals-against. And the Maple Leafs, for the first time under Imlach, finished first in the standings.

It was a close, four-way race throughout the season. With a month to go, Chicago led by eight points over Montreal, with Toronto and Detroit close behind. Imlach calls the February 27 game with the Hawks in Maple Leaf Gardens the turning point. Mahovlich scored first and later assisted Pulford and Stewart in a 6––3 win. Mahovlich got the game-winner against New York a few nights later, and the Leafs were off on a ten-game unbeaten streak. They caught Chicago within two weeks but could get only a 1–1 tie in the Stadium, although outshooting the Hawks 40–19. A tie with Montreal dropped them a point behind, as Chicago won again. When the Hawks came into Toronto, Simmons turned away all fifteen of their shots, and the Leafs got three of their thirty-six past Glenn Hall to go into first place with four games to play. Two games later they clinched the pennant by tying Montreal. Down 3–2 with only eight seconds left, they had Duff outfight big Terry Harper in the corner and center a pass to Keon, who tipped it in.

Only five points separated first from fourth place, and the playoffs promised to be close and exciting. But no series went seven games. Detroit lost two to Chicago and then swept them out in four straight. The long-awaited showdown between Toronto and Montreal was the geatest disappointment. The Canadiens had slipped back to the rest of the league and couldn't match up well against the strong, methodical, defense-minded Leafs. Toronto took the first three games, lost one, and finished off the series with Bower's second shutout. The only close game had been the second, when, with a 3–2 lead, Imlach sent onto the ice for the final shift a line consisting of Keon, Pulford, and Kelly, his three centers, because they were all better defenders than their wings.

Toronto never trailed in the finals. Dick Duff got them off to a quick start, scoring twice in the first sixty-eight seconds of the game. Nevins scored the other two in a 4–2 win. The second game had the same result, as slow-skating Eddie Litzenberger filled in for Mahovlich, scored first, and assisted Stewart twice. Detroit won the third game but no more, as the Leafs got another 4–2 and a 3–1 win to close it out, Keon scoring three, Kelly two, and Armstrong one with two assists in these games. The Cup-winning goal, however, came off the stick of the irrepressible Eddie Shack, who insisted that Douglas's shot had deflected off a Detroit skate, onto his stick, and into the net when he was "just trying to get the hell out of the way."

The Leafs had been predominantly a group of senior citizens when they won the Cup in 1962, and they were substantially the same team, just older, as they set out for their third straight Cup in 1964. But they were not the dominant power they had been the previous spring. Imlach blamed complacency, a lack of aggressiveness, a falling-off by Duff and Nevin, a lot of sulking by Mahovlich, and too much interest in his Parliament activities by Red Kelly (the Liberal Member for York West in Toronto). Stafford Smythe, always looking for the opportunity, blamed Imlach for not making proper use of his personnel. Others thought that the Leafs were just over the hill.

Imlach tinkered with changes to shake them up. Douglas, Calder-winner as a rookie, spent half his sophomore year in Rochester and didn't play in the playoffs. Litzenberger was sent down for several games, and veteran Bronco Horvath was brought up for a few games. The big change was made in February, a major deal involving seven players. The Rangers, who had slipped back into fifth place, knew they had to give up quality front-line players for youth and competence in quantity. Toronto, in third place, wanted the man who might single-handedly dominate a Cup series. Imlach had earlier rejected an even swap of Duff for Don McKenney, but this trade now became part of the package. The key figures were Andy Bathgate, the Ranger captain and four-time all-star, and Bob Nevin, whose future was still bright despite his poor year. The Leafs also gave up minor-leaguers Arnie Brown and Bill Collins and perhaps their most promising junior, Rod Seiling.

In the long run New York made a good deal, but for the nonce Imlach had dealt for a third straight Cup. McKenney skated opposite Armstrong on Keon's line, and Bathgate formed an imposing unit with Kelly and Mahovlich. Strong down the stretch, Toronto finished third. Horton (first) and Mahovlich (second) were all-stars, but second-place Chicago dominated the squad, while first-place Montreal was the leader in most statistical categories.

This time the playoffs provided the excitement that had seemed likely the year before. Detroit kept coming from behind to beat Chicago in seven games. After the Hawks won the first game, Ullman's hat trick in the second got the Wings even. After Chicago led three games to two, Ullman had another hat trick to pace the sixth-game win, and Detroit won the seventh game, 4–2. The

Checking Back

Montreal-Toronto series was almost identical. Hodge shut out the Leafs in the first game, but Mahovlich got them even with a goal and an assist in a 2–1 game. In Game 3, Henri Richard and Tremblay scored third-period goals for a 3–2 win, only to have Big M dominate the fourth game, scoring twice and assisting on Toronto's other three goals in their 5–3 win. After Montreal went ahead by winning the fifth game, Bower shut them out in the sixth. And in the seventh. Keon's hat trick was the story of a 3–1 game, despite the Canadiens' ability to lure the Leafs into a fire-wagon style of play.

The finals also went seven games. The first went to Toronto, 3–2, on a solo dash by Pulford at 19:58 of the third period. Detroit got even in overtime of the second game when Ullman and Howe fed Larry Jeffrey. In Game 3, Toronto came from 0–3 to tie the game at 18:47 of the third period, only to have Howe take the puck from Mahovlich and feed Delvecchio for the winning shot with only seventeen seconds left. The Leafs came back to win the fourth, 4–2, the game-winner going to Bathgate on passes from Kelly and Mahovlich. Game 5 went to Detroit, 2–1, as Sawchuk was superb. The sixth game was tied, 3–3, through a scoreless third period. In overtime, Bobby Baun came out of the dressing room, a cracked bone in his ankle frozen so he could play, and cracked a shot from the blue line off Gadsby's stick and over Sawchuk's shoulder.

Baun insisted on skating in the seventh game, and Armstrong, Brewer, and Kelly were all playing hurt. McKenney's torn knee ligaments kept him out of uniform. That was the price the Leafs had to pay for Imlach's insistence on arduous practice sessions, two hours with contact, even on travel days during the Cup series. Again it was a policy of short-term strength at the expense of long-range weakening. But Punch was consistent, and he won again. Bower, whom Imlach called "in his time, the world's greatest athlete," shut out Detroit. Bathgate's unassisted goal was the only one through two periods, though Keon, Kelly, and Armstrong (with two assists by Mahovlich) got insurance goals in the third.

From that peak of three straight Cups, Imlach presided over the demise of the Leafs through the next four years. They slipped to fourth place in 1965, then were eliminated from the playoffs by Montreal in six games. Their point production had fallen off badly, they didn't have a scorer in the top eleven, and dissension was becoming apparent. Brewer and Mahovlich, both second all-stars, were among the troubled players (Big M actually missed two weeks early in the season because of severe depression), but Bathgate was the most outspoken critic of Imlach on the club—except for Stafford Smythe. They only did as well as they did because of remarkable goaltending. Imlach had picked up Terry Sawchuk, and he and Bower divided the games almost equally as they became the first tandem to win the Vezina in a system that has become standard since.

Once the season was over, Bathgate blasted Imlach for pushing players past the limit of physical and mental endurance, especially the older players and the more sensitive (thus including practically all of the Leafs' stars). Punch had carried his theory of "team" to a point where no individualism such as Bathgate's, whether on the ice or off, could be tolerated—no free-wheeling skating, no mouthing off. He even instituted a team policy of endorsements where all players shared in revenue from public appearances and commercials. Bathgate had to go. He went to Detroit with Harris and Gary Jarrett for Marcel Pronovost, Ed Joyal, Larry Jeffrey, Lowell MacDonald, and Autry Erickson. Ron Ellis and Pete Stemkowski had been brought up from the farm, Brian Conacher and Mike Walton seemed ready, Hillman was back for another stint, and Jim Pappin had come along well. On paper, the Leafs looked ready to come back.

With Baun holding out, Brewer was unhappy in training camp. He fought with Bower, and Imlach seemed to take the goalie's part. When Punch pulled him from a scrimmage, Brewer took the opportunity to tell the manager what he thought. He then accepted Imlach's invitation to turn in his uniform. Rather than play for Punch, he quit hockey and didn't return to the NHL until 1970, when he played a full season for the Red Wings. During the 1966 season, things got worse instead of better. Mahovlich told a reporter that on his doctor's advice he simply tuned Imlach out whenever possible. The team played erratically but hung on in third place, only to go out of the playoffs in four straight, outscored 15–6 by Montreal. Again they had no scorers among the leaders, though Stanley and Mahovlich were second all-stars. The one bright spot was Calder-winning play by rookie Brit Selby.

Again in 1967, Toronto was third, barely beating out the Rangers. Their Stanley Cup triumph, which is recounted in the next chapter, was essentially an aberration in their steady drift toward mediocrity. Tim Horton was their only all-star (second team), and again they had no one among the scoring leaders. In the following season, the dissatisfaction Mahovlich felt in playing for Imlach was increasingly apparent in his on-ice attitude, and Toronto fans were booing him even when he starred in a game. In midseason he could stand it no longer and walked off the team for a few weeks. When he came back and showed he could still play, Toronto concluded a huge deal with Detroit, the only team behind them in the standings. Big M went, along with Stemkowski and rookie Garry Unger, besides the right to deal with Carl Brewer, for Ullman, Floyd Smith, and Paul Henderson.

But the divisiveness in the club went much deeper than pro- and anti-

Checking Back

Mahovlich factions. The rift between Players' Association members and non-members was encouraged by Imlach, who split the team in scrimmages according to their union sympathies. Conacher, Walton, Pulford, and Pappin were all outspokenly against Imlach and for the union. Conacher said that the practices were punitive devices, having nothing to do with hockey. But Punch said that the team was losing and all he could think of to do was work them harder.

It didn't help. They finished fifth and out of the playoffs for the first time in Punch's tenure. In the following season, Stafford Smythe moved to oust Imlach, bolstered by a radio poll in which fans had voted for Imlach's firing after the Mahovlich deal. The club was floundering. Imlach traded Pappin to Chicago for Pierre Pilote. Conacher and Stanley had been left unprotected and were drafted by Detroit and Philadelphia. The Hockey Committee gave Punch an ultimatum: be in contention for the playoffs by December 1 or be replaced as coach. They were in fourth on December 1. Smythe tried to change the terms to first or second or out, but backed down, and the team slipped again as controversy raged over Mike Walton. Walton, high-strung, inventive, and offense-minded (not to mention friendly with Alan Eagleson and related by marriage to Stafford Smythe), was the antithesis of an Imlach player. The coach handled him the way he handled everyone, equally—that is, equally badly—and Walton not only walked out but went public about the dispute in the Toronto *Globe and Mail*. The team supported Walton and he was back in six days, though Imlach saved what was left of his face by attaching a condition of "right attitude."

Walton helped in the stretch drive for fourth place, and the Leafs made the playoffs. Had they performed another miracle for him, Imlach might not have been out and Walton could have been traded. But the Bruins settled the issue, delivering the knockout to Punch by beating Toronto, 10–0 and 7–0, at Boston Garden, and completing the sweep, 4–3 and 3–2, at Maple Leaf Gardens. Before all the players had reached the dressing rooms, Stafford Smythe had shaken Imlach's hand and fired him.

22

The Curse Ends with the Era

As the National Hockey League entered its 1967 season, everyone knew that the closed-circuit era was coming to an end in its twenty-fifth year. The idea of all subsequent records being marked with asterisks had occurred to a few, and there were many who expressed misgivings about the plans for expansion—long overdue to some, too hasty to others; too radical to some, too protective of existing structures to others. Yet the six clubs were all aware that it was the last chance to perform under the old, established conditions, and whether because of or despite the uncertainties about the future, the season was distinguished by outstanding play, particularly by veterans.

For a quarter of a century the six-team league had been dominated by the powers enthroned in Toronto, Montreal, and Detroit. Occasional approaches to equity were made in Boston, New York, and Chicago, but they were rarely sustained. Now a final surge, while the old order still obtained, could be expected in those three cities.

Things were worst in Boston, where the Bruins had not been in the playoffs since 1959. During the fifties, when they made the playoffs eight out of nine years, they were surviving on the strength of their veterans. In 1953, when they upset the Red Wings in the Cup semis, it was because Dumart, at thirty-six, effectively defensed Gordie Howe, while Sugar Jim Henry, at thirty-two, was splendid in goal. Losing Cup finalists in 1957 and 1958, the Bruins had simply not found or developed the young players to take them all the way or sustain a resurgence.

Lynn Patrick had taken on the Boston coaching job after resigning at New York in 1950. He had the satisfaction of beating out the Rangers for the last playoff spot by a single point in his first year. In 1954, with New York and Boston in their usual fight for fourth place late in the season, he told Cal Gardner to needle Max Bentley, the hypochondriac veteran playing his last NHL season as a Ranger, about the condition of his health. There were no stones unturned in this traditional rivalry. The 1958 playoff series in which Boston beat

Checking Back

New York four games to two in the semis, led by Gerry Toppazzini's eight goals, was the high point of the decade for the Bruins.

During the 1955 season, Milt Schmidt played his last games (Bauer and Dumart had already retired) and took over behind the bench. But he couldn't find a replacement for himself on the ice. Rookie Don McKenney was a bright prospect, but though he was among the top ten scorers from 1957 to 1960 and won the Byng in 1960, he was never an all-star. Throughout the fifties, except for Schmidt and Quackenbush before they retired, the Bruins had only Fleming Mackell, the ex-Leaf, as a first all-star, in 1953. Ed Sandford made the second all-star team in 1954, Real Chevrefils in 1957, and veteran Fernie Flaman in 1955, 1957, and 1958. Bronco Horvath, picked up from Montreal and sent to Chicago four years later, had one second all-star season in Boston (1960), but he was the only other until the advent of Bobby Orr.

The Bruin rookies never seemed to fulfill their promise during this period. Goalie Jack Gelineau, the Calder-winner in 1950, despite a 3.28 average, improved to 2.81 the following year, and then was gone. He didn't make anyone forget Brimsek. Larry Regan, the 1957 Calder-winner, had a fairly good second season, was shipped to Toronto in his third, and was finished as a player in his fifth (he is now general manager of the Los Angeles Kings). Their most consistent performers in the early and mid-sixties were Murray Oliver and the Chief, Johnny Bucyk, both of whom had come up with Detroit. Bucyk played on a popular Uke Line with Horvath and Vic Stasiuk, another former Red Wing. The unspectacular Chief always seemed to be in the right place at the right time, deflecting a pass or stroking a rebound into the net, and he continued to do so through the 1977 season. The line was broken up in 1961 when the disenchanted Schmidt and Patrick, then manager, sent Stasiuk back to Detroit along with Leo Labine in the deal that brought Oliver to Boston along with Gary Aldcorn and Tom McCarthy, two forwards who could not make the team a year later. When Phil Watson moved from New York to Boston as coach for 1962, he promptly let Horvath go, too. That was the year the Bruins, with Ed Chadwick, Don Head, and Bruce Gamble in goal, allowed 306 goals, not quite a record thanks to the 1944 Rangers, but bad enough for a last-place finish twenty-two points behind fifth-place Detroit.

Fourteen games into the 1963 season, Boston had only one win, and Schmidt came back to replace Watson as coach. Hap Emms was the manager, and though they didn't escape the cellar until 1966, some signs of renascence could be seen, not often on the ice (though they beat the Leafs in Toronto, 11–0, in January 1964) but in the deals they were making. They gave up Doug Mohns, Toppazzini, and Matt Ravlich to Chicago for Reg Fleming, Ab McDonald, Murray Balfour, and Mike Draper. There were other trades involving mostly veteran players, but it took a strong youth movement to break them out of the rut that had kept them in last place six out of seven years through 1967.

Central to the movement was the coming of Bobby Orr, the wonder who was to save the franchise. Represented by Alan Eagleson, who proceeded to organize the Players' Association, Orr arrived in Boston with a contract to match his press notices. And then he went on to live up to both. He won the Calder, despite missing several games because of injuries, was second all-star, and prompted Harry Howell, New York's Norris-winning defenseman, to say, "I'm glad I won this award now because I expect it's going to belong to Bobby Orr from now on."

But the team still finished last. Another part of the youth movement had been the installation of thirty-three-year-old Harry Sinden behind the bench, while Schmidt replaced Emms as manager. The Bruins took a verbal beating throuogut the season. "Get rid of Orr," the Boston fans yelled. "He's making the rest of the team look bad." And anticipating expansion they cried, "At least we're sixth now; next year we'll be twelfth."

They allowed the most goals in the league, yet goaltending seemed one of their promising strengths for the future. Eddie Johnston, at thirty, was still improving; Bernie Parent, just twenty-two, showed flashes of brilliance; Gerry Cheevers, at twenty-six, looked like a potential all-star when he got a chance to play; and Doug Favell, two days younger than Parent, but just as good in the eyes of some observers, was still developing on the farm. So even when they lost Parent and Favell, both to Philadelphia, in the expansion draft, the Bruins felt they could man the nets effectively.

Schmidt then made the moves that made Boston a contender. He brought up Derek Sanderson from the Niagara Falls Juniors; he sent Oliver to Toronto for Eddie the Entertainer Shack; and he swung one of the most one-sided trades in NHL history, giving Chicago Pit Martin, Gil Marotte, and minor-league goalie Jack Norris for Ken Hodge, Fred Stanfield, and Phil Esposito. At the end of the closed circuit, after suffering through a quarter-century of defeat and disappointment, the Bruins entered the new era with high hopes and expectations.

So did the New York Rangers. But then the Rangers had been suffering from disappointed expectations throughout the period. They climbed all the way up to fourth in 1948, actually pushing the Bruins for third, as Neil Mac-Neil Colville, one of three remaining Rangers from the 1940 Cup-winners, had a second all-star season in his next to last year but his first as defenseman. The other two, Hextall and Watson, retired after the six-game playoff loss to Detroit. The team was led by Buddy O'Connor, winner of the Hart and the Byng trophies in his first year as a Ranger, who was second in scoring in the league; by Edgar Laprade, the 1946 Calder-winner, a master at ragging the puck, in his most productive season; and by Tony Leswick. But with Jim

Checking Back

Henry playing most of the year in goal instead of Chuck Rayner, New York allowed more goals than anyone but Chicago.

Billy Taylor, a center who had played for Toronto, Detroit (where he had led the league in assists in 1947), and Boston, did not finish the season for New York. He was expelled for life from the league by President Campbell, who also indefinitely suspended Boston's Don Gallinger. The charges were gambling and association with gamblers, and the league's summary sentences brought instant approval from Governor Kim Sigler of Michigan, who said, "I like the way you do things."

It seems that law-enforcement officials in Detroit had set up a wiretap on James (Occo) Tamer, a paroled bank robber and gambler. He knew Gallinger, and through him Taylor. There was evidence that Taylor had bet five hundred dollars on Chicago against Boston. In the event, Gallinger went scoreless but the Bruins won, 4–2, Taylor lost the bet—and then his job. Clearly, there was no fix, but the NHL press releases kept emphasizing the fact so much that suspicions were actually aroused. It must be remembered that this was a period of widespread, publicly condoned (though not legal) betting on sporting events, leading up to basketball and football scandals shortly thereafter. The New York *Times,* reporting the incident, said, "Anyone possessing even casual acquaintance with the league [NHL] did not drop dead in surprise at the findings." But the suggestion of a sporting wager by a player could not be tolerated, because of the possibility that a public image that is touched with gambling could in turn be tarnished with corruption. It is almost (one is tempted to follow Campbell's reasoning) as if one of Conn Smythe's horses were to bet on other races.

In any case, hockey, by virtue of its scoring structure, is not an attractive proposition for gamblers, and the sport has been since that incident remarkably free of gambling scandals.

In 1936 in *Maclean's* magazine and again in 1939 in *Canadian* magazine, H. H. Roxborough had examined charges of dishonesty in the league. He listed the reasons for suspicion as (1) reversals of form, (2) the playoff structure, (3) closed meetings of the NHL Board of Governors, and (4) the reticence of President Calder. But he concluded that there was honest effort even in meaningless games, that games were won or lost by inches, and that "hockey betting is very small, most of it is personal and none shows any indication of organization or backing." The conclusion stands up resonably well forty years later.

The Rangers' fourth-place finish in 1950 was the only time they made the playoffs in the next seven years, despite the arrival of Pentti Lund, rookie of the year in 1949, of Gump Worsley, rookie of the year in 1953, and of Camille Henry, rookie of the year in 1954. They had good scoring seasons from Bones

Raleigh (fourth in 1952) and Wally Hergesheimer (fourth in 1953), and second all-star selections for Leswick (1950), Hymie Buller (1952), and Rayner (1949–1951). But even 1950, when Laprade won the Byng and Rayner the Hart, was disappointing. After upsetting Montreal in five games, the last a shutout by Bonnie Prince Charles, they had a chance to go all the way when overtime goals by Raleigh in the fourth and fifth games gave them a 3–2 lead over Detroit in the finals. Detroit came back to win the sixth game, but even then the issue was in doubt until the second overtime period of the seventh game, when Babando sent the Rangers home Cup–less.

Their next playoff appearance was 1956, when Andy Bathgate arrived as a star. He had finally made the team the year before, on his third try, when put on a line with Larry Popein and Dean Prentice. Most other experiments by the Rangers had failed for several years, and they included the sentimental—reuniting the Bentley brothers in New York uniforms—the desperate— using a team hypontist—and the bizarre—ceremonially drinking a magic potion concocted by restaurateur Gene Leone. Phil Watson, in his first year as coach under manager Muzz Patrick, had a talented team, with Bill Gadsby and Dave Creighton, who had come over from Chicago, Danny Lewicki from Toronto, and rookie Andy Hebenton, along with captain Howell and Ron Murphy. Gump Worsley was firmly entrenched in goal, having been temporarily displaced by Johnny Bower in 1954. Edged by Detroit for second place in the league, New York had to face Montreal in the playoffs and were blown out in five games.

A year later, back in fourth place, they were again eliminated by the Canadiens in five games. In 1958, Gadsby and Bathgate led them to second place as Worsley had his best year alternating with rookie Marcel Paille, and the team went from last to second in goals-against average. But this time the Bruins took them out in six games. Bathgate and Gadsby, who won the Hart, were first all-stars the following year, and Red Sullivan and Hebenton joined Bathgate among the top ten scorers, but the defense collapsed and they were out of the playoffs again.

Sixth in 1960 and fifth in 1961, they didn't make the playoffs again until the fourth-place finish in 1962, when Harvey replaced Alfie Pike, who had replaced Watson as coach. Bathgate continued to be their leading scorer, fourth in the league in both 1960 and 1961 and now tied for first with Hull (Bathgate led in assists but Hull, by virtue of most goals scored, won the Ross Trophy). Dean Prentice, who had been second all-star in 1960, had another good scoring year. However, he finished the 1963 season as a Bruin.

The major difference in the team was Doug Harvey. To get him the Rangers had given up Lou Fontinato to Montreal. In other changes at defense they traded John Hanna for Montreal's Junior Langlois, and Gadsby for Detroit's

Checking Back

Les Hunt. They had thus lost their two outstanding defensemen but had gotten the league's best, who was first all-star along with Bathgate and won his seventh Norris Trophy in eight years. Harvey was more than just a great backward skater (only Gadsby and Toronto's Tim Horton were his equal in this regard), more than just proficient at every aspect of the game (Red Kelly comes to mind as the only legitimate comparison here). As player-coach he was an inspiring model for the Rangers and seemed to raise the level of play for the whole team as he made each individual play up to his standards. New York was turned into an exciting, crowd-pleasing team, imitating the Canadiens' style, but with less talent and little success. Their power play, for example, was the mirror-image of Montreal's: keeping the puck moving with passes, until the good shot was set up, unlike Detroit's idea of shooting as often as possible, Toronto's idea of feeding Mahovlich for the heavy shot, or Boston's idea of breaking fast on the wings before the defense could set up.

The Rangers just didn't have the abundance of shooters to make the style work. Other than Bathgate, there was no real scoring threat except Camille Henry, and his best shot was the tip-in, at which he and ex-Ranger Parker McDonald were equally skilled (though neither had proved worthy to wear the crown of Toronto's retired Sid Smith). Harvey's frustrations with New York were climaxed in the playoff against Toronto. The first game was lost on a short-handed goal by Tim Horton. Then, after the Rangers had battled back to even the series at two games each, came that double overtime loss, despite Worsley's heroic efforts, followed by the sixth-game collapse.

The most encouraging thing in the series was the sudden arrival of Rod Gilbert, not yet twenty-one, who scored five points in four games, including two goals in the first minute of the fourth game. By the next season he was a starter, but not for Harvey. Doug had had enough and backed out of his three-year contract to concentrate on playing. Manager Muzz did double duty as coach for most of the season before Red Sullivan, a vigorous hook-checker and clubhouse lawyer in his playing days, took over behind the bench.

Sullivan's tenure was hardly satisfactory. Through the 1965 season New York only could beat Boston to stay out of the cellar, but not by much. Bathgate was second in scoring and second all-star in 1963, and in 1964 during a rare slump suddenly became a Maple Leaf along with McKenney in the deal that brought Duff, Nevin, Brown, Seiling, and Collins to New York. They had lost Hebenton, one of the league's all-time iron men, to Boston in the draft, and now would be victims of his trick of rapping the ice while backchecking for drop passes from opposing forwards. They had released Doug Harvey, and Gump Worsley, who had once made 269 saves over a six-game span for the beleaguered Rangers, got the break of his life—he was traded to Montreal for Plante in a seven-man deal. The Snake was not the answer to New York's problems; the Rangers allowed the most goals in the league during his two years in their goal. But the rest of that deal paid off, as Phil Goyette and Don Marshall joined Gilbert as their scoring threats.

Despite the disappointing overall performance there were other areas of promise, particularly the play of Howell and Jean Ratelle as they moved toward all-star stature. Vic Hadfield was improving, too, not only as a scorer but as a brawler who could command some respect for his police work throughout the league. But patience was in short supply at the new Madison Square Garden. Muzz was kicked upstairs to a vice presidency and his assistant, Emile Francis, became manager. Then, with the team in the cellar during the 1966 season, Francis himself replaced Sullivan as coach, but they remained in sixth place.

Emile the Cat was the first and only ex-goalie (a total of ninety-five games over a six-season career, with an unimpressive 3.74 average) to return to the NHL as coach. At 5′ 7″ and less than 140 pounds, he was not an imposing figure, but he was a leader. Early in the season, before he had taken over as coach, he had charged out of the stands to dispute a decision by goal judge Arthur Reichart. Before long he was involved in a punching, wrestling mêlée with three burly antagonists. From the rink, Vic Hadfield led a rescue party of ten Rangers who scaled the Plexiglas wall to rout the enemy, but not before the boss had lost a TKO because of cuts.

Francis claims his most important move as manager was to bring Ed Giacomin up from Providence, at the cost of four players, including Paille, although Cesare Maniago and Simmons shared in the Rangers' goalminding chores in 1966. In 1967, Giacomin was installed as a regular, and for the first time since 1958 the Rangers won more games than they lost. In fact they were in a three-way battle for second place through most of the season before finishing fourth.

In the playoffs, nine minutes into the third period of the first game, the Rangers were sustaining their high hopes of going all the way, leading the smaller Montreal team, 4–1. The Canadiens then exploded for three goals within two minutes and scored twice more for a 6–4 win. With Vachon outplaying Giaconim in goal, Montreal won the next two games, 3–1 and 3–2. In the fourth game, both young goalies were splendid, with more than sixty saves between them, and at 1–1 they went into overtime. Johnny Ferguson completed the sweep at 6:28, and the long-suffering Rangers had only the satisfaction of looking forward to a new era at the merciful close of a lost quarter-century.

In America's second city, however, the Black Hawks were posed to finish on the highest possible note, having pulled even with Toronto in their semis after dominating the league throughout the season. Chicago's fortunes had been on the rise for a decade, after a miserable period of cellar-dwelling. In the eleven-season period 1947–1957 they had been out of last place only twice and in the playoffs only once. Through these years they had continued their tradition of high-scoring forwards, from the Bentleys and Mosienko, through Roy Conacher and Litzenberger. They also continued their traditional parade of coaches. Johnny Gottselig replaced Paul Thompson early in the closed-circuit era, earning Bill Chadwick's scornful remark that he "didn't know which end of the stick was up." Charlie Conacher followed, lasting less than three years, Eb Goodfellow for two, Sid Abel for two, Frank Eddolls one, Dick Irvin one, and Tommy Ivan less than two, before Rudy Pilous took over.

At least one Chicago tradition went by the boards. After three straight Lady Byng winners, Max Bentley in 1943 followed by Snuffy Smith and Mosienko, they didn't have another until the mid-sixties, when Ken Wharram, Hull, and Mikita won it four times in five years. But for the first fifteen years of the era, their most harmful tradition persisted: no defense. Compared to the other have-nots, over the decade and a half, Chicago allowed 250 more goals than New York, 335 more than Boston.

The turnaround began in 1958. Glenn Hall was acquired from Detroit and for nearly a decade was rarely out of the Chicago goal. They hadn't had outstanding goaltending since the early thirties, when Gardiner and Chabot had won three Vezinas in four years for them. Now they had one of the best, called by many the greatest of the modern era, credited by Plante with inventing the "V" or "butterfly" style, and chosen as an all-star eight of the next ten years (five first-team, three second) despite only two Vezinas, 1963 and 1967, the latter shared with Denis DeJordy. For all his skills, Hall was most impressive for his durability. He played 503 consecutive NHL games, plus 50 in playoffs, before his unprecedented streak was broken early in the 1964 season.

Pilous had more than Hall to build dreams of glory on. Two young defensemen looked good: Moose Vasko in his second year and Pierre Pilote in his third. Up front along with Litzenberger and Nestorenko there were Glen Skov who had come over from Detroit two years ago, Ron Murphy newly arrived from New York, and the newly acquired all-timer Ted Lindsay. Best of all, there was an eighteen-year-old golden boy from St. Anne, Bobby Hull. He did not win the Calder that season, but it's hard to justify the oversight. Frank Mahovlich, the winner, had a good season for last-place Toronto, but Hull's was better for fifth-place Chicago. And he was the sensation of the league, exciting fans and sportswriters in all six cities.

At the beginning of Hull's second season, Chicago looked ready to challenge for leadership in the league. Pilous moved to strengthen immediate possibilities. He picked up three capable defensemen: Tex Evans from New York, Al Arbour from Detroit, and Dollard St. Laurent from Montreal. Giving Hall some hope and help, this crew moved the Black Hawks up to third in goals-against average. At forward, too, they were much stronger, having acquired Murray Balfour from the Canadiens, Tod Sloan from the Maple Leafs, and Dan Lewicki from the Rangers for his final season. In addition, Ken Wharram, up for his fourth try, finally made it as a regular on his way to being first all-star right wing ahead of Gordie Howe in 1964 and 1967.

The Hawks soared to third place, just four points behind the Bruins, and drew the reigning Canadiens in the playoffs. The only other times in the era that they had qualified for postseason play they had drawn the Canadiens, who had overwhelmed them in four straight, scoring twenty-six goals to their seven in 1946, and then outlasting them in seven games in 1953. The jinx held in 1959. In six hard-fought games Chicago was eliminated, the decisive goal coming on a short-handed solo play by Claude Provost just when it looked like Montreal might be carried to a seventh game.

And it was extended through 1960, though the Hawks had acquired even greater strength. For once Chicago was strengthened not by picking up expendable talent from other teams but entirely by their own young players. They brough up the rookie of the year, Red Hay, a fine stick-handling center from Saskatoon who had been a collegiate All-American at Colorado College. He scored fifty-five points his first year, largely because of Pilous's best move, shifting Hull to left wing and teaming him with Hay and Balfour, who soon were known as the Million-Dollar Line. The rookie yield was even better than that, however, as Chicago made a regular of Stan Mikita, who had been born nineteen years earlier in Sokolce, Czechoslovakia.

In time a new Scooter Line was formed, with Mikita centering for Ab McDonald, who came over from Montreal in 1961, and Wharram. By 1962 Mikita had gone far beyond Hay, but for the present it was Hay who got almost as much attention as Hull. At twenty-one, Hull had already become the most feared forward in the game. Described as a perfect mesomorph, he had incredible stamina, speed, strength, and coordination. His skating speed was measured at over 29 mph, his slapshot at 119.5 mph, his forehand wrist shot at 105 mph, and even his backhand shot at 96. His stick seemed to hold contact with the puck longer than other shooters.

In 1960, Hull's thirty-nine goals and forty-three assists won him his first of three Ross trophies and first all-star selection. Through 1972 he was first all-star left wing ten times, second twice, while the Big M, to whom he had lost the Calder in their rookie year, played second fiddle. In 1965 and 1966 he was the MVP, and from 1960 through the end of the closed-circuit era, he was out of the top four scorers only in 1961 and 1963, winning the Ross again in 1962 and 1966. He hit the magic mark of fifty goals the year after Geoffrion did it and then was the first to break it, in 1966 and again in 1967. The fifty-first goal came on March 12 on a power play against the Rangers and Maniago. Maniago had been the victim of a four-goal night by Hull earlier in the season, and so had Gerry Cheevers, but Hull played no favorites. He had hat tricks against Bower and Sawchuk during the season, and two-goal games against Roger Crozier twice, Giacomin twice, Sawchuk twice, Simmons, and Worsley.

When the third-place Hawks drew the first-place Canadiens again for the 1961 semis, Pilous determined that his team should beat the jinx by beating up on Montreal. Chicago had the muscle to do it against a tired, Rocket-less, injury-ridden team. The Hawks lost the battle for the first game but probably won the war at the same time. The Canadiens scored six goals but sustained injuries to Beliveau, Marshall, and Hicke, the latter rushed to the hospital with a concussion. In the second game, Eddie Litzenberger scored his last goal as a Black Hawk, three minutes before the end of the 4–3 game, to even the series.

The third game marked the shifting of advantage over to Chicago. Murray Balfour's goal was the only one of the game until well into the third period, as Hall and Plante stopped everything else. Blake pulled the goalie in the last minute, Goyette won the draw in the Chicago end, and Henri Richard tied the game at 19:45. Through two overtimes Hall and Plante kept it going, but in the twelfth minute of the third extra period, a tripping penalty to Dickie Moore presaged the end. Less than half a minute later, Mikita topped a slapshot that dribbled toward the crowd in front of the crease. Balfour got to it first, whirled around, and finessed the puck through Plante's legs. The action wasn't over, though. Toe Blake stormed onto the ice and swung at referee Dalton MacArthur, thereby earning a record two-thousand-dollar fine levied by Clarence Campbell.

Montreal was not about to give up their crown without a fight. They stormed out in the fourth game in an all-out offensive effort, getting 52 shots at Hall in the first two periods, and evened the series with a 5–2 win. But they didn't score again. Hall regained his composure, got some help from the hungry Hawks, and recorded consecutive 3–0 shutouts. Geoffrion had disregarded his doctor's advice, taken the cast off his knee, gotten a shot of novocaine, and tried to play in the sixth game. But it was a vain, even feeble effort to forestall the inevitable end of Montreal's skein.

Detroit had upset Toronto in five games in the other semis and were waiting in Chicago. The Hawks didn't keep them waiting long, scoring three times in the first period (two by Hull with two assists each by Mikita and Balfour) and then holding on to win, 3–2. Game 2 went to Detroit at Olympia, 3–1, as Delvecchio scored twice with Howe picking up his third and fourth assists of the series, and Hank Bassen replacing the injured Sawchuk in goal.

Game 3 at Chicago Stadium repeated the pattern. Three second-period goals for the Hawks (Hull and Pilote getting two assists each as Mikita, Murphy, and Balfour scored) were enough, Howe getting the only Wing goal in the third. It was Hay from Balfour and Hull to open the scoring in the fourth game, but Bruce MacGregor and Howe assisted Delvecchio to tie it up, and MacGregor scored the winner late in the third period.

Hoping to stop the string of home-ice victories, Abel sent Sawchuk back in for the fifth game. It was a high-scoring affair, with goals by Labine, Howie Glover, and Stasiuk matching Balfour's two and Murphy's at the end of two periods. But the third period was all Mikita as he scored twice and fed Pilote for the 6–3 margin. Then for the sixth game in Detroit, Bassen was the beleaguered Wing goalkeeper. Detroit led, 1–0, and had a power play going in the second period when Delvecchio's pass to Howe was intercepted by Reg Fleming, who beat Bassen to tie the game and take the heart out of the Wings. Mikita and Hull assisted McDonald for the Cup-winner before the period ended, and then Nestorenko, Evans, and Wharram made it a rout in the third.

Hull, the Golden Jet, was the charismatic star of this team, and Hall the venerable hero, but by 1962 it was clear that there were two other outstanding Hawks in the line-up. One was Pierre Pilote, who made up for comparative lack of size for a defenseman by his cleverness and determined thoroughness on defense and his playmaking ability on offense (though Bathgate said he *always* went to his left). Three times second all-star in 1960–1962, he moved up to first-team selection in 1963 (when teammate Moose Vasko was second-team) and stayed there through five straight seasons while winning three consecutive Norris trophies.

The other star, of course, was Mikita. At eighteen, just ten years after leaving Czechoslovakia, he had his first NHL face-off against Jean Beliveau in November 1958. From the beginning, Stan was a pugnacious scrapper, a center in the Milt Schmidt mold, but he overcompensated for his lack of size by taking a lot of penalties, earning the sobriquet "Le Petit Diable" in Montreal as much by his troublemaking as by his playmaking. His skills were unquestionably great. Plante said that, in close to the crease, only Rocket Richard was comparable. On the power play along with Hull, Mikita's stick-handling à la Max Bentley gave Chicago an overpowering freelance attack that was unlike the set pattern play of other clubs.

Mikita became an even more prodigious scorer than Hull, finishing ahead of the golden one five of six years in 1963–1968; leading the league in 1964, 1965, 1967, and 1968 (the two Hawks were 1-2 in 1964, 1966, and 1967); and winning the Hart in 1967 and 1968. He was first all-star center six of the seven years 1962–1968 (second behind Ullman in 1965). When Doug Mohns came over from Boston in 1965 to replace McDonald on the Scooter Line with Mikita and Wharram, they became the most prolific line in history. In 1967 they had 222 points among them.

Checking Back

Clancy called Mikita the "latter-day Howie Morenz." He is credited with introducing the curved stick to the NHL after accidentally discovering in a practice session in 1962 what it could do with a shot, though Hull wrote in 1967 that a puck (like a thrown baseball, I suppose) *cannot* curve, never mind drop or lift—curved stick or not. Most goalies side with Mikita on the issue. The Czech was not very popular with other players, however, and not entirely because of his on-ice belligerence. Writing for *Hockey Illustrated* in 1963, he had broken an unwritten code by naming names in a discussion of roughness and dirtiness. He went on getting penalized, usually in retaliation for what he considered deliberate affronts. In 1964 he earned 146 penalty minutes, then 154 the following year. Yet two years later, after a virtual overnight character change, he became a Byng-winning sportsman, repeating his Hart-Ross-Byng triple crown in 1968.

In 1962, Mikita set the first of his scoring records in the playoffs. Chicago had come in third during the season and faced off against the Canadiens yet again. A Montreal fan, Ken Kilander, was arrested for taking the Cup from its glass case in Chicago Stadium, explaining to the arresting officer, "I want to take it back where it belongs, to Montreal." But the Hawks proved him wrong. Chicago lost the first two games, but Mikita turned them around in the third. Twice in the first period his pesky forechecking taunted Lou Fontinato into charging penalties, and twice the Hawks scored on the power play. They went on to win, 4–1, and swept the next three games, 5–3, 4–3, and 2–0. Mikita had ten assists.

Against the Maple Leafs in the finals, the Black Hawks were beaten at their own game. Toronto matched their heavy bodychecking, and their pressure on goal made Glenn Hall look bad. After 4–1 and 3–2 losses in Toronto, Chicago got a shutout from Hall and a 4–1 win to tie the series. But the Leafs' five straight goals to turn the fifth game into an 8–4 rout settled the issue, Toronto winning the sixth game 2–1 on Duff's goal. In this series, Mikita added three goals and five assists to his semifinal totals for a record twenty-one points.

The Hawks faded in the stretch again, as had become traditional, during the following season and were barely edged by Toronto for the pennant. But then Detroit knocked them out of the playoffs in six games. Ivan replaced Pilous with Billy Reay, but the same thing happened in 1964: they were beaten to the pennant by Montreal by one point and knocked out of the playoffs by Detroit in seven games. That precipitated significant changes for 1965. They gave up Fleming and McDonald for Mohns and also dealt Balfour and Mike Draper to Boston for Toppazzini and Matt Ravlich. (Before the year was over, Balfour, at twenty-nine, was dead of cancer.) They sent Murphy and Erickson to Detroit for John Miszuk, Ian Cushenan, and Art Stratton. The most significant changes, however, involved young players brought up from the minors: Denis

DeJordy, to give some relief to Glenn Hall, and Phil Esposito and Dennis Hull (Bobby's kid brother), to give some additional scoring punch. A year later they drafted Pat Stapleton from Toronto to shore up the veteran defense.

The result was a good goals-against average, a tie for the lead in point production, and a third-place finish. But this time they got by first-place Detroit in a seven-game series. The Red Wings won the first two games, but the Black Hawks came back as the Golden Jet shook his defenders to score eight goals and five assists. Hall's shutout in the sixth game was one of the finest efforts, showing up Calder-winner Roger Crozier in the opposite goal, and thoroughly demoralizing the high-scoring Wings.

The finals against Montreal had home-ice victories in every game. Blake assigned Claude "Pete" Provost to shadow Hull, and he did the job so effectively that in the four games Montreal won Bobby had only one assist. Actually the Black Hawks scored only two goals in the four games at the Forum, both in the 3–2 loss in the first game. Rookie Yvan Cournoyer won that one in the third period, and Gump Worsley got a 2–0 shutout in the second game on goals by Beliveau and Duff.

Chicago beat Worsley, 3–1, at the Stadium—Esposito, Wharram, and Chico Maki getting the Hawk goals—then beat Charlie Hodge, 5–1, as Hull got two goals including the game-winner. Hodge recovered to get a 6–0 shutout at home, Beliveau scoring twice and assisting twice, but the Hawks came from behind to win, 2–1, in the sixth game, Vasko scoring from Mohns and Ravlich, and Mohns from Mikita and Ravlich.

Game 7 was all Canadien. Beliveau scored after just fourteen seconds and that was all Worsley needed, though Duff, Cournoyer, and the Pocket Rocket added to the first-period onslaught. Le Gros Bill was the first winner of the Conn Smythe Trophy for playoff MVP. He had scored four game-winning goals during the two series, but Montreal had actually won by their unusual success in defending against Hull and Mikita.

The Hawks' second-place finish in 1966 was disappointing, and the six-game loss to Detroit in the semis was even harder to take, with Bryan Watson aping Provost's success in shadowing Hull. But in 1967, for the first time, in their last chance of the closed circuit, they led the league from start to finish. They won forty-one games and finished with ninety-four points, seventeen better than second-place Montreal, breaking the Canadiens' scoring record with 264 goals. Mikita was first, Hull second (with 52 goals), Wharram fourth, Esposito seventh, and Mohns ninth. Hall and DeJordy shared goalkeeping chores, and they easily won the Vezina with a combined 2.43 average. Thus, at the last possible opportunity, a combination of extraordinary skills proved stronger than the Curse of the Muldoon.

Yet the Black Hawks, who had come so far as to be a dominant power in the league through the sixties, though without many team titles to show for it, could not close the era on top. They took the first game from Toronto, 5–2, came from behind to win the fourth game, 4–3, and tie the series at two games each, but were eliminated, 4–2 and 3–1. Montreal meanwhile had swept New York in four straight with rookie Rogatien Vachon in goal. Fittingly, the last Stanley Cup of the era was to be contested by those ancient adversaries, the Maple Leafs and the Canadiens.

Ancient is right. Montreal was basically a veteran team, with such familiar names as Worsley, Beliveau, Richard, Duff, Ferguson, Harris, Bobby Rousseau, and Jean-Claude and Gilles Tremblay. But they were raw recruits compared to Punch Imlach's senior citizens. Goalies Sawchuk and Bower were thirty-seven and forty-two, Allan Stanley was forty-one, Kelly thirty-nine, Shack and Horton thirty-seven, Armstrong and Pronovost thirty-six, and Baun, Hillman, and Pulford all past thirty. Of those under thirty, Mahovlich had ten seasons behind him, Larry Jeffrey six, and Dave Keon seven. Their "kid" line of Pappin, Pulford, and Stemkowski averaged more than twenty-seven years and almost six NHL seasons.

Both teams had had early slumps during the season. The Leafs' came in midseason when they slipped to fifth. Imlach had worked them harder and seemed to have them out of it but worked himself into the hospital. Under Clancy they won nine of twelve games, and the stretch drive under Imlach brought them to third place. The Canadiens had also rallied late in the season, from fourth to second, and streaked into the finals after Toe Blake brought in Vachon to replace Gump Worsley.

Favored and with the home-ice advantage, Montreal won the first game, 6–2, Richard scoring a hat trick and Cournoyer two goals including the game-winner. Sawchuk was apparently worn out—he had played all but one period of the Chicago series because of Bower's injuries—so Punch started Bower in the second game. Stemkowski, Mike Walton, and Horton scored in a 3–0 shutout that sent the series back to Toronto all even. In Game 3 Bower matched Vachon through regulation, making forty saves in the 2–2 game. In overtime, Montreal bombarded him with twenty more shots on goal, but he stopped them all until Pulford won it at 28:26 with assists to linemates Stemkowski and Pappin.

Before the fourth game started, Bower pulled a leg muscle and was through for the season. Sawchuk was again victimized as Cournoyer and Richard duplicated their first-game production in another 6–2 win. In the fifth game, however, Sawchuk was his old self while Vachon made some rookie errors. Toronto won, 4–1, the game-winner going to rookie Brian Conacher, who had replaced injured Chief Armstrong at wing. The last goal went to center Dave Keon, whose forechecking and penalty-killing were so impressive throughout the playoffs that he was selected the third winner of the Smythe Trophy after Beliveau and Crozier.

The sixth game began with a close-checking, scoreless first period, Sawchuk and Worsley getting ample protection. In the second period, young Ron Ellis scored on passes from veterans Stanley and Kelly. Then the Pappin-Stemkowski-Pulford line clicked again for a 2–0 lead. Back came the Canadiens in the third with a goal by Duff from Harris, but Sawchuk kept them at bay with a total of forty-six saves. With a minute to play and a face-off in the Leaf end, Blake pulled Worsley for a sixth shooter. Imlach responded by sending out Stanley, Horton, Kelly, Armstrong, and Pulford in front of Sawchuk, making up ninety-eight years of NHL experience. Stanley muscled Beliveau off the draw and pinned his stick. Kelly hustled in to pick up the puck and hit Pulford with a sure pass on the left wing. Pulford calmly sent it across the rink to Armstrong, who was open on the right side. The captain carefully took it across the red line, so that there would be no icing call in case he missed, and shot the puck into the open net.

Even Punch Imlach might have been accused of making a sentimental gesture with this clinching line-up, but as he said, "We needed to keep those guys from scoring in the last minute. Where better to turn than to my old guard?" And so as the league looked forward to the uncertainty of a new era, the final championship of the closed circuit looked backward; twenty years after the Toronto Maple Leafs had been the youngest squad to win the Stanley Cup, they became the oldest to do so. Winning the trophy for the eleventh time, they delayed for a year Montreal's fifteenth—and the final Cup score for the quarter-century was Canadiens ten, Maple Leafs nine, Red Wings five, Black Hawks one.

PART *IV*

Road to Ruin and Redemption

In the provincial world of the closed circuit, the National Hockey League was hockey and hockey was the NHL, and that meant six cities in the Northeast of the continent. If the game was getting dully repetitious, well, let it—it was still theirs. But it could not remain so.

Hockey was being played with escalating skill all over the world. Hockey players were becoming more sophisticated about their prerogatives. The old breed of hockey executives was passing, and a new breed was aware of contemporary marketing concepts. If the league was not responsive to opening up to new franchises, it would be opening the door to a rival league.

Expansion was the answer, if not the solution. Many feared it would destroy hockey—i.e., the NHL—and when it came most of those believed that their fears had been justified. But at the end of a short decade of the new era, it begins to appear that hockey has been preserved after all.

The league exploded to twelve teams, then swelled to fourteen, sixteen, and eighteen. A rival league was organized anyway, and in 1977 there were thirty major league teams altogether. The quality of play fell off sharply. The expansion teams could not compete with the original six. In Stanley Cup play, a new team didn't win a single game from an old for almost four years and not until there were adjustments in the divisions and the playoff structure. It was another three years before an expansion team could win a playoff series from one of the established six—and then it went all the way.

The Flyers' 1974 Stanley Cup proved that expansion had worked in one way: an equity in competition had been achieved. But the brand of hockey played in Philadelphia was not mistaken by anyone for that of the great preexpansion teams. Meanwhile, national teams from Eastern Europe were demonstrating a mastery of the game and a style of play that *were* reminiscent of a golden age of hockey.

Postexpansion parity was only a step. The upward leap that was needed was postexpansion excellence. In the 1976 and 1977 seasons a team cohered with the depth and brilliance to rival the great ones of the past. Not surprisingly, the team was the Montreal Canadiens, and their emergence as dominant champions marks the real success of expansion and looks forward to the possibility of a new golden age. The dilution of talent, the diminution of quality, the leveling out for competitiveness have passed; the achievement of excellence has recommenced. The following four chapters examine the processes by which the road to ruin has paved the way for redemption.

23

The Short View and the Long Haul

Many forces built up pressure for expansion in the National Hockey League. For a long time the league's response to the pressures was to keep the lid on. And so naturally, when in time the forces were released, the result was not expansion but explosion. Overnight the closed circuit of six clubs in a tight geographical area became a transcontinental entity with twelve units, and a few short years later it was three times its traditional size with eighteen teams.

Contemporary critics of hockey, and they are many and vocal, generally agree that expansion thus implemented ruined the game. Rocket Richard, after two years of watching the twelve-team league, reduced the matter to eloquent simplicity:

> The game of hockey is simply not the game it was in my day. Shooting was more accurate then. Passing was cleverer. Stickhandling was an art practiced not by just a few but by many. And, most important, there was much more individuality. In short, the game is hurting today, and if you want to find the causes, you have to start with the biggest one: expansion.

Yet a case can be made that some of the very factors that led to expansion had in fact already contributed to the dimmed luster of the sport. Without question, a radical change that by fiat made major-leaguers of twice as many players as had staffed the six old clubs had to lower the general level of individual skills. But if the nature of the game as played in the NHL suffered at the same time, it may be a matter of coincidental effects rather than simplistic cause.

There was indeed a sameness about the play, even the most exciting of play, in the NHL hockey of the sixties. With the exceptions already described in terms of personnel, most managers and coaches and players had fallen into established, proven patterns of strategy and technique. What worked for one was supposed to work for all. And with the monolithic control of just six teams, all Canadian and American hockey followed suit. Moreover, there was a sameness about the competition, so that year after year the haves got and the have-

Checking Back

nots did not get, as the dominant powers reached far down into and across the minor and amateur leagues. The sameness both of play and of competition could be remedied over the long run by opening up the major league to other franchises and at the same time dividing and limiting the control of minor-league personnel with a universal draft system. At first there would be a leveling process that would attenuate the sameness, but inevitably, with diversification would come, in time, variety.

To the factor of sameness, however, there was a paradoxical reverse side. The sixties saw a phenomenal development of international hockey, particularly in eastern Europe, and the game was nurtured in a mold that was consciously and deliberately different from that of the NHL. Anatoli Tarasov, one of the architects of the Soviet Union's hockey triumphs, succinctly described the NHL's checking style in his *Road to Olympus:*

> One of the peculiar features of Canadian tactics is body checking on a wide scale, within the framework of picking off a player, their own peculiar brand of pressing. If all this power were put to work only in defence, it would only be half as bad, but this power play in duels is also employed in attack, and on account of this, hockey, as a spectacle, becomes unpleasant to watch.

The Russian way, which he calls "the attacking style," was designed as an antidote and an improvement over the other:

> The attacking style of hockey actually eradicates power hockey because it requires speedy manoeuvres, it requires profound thought, decisions which contain more craftiness, common sense, coordinated actions, superior technique than brute force. And the future is with this type of hockey.

Parenthetically it should be added that the growth of hockey in the USSR is one of the great sports success stories of all time. I find it significant that the first hockey school in North America was opened by Emile Francis and George Vogan at Moose Jaw, Saskatchewan, in 1950, followed shortly thereafter by one in Grand Forks, North Dakota. Now there are scores of summer hockey camps from which NHL personnel derive additional income, but the recognition that new ways of developing talent were needed in changing times was long overdue. By contrast, in the Soviet Union, once the commitment to excellence in hockey was made, hundreds of hockey training schools were established, virtually overnight, all across the country.

Hockey fans, like hockey players, are inclined to be chauvinistic types. There may be some black-white animosity in or about the game (there are very few black hockey players), but there is strong Canada-vs.-U.S. feeling, as well as Anglo-vs.-French, not to mention specific stereotyping attitudes toward Newfies, western rednecks, Toronto snobs, West Coast nuts, and the like. But though feelings ran high against the "foreigners," there had to be a growing, grudging recognition that the Russians, the Czechs, the Poles, and the Swedes had something other than political nationalism going for them.

International competition also provided an impetus for amateur hockey, particularly at the university level, with collegians called upon to staff national teams and with a remarkable improvement of play and growth of competition in the NCAA ranks and tournament, for example, that persisted throughout the sixties and into the seventies. One side effect of that development has been the gradual rise of literacy and articulateness among hockey players. Eddie Shack may have been exceptional as an NHL player at the time who could not, according to Eskenazi, read or write, but a prevailing antiintellectual attitude was typical. Red Berenson, a Michigan graduate, was regarded with great distaste by Emile Francis, who told a reporter, "If I ever see him read a book on the bus again, I'm going to throw him off," and shortly afterward dealt him off the Rangers to the Blues. Ken Dryden, who was working toward his law degree while tending goal for the Canadiens, experienced the old NHL mentality firsthand when Peter Mahovlich—as a prank—tore up a paper he was writing for one of his courses. And Jim Krulicki, retiring from the Wings at twenty-three, talked about being ridiculed for reading "heavy" stuff as one of the signs that athletes are not accepted as persons, that there was no fun or freedom in the ruthless business of hockey, and that he didn't want to be a machine.

That ancient hockey stance may help explain the traditional attitude of NHL management toward contemporary media types. When Stan Fischler incurred the wrath of Phil Watson by criticizing the Ranger coach, a magazine with a Fischler article was banned from sales at Madison Square Garden. A few years later, Fischler was banned from the Rangers' dressing room and postgame conference room for criticizing Muzz Patrick; Fischler was reinstated only when the *Journal-American* threatened to boycott Ranger news in its sports pages. Perhaps more revealing is the case of Dave Marash, who as recently as 1972 was turned down by both the Rangers and the Islanders as their play-by-play announcer because he wouldn't shave his beard.

In any case, the changing conditions which brought about expansion included a raised level of awareness among the players. The proof of this advancement was the acceptance of the Players' Association by the league just a few months before the expansion went into effect. In a sense, recognition of the union was one of the prices the NHL had to pay for expansion, since players—especially the stars—now had new leverage in their bargaining positions. This was recognized by Alan Eagleson, the organizer, a Toronto lawyer who had overseen Bobby Orr's precedent-making contract, and who in the

Checking Back

spring and summer of 1967 brought most of the NHL rosters into the union camp. But in a larger sense, it was the drive toward a players' association—as old as the league itself, but fought, stymied, aborted, and outflanked by management over the years—that in a newly enlightened era required an enlightened adjustment by the league to the times. The players' movement could no longer be checked, and a larger league with broader policies would provide the wherewithal to encompass, among other by-products, a union and acknowledgment of players' rights.

Eagleson has been branded by some shortsighted viewers as the man that ruined hockey, when he has simply been the one to help open hockey's eyes to its contemporary world. Similarly, myopic critics have labeled Don V. Ruck as a destroyer, but even more than Eagleson, he has made the NHL a viable, contemporary, professional sports-entertainment operation. Although he had spent some years as a sportswriter, Ruck's real game was marketing, and that was the very area in which the NHL needed leadership. Hockey needed to expand its markets along with its horizons, and to anyone with even limited vision this meant television. Ruck joined the league as a vice president in 1965, with offices in New York (an insult to some Canadians, a necessity for new media-awareness in the league), at the time when the first expansion plan was approved but a network television contract was only in preliminary, wishful stages. A year later there was a $3.5-million deal with CBS for coverage of a Game of the Week. In addition, Ruck became president of National Hockey League Services, which takes advantage of all the adjunct marketing capabilities of a major sports league.

A mixed blessing as with any superimposition of nonsporting policies upon sport, televising hockey has also been an inconsistent success at best. In Canada, the Wednesday night program, "Hockey Night in Canada," gets the second highest ratings in the country, second only to Saturday's "Hockey Night in Canada." In the United States, the "Game of the Week" suffered poor ratings, and CBS eventually canceled. There were problems with sixty-second commercials interrupting the flow of play, until Ruck persuaded advertisers of the wisdom of thirty-second breaks. There were problems with camera crews who were not sophisticated enough about hockey to anticipate action. There were problems with the game itself; its speed, its rules, and its sudden rush of exhilarating instants were unfamiliar to the mass markets. But local telecasts continue to do well in selected major markets, and now there is optimism that when the level of popular understanding rises along with the level of play, network telecasts will return.

Among the factors building up the pressures for expansion, the management shifts within the old clubs and the shifting balance of political power in the league should not be minimized. Back in the twenties, in the first great expansion when six of the ten teams were in the United States, the four Canadian owners had been forced to revise their thinking and the rules of the game in recognition that American fans liked rugged competition and sustained speed but cared little for the fine points. Led by Lester Patrick and Art Ross, the league, as Frank Selke has observed, made pragmatic compromises that assured progress without undermining the basic structure of the game. Comparable leadership was not clearly forthcoming in the sixties.

The old guard, Conn Smythe in Toronto and the Norris brothers in Chicago and Detroit, steadfastly resisted any change. Their personal antipathies were colored with a kind of mindless chauvinism. They could not appreciate the point of view of Brian Conacher, for example, one of the most articulate and sensitive spokesmen to come out of the world of hockey, who said in 1970:

> A game which is intimately linked to the whole cultural reality of a society as hockey is to Canada's must adapt to major changes in that society or find itself rejected where it has been most cherished.

Among the major changes was the concept of sports management as a type, even a model, of modern corporate enterprise. Bill Jennings, president of the Rangers, emerged in this period as the leading exponent of the image, and finally it was he who led the expansionist party. But support came slowly and reluctantly from within, among a group that found any cohesiveness hard to come by.

As Andy O'Brien described the league,

> The N.H.L. itself is an anomaly. Its name is not even registered. It is a partnership of corporations, all independent, operating under terms of a contract among them. There is only one "signing" executive officer, Campbell. The governors give him a set of by-laws with very specific powers, including absolute power in the touchy matter of enforcing discipline.

What keeps it together and makes it strong is the very competition among the separate units. And the league has encouraged the integrity of that competition wisely by providing incentives for players and teams throughout the regular season and cannily by blinking cutthroat off-ice manipulations. But Fischler's depiction of the board of governors is more appropriate here. He cites one governor who is supposed to have said:

> I could take a broad, strip her, and put her on the governors' table, and everybody would think of something different to do. One guy would want to stick it in her ear. Another guy would want to stick it in her tail, and then there'd be one who'd say, "The hell with this, I want to go out and jump the bellboy."

Checking Back

Nevertheless Jennings soon had support in unexpected places: Toronto, when Stafford Smythe began to have things his own way after his father's retirement; and Montreal, when David Molson, the sensitive president, became the policy-maker after Selke's retirement. Even Bruce Norris was wavering (along with ever-neutral Weston Adams in Boston) while only his brother Jim, Jr., held firm in Chicago. Clarence Campbell shifted with the balance of power, like the proverbial supreme court following election returns, and the plan was formulated, with the bargain price set at two million dollars for a franchise.

Perhaps the most telling factor that led a basically reactionary group to support such a forward-looking piece of radical change as Jennings advocated was simply self-protection, a kind of limited enlightened self-interest. Though they did not believe it, they were at least fearful that a rival league would fill the vacuum their intransigence had created (the players' movement had taken advantage of that fear). There was talk of a Canadian community-owned league. There was agitation in the halls of Parliament for new Canadian franchises. And especially in the Pacific Northwest, a traditional stronghold of professional hockey, there was increasing activity toward major-league involvement. In the event, the NHL expansion may have delayed the formation of the World Hockey Association only slightly, while ironically it demonstrated that a diluted form of major-league hockey would be welcomed in many franchise-hungry communities.

Dictated primarily by the media marketplace and secondarily by a perception of financial capability, the choices for five of the six new franchises were Los Angeles, Philadelphia, Pittsburgh, the Twin Cities of Minnesota, and the San Francisco Bay area. Vancouver had the inside track on the remaining spot, but questions were raised about the financing, prompted in the minds of most by the fact that Vancouver *already* was a TV hockey market (the "Hockey Night in Canada" shows). Besides, the Black Hawks owned the St. Louis Arena and hoped to sell it to a new NHL franchise to make the expansion a bit more palatable. Several months after the original five were approved, the remaining slot was filled by a group headed by Sidney Salomon in St. Louis. Though there were anger and resentment in Vancouver and throughout Canada, that decision proved to be one of the wisest. It gave the league experienced and forward-looking sports management, a team that would be the class of the division for several years, and the reluctant Chicago owners an extra four million dollars for the old rink.

For the two-million-dollar initiation fee, the six new clubs were allowed to draft twenty players each. The event occurred, appropriately enough, on the twenty-third anniversary of D-Day, and the procedures were as carefully prearranged as an invasion plan. The old clubs could protect eleven players plus one goaltender. As the new franchises first took one goalie each (Sawchuk was the first choice of all), the established teams could protect a second goalie; then a second goalie each was taken. The draft of all other players followed. When a team lost a player it could add another to its protected list, then a second when it lost a second. Only after three more were taken could three additional players be protected. That was repeated for another three, after which it became a one-for-one arrangement until each expansion team had its quota.

There followed an unprecedented flurry of trading activity. Many of the deals which had been set up before the draft explained some surprises in the choices both of the drafters and the protecters. The Canadiens seemed to suffer least of the old teams, because of their great depth and the cleverness of their predraft arrangements, and the Bruins most. The Philadelphia Flyers seemed to have chosen most wisely, while the Los Angeles Kings' selections raised the most eyebrows.

It is difficult to measure quantitatively the extent of the lowering of standards of quality. It may be illustrated, however, by the case of Larry Zeidel. He had played in the NHL in parts of three seasons for Detroit and Chicago, 1952–1954, and then bounced around the minors since, mostly with Seattle and Cleveland. At thirty-nine, with a promising career as a stockbroker, Zeidel reacted to expansion by saying, "I'm better than half the guys they've selected," and putting together a brochure to sell himself as a viable commodity on the NHL market. Only one team responded, but given a tryout, Zeidel not only made the Flyers' squad but became a mainstay of their rugged corps of defensemen. His NHL playoff appearances in 1968 came after a sixteen-year hiatus.

A new era was about to begin. There was a twelve-team NHL. There was a Players' Association. There was an end to the domination of minor-league talent by a few clubs—a universal draft system had been adopted along with expansion plans in 1966, but now the draft age was lowered from twenty-one to twenty. There was a network TV contract. There was a reduction in the threat of a rival league. And if the game was the same, just not as good, there was the hope that quality in time would be restored while the integrity of competition was maintained.

24

Programmed Second-Class

With a nice mixture of openness and hypocrisy, the National Hockey League devised a way to keep its cookies while eating all available crumbs. It succumbed to the pressures and expanded into six new markets, doubling its size and diluting by half the major-league caliber of its personnel. But the expansion draft was designed, as expansion drafts always are in professional sports, so that existing teams maintain substantial superiority over expansion teams. The NHL, however, added its own new wrinkle to expansion tactics. It put all six new teams in one division, called the West, devised a schedule in which most of the games would be played within divisions, and lo the East was merely a somewhat diminished extension of the old closed circuit: New York, Boston, Detroit, Chicago, Montreal, and Toronto.

It was almost as if expansion were to be treated as a set of minor inconveniences—some extra games, some extra travel, a lot of extra money, a lot of new faces, likely longer careers—but where it counted, the NHL would be relatively unchanged. Four teams in the East would play off for the Stanley Cup. The winner would have the additional inconvenience of an extra series of exhibitions against the winner of the West, but the result was taken for granted. For the cynical fans, there were few surprises in the 1968 season. All the leading scorers played for the old franchises: Mikita, Hull, and Wharram in Chicago, Esposito and Bucyk in Boston, Howe and Delvecchio in Detroit, Ratelle and Gilbert in New York, and Ullman in Toronto. Without an individual leader, Montreal was second in team scoring, with 236 goals. The all-star teams were solidly old-franchise: Worsley, Orr, Horton, Mikita, Howe, Hull; Giacomin, Tremblay, Tim Neilson, Esposito, Gilbert, Bucyk. Almost all trophies stayed east: the Hart, Ross, and Byng to Mikita, the Norris to Orr, the Vezina to Worsley and Vachon. Even the Calder went to Boston's Derek Sanderson, while the only exception was that veteran Glenn Hall's valiant playoff efforts in the St. Louis goal took the Smythe Trophy west.

Although West teams won 40 and tied 18 in 144 head-to-head meetings with the East, no expansion team won as many games as it lost overall, and only

Detroit of the old six played under .500. That the new teams won as many games as they did could be explained by two factors, one old, one new: the relative unimportance of individual regular-season games; and the overall level of play, in which, as Brad Park put it a few years later, "Expansion clubs just have a way of dragging the better teams down to their level."

Changes in planning game strategy were inevitable. Because teams played each other far fewer times, and because the turnover in lineups was continual, there was less concentration on matching up against opponents and more emphasis on each team regularizing and standardizing its own play. Writing four years before expansion, Andy O'Brien said:

> For some years I've suspected that NHL players are getting over-coached. The parent team trains its coaches in minor pro and amateur sponsored clubs to follow a set pattern. They all stress positional hockey; players mainly stay in their allotted lanes, skate fast and faster, repeat their own pet tricks and depend on the percentage in clicking. Defencemen also follow a pattern. The result is such a sameness that all NHL teams look alike, and the players are so alike that one can shift to another team and almost overnight look as if he always wore the new sweater.
>
> The only real difference is that in some positions some teams have better craftsmen than others. But when they face something "different," too often the patterned players are stymied—until they and their coaches work out a new technique in practice.

Expansion solidified O'Brien's perceptions into prophecies. As the level of skill dropped throughout the league, the degree of sameness rose in direct proportion. Relative changes of excellence were few but pronounced. For example, the new Los Angeles Kings were designed for as wide-open a style as contemporary hockey allowed, while the new Philadelphia Flyers were from the beginning defense-oriented. Those were management decisions, implemented by the purchase of minor-league personnel (Los Angeles buying the Springfield Indians, Philadelphia the Quebec Aces) as well as by their draft choices. Thus the established teams that were most rigid in their patterns would fare relatively poorly against the new clubs, while the more mobile offenses and defenses would best adjust according to their opposition. The Toronto Maple Leafs, from a third-place finish and a Stanley Cup in 1967, dropped to fifth in the East and out of the playoffs in 1968, while the New York Rangers, from fourth place and quick elimination from playoffs, rose to second best in the league, with ninety points.

The primary rationale for putting all six new clubs in one division was to make them competitive with one another, regardless of their second-class status vis-à-vis the old six. The initial season seemed to justify that thinking, as five of the six newcomers battled on even terms throughout the season. Oakland, plagued with management problems, was the exception, winning only fifteen games and finishing twenty points behind fifth-place Pittsburgh. The Penguins missed the playoffs by only two points, and a total of four points separated first-place Philadelphia from fourth-place Minnesota.

That balance persisted throughout the West playoffs where each series went a full seven games. Twelve of the twenty-one were won by one goal, and seven went into overtime. In the St. Louis Blues, Philadelphia was facing a team that had been selected with playoffs in mind. Lynn Patrick and Scotty Bowman had taken Glenn Hall first and then gone mainly for players with experience in Stanley Cup play, including Dickie Moore, Al Arbour, Don McKenney, Jim Roberts, Ron Stewart (later traded to New York in the deal that brought Red Berenson and Barclay Plager to St. Louis—called his "most controversial move" by Francis), and Rod Seiling (traded back to New York before the season started for Bob Plager and Gary Sabourin). During the season they picked up Jean-Guy Talbot from Detroit on waivers. The Flyers, on the other hand, under Bud Poile and Keith Allen, had stressed youth, beginning with Boston's kid goalies, Parent and Favell, and following with Ed Van Impe, Joe Watson, Brit Selby, Lou Angotti, Leon Rochefort, Don Blackburn, John Miszuk, Gary Peters, Dick Cherry, Fern Gauthier, Gary Dornhoefer, and Pat Hannigan, all in their twenties.

Hall began the series with a shutout, Roberts getting the only goal past Favell. Philadelphia got even with a 4–3 win on Rochefort's goal in the second game. The third went into a second overtime before Larry Keenan, a former Leaf prospect, won it for St. Louis. The Blues won the fourth game, 5–2, but lost the fifth, 6–1, in a game marred by a 20-minute brawl that brought 49 minutes in penalties and $3,800 in fines to players and coaches. The Flyers tied the series with a 2–1 overtime win on a goal by Blackburn at 31:18, but the veteran Blues, led by Moore and Doug Harvey, who had been player-coach for their Kansas City farm club during the season, won the decisive game, 3–1.

Farther west, the Minnesota North Stars were being entertained at the eighteen-million-dollar home of the Los Angeles Kings, Jack Kent Cooke's Forum. Cooke's choices in assembling his team, with the single exception of Terry Sawchuk, had all been questionable. Larry Regan as manager and Red Kelly as coach were relatively inexperienced, and the players they chose were hardly household familiars. Yet they were the surprise success of the new hockey world. Minnesota, on the other hand, playing in the magnificent new Metropolitan Sports Center in Bloomington, at the heart of the most dedicated hockey world outside of Canada, was something of a disappointment. Under Wren Blair and John Mariucci, they had apparently drafted well— Cesare Maniago, Pete Goegan, Moose Vasko, Parker McDonald, Bill Goldsworthy, Wayne Connelly. They had passed up Montreal's Claude

Larose for Dave Balon on the first round after the goalies' draft, but this was part of an agreement leading to a set of subsequent deals with the Canadiens. And they had also bought from Toronto the rights to six members of the Canadian national team. The veterans did not come through as hoped, and the team was shocked and weakened by the death of Bill Masterson, who never regained consciousness after his head hit the ice in a January game against Oakland. It was the first NHL-action death in the league's history and led to widespread adoption of helmets by the players.

Sawchuk stopped the North Stars, 2–1 and 2–0, in Inglewood, but back home Minnesota came back with 7–5 and 3–2 wins. Wayne Rutledge took over in goal for the Kings and won, 3–2, but lost in overtime, 4–3, on a goal by Milce Marcetta, a young winger drafted from the Toronto system. Sawchuk came back for game seven but was bombarded with forty-two shots and shot down, 9–4, in his last game as a King. The North Stars went straight to St. Louis to begin the semis and lost, 5–3. They got even at home on an overtime goal by McDonald and then went ahead with a 5–1 win at St. Louis.

The fourth was a home game for Minnesota, but with the Ice Follies booked into Metropolitan Sports Center, it was played in St. Louis. It was won, 4–3, by the Blues on an overtime goal by rookie Gary Sabourin, after they had come back from a 3–0 deficit in the last nine minutes of play with Roberts scoring twice and Moore once. By the time the North Stars got back on home ice they trailed in the series, thanks to another overtime loss, this one 3–2 on Bill McCreary's goal at 17:27. A 5–1 Minnesota win sent the series to a seventh game, and it was vintage Stanely Cup play.

Maniago and Hall were perfect through two periods and well into the third. Walt McKechnie scored for Minnesota with only four minutes left, but Dickie Moore tied it up less than a minute later. A full overtime period was also scoreless, but at 2:50 of the second extra period, Ron Schock took passes from McCreary and Gerry Melnyk, split the defense, and beat Maniago head-on. The Blues had a day of rest at home and then took on the Canadiens, who had been waiting a week to go through the motions of polishing off their fifteenth Stanley Cup. The decisive series, most believed, had taken place a month ago, when Montreal took out Boston in four straight.

The Canadiens had stood to lose the most in the draft, but they had by far the most to lose. And every time one of their number was chosen they protected one more valuable property for the future, like Serge Savard, Carol Vadnais, and Claude Larose. Toronto and Detroit could not recover from their losses. Both finished out of the playoffs (the first time that had happened since 1930) and were driven to the midseason extreme of swapping major stars: Mahovlich, Stemkowski, and Unger for Henderson, Ullman, and Floyd Smith.

The Black Hawks and the Rangers came through the draft with relatively slight losses, while the Bruins, hard hit, more than compensated by Milt Schmidt's vigorous dealing. Boston led the league most of the way, but injuries to Orr and Teddy Green weakened them in the stretch, and they faded to third. Eddie Shack, for whom they had sent Murray Oliver and $100,000 to Toronto, missed three games when Campbell suspended him following a stick-swinging affair with Larry Zeidel. Boston scored many more goals than anyone else and also amassed a record number of penalties, going over a thousand penalty minutes for the first time.

With Beliveau out of the lineup, Montreal slumped to sixth place before Christmas. But a string of sixteen games without a loss, including twelve straight wins, brought them to the top. New York was giddy with its rare second-place finish and skated well against Chicago to open the playoffs. Harry Howell got the game-winner in the 3–1 opener at the Garden, and Don Marshall won the 2–1 second game for a two-game lead. Mikita and Hull then got their act together and blasted the Rangers, 7–4 and 3–1, in Chicago. The fifth game was tied in the third period when Bobby Schmautz, who would still be a rookie next season, slapped a shot past Giacomin from the blue line at 16:46, and the Black Hawks closed out the Ranger season with a 3–1 win at the Stadium.

Montreal skated around and past Chicago as easily as it had done Boston. The Canadiens beat the Bruins, 2–1, 5–3, 5–2, and 3–2, and the Black Hawks, 9–2, 4–1, and 4–2, before losing a playoff game in 1968. Chicago got a 2–1 win at the Stadium and then held Montreal even at the Forum into overtime before Jacques Lemaire got the series-winner. Beliveau had seven goals and four assists in these series, Cournoyer four and six, Provost seven assists, the Tremblays five assists each, and Backstrom, Lemaire, Ferguson, and Larose three goals each.

The balanced attack would be needed in the finals, because Le Gros Bill was sidelined with a bone chip in his ankle. St. Louis fans were apparently resigned to defeat, only 10,231 showing up for the smallest Stanley Cup crowd since the war. They saw a good show. Barclay Plager put the Blues in front in the first period, but Pocket Rocket tied it 23 seconds later. Dickie Moore scored in the second, against the team for which he had scored thirty-eight playoff goals, only to have Cournoyer tie it before the period ended. After a scoreless third, Lemaire repeated his overtime act, winning this one unassisted at 1:41. In Game 2, Glenn Hall was even better, smothering every Canadien assault through two periods. But Savard's goal, with an assist to Provost, won the game, since St. Louis could not beat Worsley at all.

At the Forum, the Blues refused to fold. Again they led in the first period on rookie Frank St. Marseille's goal, only to have Cournoyer tie it. Then Berenson matched Savard's goal in the second and Backstrom's in the third to send this one, too, into overtime. Again, in less than two minutes, Montreal won, Duff feeding Rousseau. Still the Blues came back. They led in the fourth game, 2–1, after two periods on goals by Craig Cameron and Sabourin, only to have Richard tie it and J. C. Tremblay win it in the third.

They had played the Canadiens tough in all four games, and Hall surely deserved his Smythe Trophy. The Bruins and the Black Hawks had fallen far more easily to these Canadiens. The games never appeared to get out of Montreal's hands, however. Never had St. Louis been more than one goal in front, and it seemed that the Habs could tie or win whenever they put on full pressure, Hall notwithstanding. Still, the closeness of the scores seemed to give credibility to the new structure and justify the planning. The league was officially pleased, and the arrangement of two divisions—the old established powers in one, the second-class citizens in the other—was perpetuated for another two years.

This was the period in which the Bruins came to power, supplanting the Canadiens at the summit, but far more dramatic was the demolition of scoring records. The effects of expansion were felt much more keenly in the second and third years than in the first, and the reason was a change in the scheduling policy. In 1968, in a seventy-four–game schedule, each team played ten times against the teams in its division (fifty games) and only four times (twenty-four games) against the teams in the other division. That achieved the desired result of competitiveness within divisions and actually exceeded the desired result of 25 percent success of new teams versus old. Unfortunately, one anticipation was disappointed: competitiveness did not necessarily generate fan interest, particularly in California and Pittsburgh, because of the limited opportunities (twice in each new market) for seeing the major attractions: Hull and Mikita, Howe and Mahovlich, Beliveau and Cournoyer.

For 1969, on the basis of the programmed and predictable "success" of the expansion clubs, a new seventy-six–game schedule was designed whereby each team played teams within the division eight times (forty) and the others six times (thirty-six). The results of that arrangement were predictable too. The more the old teams played against the new, the more the disparity was exposed and exploited. Even the last-place team in the East, the Black Hawks, won more games than they lost, and fourth-place Toronto's eighty-five points would have put them in first place just five years earlier. In the West only the Blues, staffed with experienced players and with veterans Hall and Plante winning the Vezina, won more games than they lost.

The dominance and inequities showed up most clearly in scoring. Inadequate defenses and the inability to clear the puck even when scoring attempts failed meant that the good shooters would have many more opportunities against easier targets. The assists record, for example, had been rising stead-

Checking Back

ily, from Lindsay's 55 in 1950 to Olmstead's 56 in 1956 to Beliveau's 58 in 1961 (tied by Bathgate in 1964) to Mikita's 59 in 1965 and 62 in 1967. Mikita raised his own record to 67 in 1967 and was *10* behind Esposito's 77. Hull raised the goals record to 58. Hull and Mikita had shared the points record at 97. Mikita tied it and was fourth in the league. Howe broke the magic 100 mark with 103 and was third. Hull had 107 and was 19 out of first, as Phil Esposito added 49 goals to his record assists total for 126 points. Berenson (the only player from the West among the leaders) and Beliveau tied for eighth with 82 points, which would have won the Ross Trophy in 1960.

Throughout the season the Bruins battled the Canadiens for the league lead, while Scotty Bowman's Blues easily dominated the West over the resurgent Oakland Seals. Orr, who scored a record 21 goals for a defenseman, won the Norris again, and teammate Teddy Green was second all-star, while Ken Hodge was fifth in scoring behind first all-star and Hart-winner Esposito. The Bruins as a team shattered two records as they scored 303 goals and served 1297 penalty minutes. But the Canadiens, with 103 points to Boston's 100, and with the fewest goals against and penalty minutes in the division, came home first, with Beliveau, Cournoyer, and Harris as second all-stars. Howe and Hull, the first all-star wings for the second of three straight years, were out of the playoffs.

In the West, Los Angeles upset Oakland in a seven-game series, but there were no serious surprises when the Blues swept the Flyers (seventeen goals to three) and then the Kings (sixteen goals to five) to await their ritual sacrifice at the hands of the old NHL. Toronto had a first all-star defenseman in Tim Horton, but no defense against a Bruin onslaught that swept them out in four games (twenty-four goals to five). With second all-star Giacomin in goal, the Rangers fared a little better against Montreal, but were also unable to win a game (total goals sixteen to seven).

The climactic series was the finals of the East, and it lived up to anticipation as a classic match between the artful Canadien champions and the tough Bruin challengers. Claude Ruel had replaced Toe Blake behind the bench for Sam Pollock's team, but it was basically the same team that had won the Cup the year before. Vadnais had gone to Oakland, Larose and Gilles Tremblay were out of the playoffs, and Danny Grant had been lost to Minnesota, where he had won the Calder Trophy, but they had acquired Larry Hillman from the North Stars.

At Boston, Schmidt and Sinden had the team of their fondest dreams, with Cheevers and Johnston in goal; Orr on defense along with Green and veterans Don Awrey, Gary Doak, and Dallas Smith; and a high-powered corps of forwards, including Bucyk, Esposito, Hodge, Sanderson, Stanfield, Wayne Cashman, Bill Lesuk, Don Marcotte, and Ed Westfall. That team rushed five men, whenever they weren't shorthanded because of penalties, and flattened anyone within reach so that no one could skate with heads down against them.

The heads-up Canadiens, however, had the solution. They allowed themselves to be pushed around but without being intimidated. They flashed their superior skating and stick-handling whenever opportunities opened up. And they took advantage of power-play chances. At the Forum, the Bruins dominated play but lost the opener, 3–2, when Ralph Backstrom scored in the first minute of overtime. The second game was a 4–3 reprise of the first, with Redmond winning it at 4:55 of overtime.

At Boston Garden, with the fans screaming their bloody approval of their Bruins' hitting, Cheevers won a 5–0 shutout and the home team evened the series with a 3–2 win. But back in the Forum—led by Serge Savard, who eventually won the Smythe—Montreal went ahead with a 4–2 win. The sixth game broke the home-ice streak as Rogie Vachon outdueled Cheevers under tremendous pressure, at one stretch making 22 saves while Cheevers only had to make eight. It was at 11:28 of the second overtime that the incomparable Beliveau won the 2–1 game and, to all intents and purposes, the Stanley Cup.

The finals were treated as perfunctory by everyone but Ruel, who was suspicious of anything that came too easily. Duff, Rousseau, and Ferguson beat Plante in the first game, as St. Marseille got St. Louis's only goal. Larry Keenan scored for the Blues in the second game, but only after Backstrom, Duff, and Cournoyer had beaten Hall, the league's all-star goalie. At St. Louis, Vachon got a shutout while Savard, Lemaire, and Duff twice beat Plante, Beliveau getting his fourth and fifth assists of the short series. In the fourth game, for the only time in the series, St. Louis led when Terry Gray scored in the first period. The Canadiens, when they finally concentrated after the distractions of golf, horse racing, and party-planning in the Gateway City, put together two quick third-period goals by Harris and Ferguson and closed out their second straight Cup championship, their third in four years, their tenth in a marvelous fourteen-year span. Beliveau, Provost, and Henri Richard had been on hand for all of them.

But the Bruins knew how to beat them. Sinden said, "You have to press them, rush them, hit them in their own end—but we're the only club with the players to do it." A year later three other clubs could do it, and Montreal was not in the playoffs, for the first time in twenty-three years. And with Toronto in last place, 1970 marked the first year ever that no Canadian team would be playing for the Stanley Cup.

It is difficult to account for the Canadiens' "collapse." With the league repeating its 1969 schedule, the East was even more dominant. Toronto, under new coach John McLellan and new manager Jim Gregory, was trying to rebuild but lost more than they won. The other five old teams all totaled more than 90 points. Montreal's 92 tied New York, with identical records of 38–22–16. The goals-scored column gave the Rangers the final playoff spot, 246–244. Detroit, under Sid Abel (who took over the coaching from Gadsby), improved to 95 points, and Chicago tied Boston at 99, winning the pennant with more wins.

Montreal had nearly the same squad that had won the Cup, except for veterans Duff and Worsley, who were picked up by Los Angeles and Minnesota respectively during the season. Perhaps their major loss was in the draft when Chicago took Tony Esposito. Pollock had made a deal with Tommy Ivan and didn't protect him. Minnesota had first pick, but Wren Blair had to agree to pass Esposito for Chicago as final payment ("future considerations") for the Danny O'Shea deal. Younger brother of the defending MVP, Tony won the Calder and the Vezina, taking the Black Hawks from last in the East in goals-against to first in the league, with a remarkable fifteen shutouts. He probably would have won the Hart as well, except that Bobby Orr could not be denied. A few years later Plante was to call him "the best goalie in the business today." So if the Canadiens had not gotten much weaker, then, except that their veterans were all a little older, four other teams had gotten stronger.

There was little change in the West. St. Louis alone had a winning record, finishing twenty-two points ahead of second-place Pittsburgh, where Red Kelly had inspired some improvement after moving over from the Kings. In Los Angeles, however, under Hal Laycoe, Jack Kent Cooke's team had sunk to the cellar. The West had taken to imitating the Bruins, hitting whenever possible, trying to intimidate physically, and piling up penalties—especially Philadelphia, but Pittsburgh and Minnesota also took over a thousand penalty minutes. The trouble was that they all lacked the skills to complement the heavy-hitting game, and the quality of play deteriorated; if anything. It was perceptibly bad enough for the league to realize that new accommodations had to be sought.

In the playoffs in the West, the Blues, led by Phil Goyette and Red Berenson, who finished fourth and seventh in scoring in the league, were extended to six games by Minnesota, led by eighth-place scorer Jean-Paul Parise. Pittsburgh swept Oakland in four and then also extended St. Louis to six games, but the Blues finished the three-year period without ever losing or even trailing in a playoff series within the division. Goyette became the first expansion player to win the Byng, succeeding Detroit's Delvecchio.

In Chicago Hull had missed thirteen games because of injuries and not been among the scoring leaders for the first time in almost a decade, but he was still the all-star left wing ahead of Mahovlich. The Hawks also had new all-star Esposito in goal, and still had Mikita, whose eighty-six points gave him third place and second all-star selection at center. They were facing the Red Wings, still led by perennial all-star Howe, Mahovlich, and Delvecchio and strengthened by the acquisition of second all-star Carl Brewer from Toronto. Chicago, however, swept the series from Detroit, winning all four games, 4–2.

Boston had a little more trouble with New York. The Rangers were much improved, with second-year man Brad Park earning first all-star selection at defense, while Giacomin repeated as second all-star goalie. On attack they had gotten seventy-seven points from Walt Tkaczuk, seventy-four from Jean Ratelle, and seventy from Dave Balon. After the Bruins bombed them in Boston, 8–2 and 5–3, the Rangers skated back into contention with 4–3 and 4–2 wins in New York, but that was the last loss for the Bruins that season.

Boston dominated the league and the playoffs that year just as they dominated the ice in every game, averaging more than forty shots on goal and taking more than fifteen penalty minutes per game. Sanderson was a celebrity as skilled with his mouth as with his stick, Bucyk steadily contributed his sixty-nine points, and Cashman and Hodge and Stanfield would have been stars on most clubs. McKenzie made second all-star, perhaps less for his seventy points than his impressive bodychecking. Phil Esposito was Schmidt's pride and joy, first all-star center ahead of Beliveau and Mikita. His speed and grace on skates and his strength in checking or shooting made him the most feared centerman since young Beliveau, and his reach seemed to get a stick on the puck anywhere near the goalmouth. But Espo's ninety-nine points were only good for second place on the team—and in the league—to Bobby Orr.

This was the first of Orr's three consecutive superstar years, the seasons when he skated through entire schedules without injury. He won the Ross, Norris, Smythe, and Hart trophies—and none was in doubt. For a defenseman to score thirty-three goals was unheard-of, and his eighty-seven assists and 120 points were simply incredible. Not since the Rocket's heyday had any player dominated games the way Orr did, and no defenseman had ever so powered an offense, not even Shore. But the fact is that only on a team that so intimidated its opposition with physical power as the Bruins did could an Orr have been turned loose in that way. And the intangible element behind the Bruins' success was the defenseman Teddy Green, whose name doesn't appear on the 1970 Stanley Cup—who missed the whole season because of a fractured skull.

Terrible Teddy had an unenviable reputation. Keith Magnuson had put him in a class by himself as a "high-stick artist." After he had speared Phil Goyette once, Bill Jennings called Green an animal and said that a bounty should be placed on his head. Green himself claims that he had stopped being Terrible Teddy two or three years before the injury, yet Brad Park said he deserved it because he still carried his stick too high. Green claims there was bad blood throughout the league involving the Maki brothers, especially ever since

Checking Back

Chico had slicked Tom Johnson in the back of his legs and took him out of hockey with a severed nerve. But it was brother Wayne who axed Green with an open shot to the head in a preseason game. And all season long, Orr would go around the dressing room tapping each Bruin with his stick before a game, ending with a ritual tap in front of Teddy's vacant locker.

The Hawks were not up to stopping the Bruins' momentum. Westfall shadowed Hull and shut him down. Phil Esposito beat his brother five times in the four games, and Cheevers was good enough in them all: 6–3, 4–1, 5–2, and 5–4 wins for Boston. Orr seemed to be everywhere on the ice, breaking up Chicago thrusts and hitting Boston sticks with every pass, and Espo was piling up points, a record twenty-seven with thirteen goals in the fourteen games.

As they carried their playoff streak on to St. Louis, there seemed little possibility that they could be stopped. Bucyk's hat trick paced the 6–1 win in the first game, two goals each by Westfall and Sanderson the second (6–2). Back in Boston, Glenn Hall stopped forty-two shots, but the Bruins won 4–2, as Cashman got a pair.

The veteran Blues came out determined to make a fight of the fourth game, struggling to win one time in their third Cup finals of the young era. Berenson matched young Rick Smith's goal in the first period, Gary Sabourin's in the second was matched by Espo, and Keenan's in the third by Bucyk. St. Louis had saved face by taking the mighty Bruins into overtime, but it lasted only forty seconds, as, fittingly and properly, Bobby Orr took a pass from Sanderson and, sailing flat out over the ice after being tripped, poked the puck into the net. The Bruins had the Cup again after twenty-nine dry years.

25

Sorting Things Out

If the noble experiment of expansion were to work, however ignoble the motives of a few expansioneers, clearly some adjustments had to be made. No sporting operation could succeed without competition, and in the expanded NHL there were far too many meaningless games among teams that were not competitive—including the final Stanley Cup series. The apparent success of the competition in the first year of expansion proved to be illusory in the second and third. In the playoffs, where every game *was* important, no new team had ever won even once against an old.

With seeming illogic, the league attempted to cure some of the inherent ills of expansion with more expansion. There were two new franchises awarded, to Vancouver and Buffalo. The price had tripled in three years to six million. Television was not permitted to dictate those choices—the one city was served by "Hockey Night in Canada," the other had access to Toronto programming. But both cities had an eager constituency for supporting hockey at the gate, and that was a primary consideration in light of attendance problems in Oakland, Los Angeles, and Pittsburgh. The admission of Vancouver would take pressure off the league from the Canadian government, while the admission of Buffalo was a bitter pill for Chicago's Jim Norris, who had said, "I don't want a town named Buffalo playing in my building."

Ironically it was Chicago, the most intransigent of the established franchises, that had to make the most radical adjustment. The two new clubs were to play in the East while the Black Hawks moved to the West. The new division got an old team with superstars Hull and Mikita, not to mention pennant-winners in 1970, and the Black Hawks got an easier route into the Stanley Cup finals. The schedule was increased to seventy-eight games, each team facing every other six times. In the playoffs, however, after the first round, there would be crossovers between divisions in the second round.

Before the season started the NHL committed an error in judgment that could have undermined all the virtues of the new arrangements. It approved the sale of the financially troubled Seals to Charles O. Finley. There was

Checking Back

another bidder—Jerry Seltzer, the Roller Derby man—who had the support of Sid Salomon, III, on the board and of several of the AFL establishment, not to mention Senator Stuart Symington, whom Finley had offended not only by moving the Kansas City baseball club to Oakland but by telling the Senator where he could shove the whole state of Missouri. But the governors had predetermined the issue, rejected Seltzer's very professional presentation, and accepted the shabby Finley proposal.

Among the hockey people who resigned rather than continue under Charlie O. were Bob Bester, Frank Selke, Jr., Munson Campbell, Garry Young, and Aldo Guidolin. Geoffrion was hired as scout with a handshake, then unhired eight hours later. Emile Francis, who had accepted Boom Boom's resignation, welcomed him back. Then he canceled a deal to lend Mike Murphy to the Seals for a season since he could no longer trust Finley. Then Finley got tough with the league, angling to move his franchise elsewhere, vetoing any further expansion until he got his way. The NHL, having learned the nature of their junior member, dealt with him in traditional fashion. They changed their rules so that a 12–2 vote was sufficient for expansion, insisted on keeping the Seals in the Bay area, and eventually bought the franchise back from Finley in 1974.

In his first year, his newly named California Golden Seals finished last, 17 and 18 points behind Pittsburgh and Los Angeles; all three were as troubled on the ice as at the box office. The Seals had allowed a record 303 goals against. Chicago as expected led the division, with 107 points, 277 goals, and 184 goals against, but they also led in penalty minutes with 1280. Hull and Stapleton were second all-stars. The real competition in the West was for second place, the Blues finally edging the Flyers and the North Stars.

The major surprise in the East was that Buffalo and Vancouver both finished ahead of Detroit, all three, of course, out of the playoffs. Toronto had come back into the playoffs with a fourth-place finish, thanks mainly to improved gaoltending. They started the season with journeyman Bruce Gamble and forty-two-year-old Jacques Plante, acquired from St. Louis after suffering a concussion against the Bruins in the Cup finals. Then in February the Leafs traded Gamble to Philadelphia for the brilliant Bernie Parent, who reminded many people of Jake the Snake with his swaggering cockiness. Parent and center Dave Keon were both second all-stars. Mike Walton went to Philadelphia in the same deal and was immediately sold to Boston. The league had backed Walton's insistence that he be traded, despite Toronto's reluctance, because of persuasive psychiatric testimony on the player's behalf.

Montreal coasted home third with 97 points, led by Jean Beliveau, who was tied for ninth in scoring in his last year, first all-star defenseman J. C. Tremblay, and second all-star right wing Cournoyer, who replied to Cheevers' joking request that he slow down one night by saying, "No Ger-ry, I have the tailwinds tonight." The Rangers had one of their finest years ever, finishing second with 109 points. Ed Giacomin, first all-star, and Gilles Villemure shared the Vezina and had a remarkable twelve shutouts. Park was second all-star defenseman, while Ratelle, Hadfield, and Gilbert led the attack.

In that season, however, when forty-eight games out of seventy-eight were played against expansion teams, Boston dominated the awards as they did the league. Orr, Esposito, Hodge, and Bucyk were first all-stars, Orr won the Hart, Espo the Ross, and Bucyk the Byng. Espo led the league with incredible totals of 76 goals and 152 points. Orr had 102 assists and 139 points. Bucyk had 51 goals and 116 points. Hodge was fourth with 105 points, Cashman seventh with 79, McKenzie eighth with 77, and Stanfield tied for ninth with 76. The Bruins scored 399 goals while allowing only 207, with Cheevers and Johnston alternating in goal.

Tom Johnson's first season as coach could hardly be faulted, though the loss of Sinden in a salary dispute after the 1970 Cup had signaled trouble to a few. The Bruins were heavily favored to repeat, but the Canadiens had a surprise in store. Instead of Rogie Vachon or his usual relief, Louis Myre, they started the playoffs with Ken Dryden, a Cornell All-American whose brother Dave preceded him as an NHL netminder but who had played less than six full games himself in the big league. A lanky standup goalie with good range and unusual cool, Dryden was impressive even in defeat (3–1 in the first game), and Al MacNeil, who had replaced Claude Ruel behind the Montreal bench in December, decided to go with him all the way.

This seemed a mistake midway through the second game, as Dryden appeared shaky and trailed, 5–1. But the mistake may have been at the other end, where the cocky Bruins had gone to Johnston in their usual pattern of alternation. Dryden settled down, and Montreal stormed back behind Beliveau, Cournoyer, Jacques Laperriere, Lemaire, Richard, Tremblay, and the Mahovlich brothers playing together in the playoffs for the first time. Peter was much bigger than big brother Big M and his opposite in temperament, but they both seemed to benefit from the teaming up. When the smoke cleared, the Canadiens had tied the series with a 7–5 win. Now it was Cheevers versus Dryden all the way. Montreal won, 3–1, Boston won, 5–2, and 7–3, and Montreal tied it, 8–3. The upset was complete when Dyrden bested Cheevers 4–2, so frustrating the Boston scoring machine that Esposito smashed a stick against a partition.

The Rangers meanwhile had just gotten by the Leafs in six games, winning the last on an overtime goal by Bob Nevin, their veteran "mountain goat," who would turn his shoulder into bodychecking defensemen and rarely lose his balance or his feet. The Black Hawks, as planned, had swept the Flyers in four games, but the Blues had been upset by the North Stars in six games.

Checking Back

Minnesota then went on to do what no expansion team had ever done, winning a playoff game from an established team.

In the Forum, of all places, Maniago stopped the Canadiens, 6–3, as Danny Grant had three assists, evening the series at one game each after a 7–2 rout of Worsley in the opener. Then they did it again, 5–2, for Maniago in the fourth game, after Montreal had beaten Worsley 6–3 in the third. The Canadiens finally beat Maniago, 6–1, in the fifth game and closed out the series at 3–2, Rejean Houle scoring the winner, while Minnesota barely missed tying the game when Ted Hampson's shot caught the net a split second after time ran out.

Chicago's easy way to the Cup finals proved difficult after all as they faced the hungry Rangers in the semis. Pete Stemkowski's overtime goal gave New York the first game, but Tony Esposito's shutout won the second for the Hawks. The Rangers went ahead with a 4–1 win at home, but Chicago got even again, 7–1. The teams then traded overtime wins on home ice, Hull winning one, Stemkowski the other, and the seventh game was tied, 2–2, in the third period when Hull beat Giacomin.

The Hawks extended their streak into the finals. Hull, shadowed throughout the series by Houle, broke away to tie the first game, 1–1, after Lemaire scored for Montreal. Dryden and Esposito matched save for save through a full overtime period, but Pappin scored from Mikita and Bill White at 1:11 for Game 1. Chicago won the second, 5–3, as Lou Angotti scored twice and assisted twice while MacNeil kept juggling lines in a panic that earned a public blast from Pocket Rocket for his "incompetence" after the loss.

The squabble put additional pressure on the Canadiens and may have helped them put it together in Game 3. Chicago led on goals by Cliff Koroll and Hull, but Peter Mahovlich scored, and brother Frank tied the game in the second period. Cournoyer got the game-winner in the third and Big M added another. Dryden seemed to have settled down, while Espo looked shaky in the fourth. Three first-period goals were enough for Montreal, though Cournoyer added two in the second in a 5–2 win that evened the series.

Dennis Hull's goal early in the fifth game, assisted by Koroll and brother Bob, was all Esposito needed as he shut out the Canadiens at the Stadium, though Hull returned the favor to Koroll later on in a 2–0 win. Then at the Forum Pappin's second goal gave Chicago a 3–2 lead and a chance to win it all in Game 6. But Frank Mahovlich tied it up five minutes into the third period and then fed brother Peter less than four minutes later for the game-winner that set up the classic seventh game.

It has been twenty-six years since a home team lost a seventh game in the finals. Dennis Hull scored in the last minute of the first period on a power-play rebound off Bobby's shot, but Dryden had made spectacular saves against Pappin, Mikita, Nestorenko, and Magnuson. Esposito was also spectacular, smothering a Lemaire shot as the Canadiens skated four men against three, and early in the second period forechecking Pit Martin dug out the puck and fed Danny O'Shea to make it 2–0. But before the period was over the game was tied.

Espo's spell was broken in a shocking way, a rising sixty-foot slapshot by Lemaire that went over the flopping goalie's shoulder. Four minutes later it was Lemaire forechecking, forcing a bad pass by Nestorenko, and feeding Richard. The Pocket Rocket got the Cup-winner just two and a half minutes into the third period, skating past Magnuson and deking Esposito to the ice before loosing a wrist shot over his shoulder. Dryden protected that lead with magic of his own, especially on a shot by Pappin at point blank range. It was an upset but hardly a surprise. Richard embraced MacNeil at center ice, and Beliveau skated around the rink with the Cup for the last time.

The addition of eight new franchises to the NHL would have seemed to take the wind out of any projected new league's sails. Instead, the general acceptance of a relatively inferior brand of major-league hockey provided the impetus for a new league. Dennis Murphy and Gary Davidson, two of the idea men behind the upstart ABA, incorporated the World Hockey Association in June 1971 and staked out Los Angeles and San Francisco for their own franchises. They found the standard NHL players' contract to be weak, so that raiding for personnel would be comparatively easy, and they hoped to recruit many European players.

Early candidates for franchises were Herb Martin in Miami, Paul Deneau in Dayton, Harold Anderson and John Syke in Chicago, Lou Kaplan in St. Paul, and Neil Shayne in New York. Thanks to sportswriter Walt Marlow, contact was made with Bill Hunter in Edmonton, Ben Hatskin in Winnipeg, and Scotty Munro in Calgary. These three brought hockey expertise and gave the project the necessary credibility in Canada. When the WHA held its first formal meeting in September, there were fourteen prospective owners in attendance, including Thomas Cousins from Atlanta, who turned out to be a pivotal figure.

The NHL had announced 1974 as the earliest date for further expansion. The WHA, though not viewed as a serious threat, was seen now as at least a nuisance if it were to establish footholds in Atlanta, a coveted market, and Long Island, where the Nassau County Coliseum was a-building. So the NHL changed its policy and its rules, gave Cousins the Atlanta franchise and Long Island to Roy Boe, and played with eight teams in each division in 1973.

But the WHA had taken hold anyway, starting play in the 1973 season with twelve teams. Murphy had his Los Angeles Sharks. Davidson had sold his option to Quebec City, where the Quebec Nordiques would be at home, with Paul Racine as trustee. Deneau could not get suitable support or cooperation in Dayton and ended up with the Aeros in Houston. Kaplan had his Minnesota Fighting Saints in St. Paul, where their new building rivaled that of the North Stars. Ben Hatskin had the Winnipeg Jets. The Chicago franchise, the Cougars, eventually went to brothers Jordon and Walter Kaiser. Hunter's team ended up as the Edmonton Oilers, instead of Alberta, when he decided not to use Calgary as an alternate home (after Munro's separate Calgary venture had aborted).

In New York, Shayne sold out to Dick Wood and Sy Siegel. A rental agreement had been worked out for the Garden, putting Jennings in the doghouse as far as most NHL governors were concerned, but the New York Raiders became the Jersey Knights in their second season, at home in Cherry Hill. Other renters were Howard Baldwin's and Bob Schmertz's New England Whalers in the Boston Garden. Herb Martin's Miami project came a cropper when plans for the building fell through, and the Screaming Eagles were transformed into Philadelphia Blazers by Jim Cooper, only to move to Vancouver after a year. Doug Michel originally spearheaded the Ontario franchise, locating in Ottawa as the Nationals for a season, before becoming the Toronto Toros. The last of the charter trustees was Nick Mileti, whose Cleveland Crusaders replaced the Calgary franchise. Rejected by the NHL in its expansion plans, Mileti gave the new league sound management and a solid financial base in a key franchise.

Surprisingly, the WHA took shape on ice with greater substance than it did on paper. Bernie Parent was the first star to jump, from Toronto to Miami, ending up back in Philadelphia. He was one of 78 NHL players among the 340 signed for the first WHA season. Finley lost the most, 10, his niggardliness in salary negotiations in hockey presaging the breakup of his championship baseball club a few years later. Punch Imlach's Sabres lost nine players, as did the Red Wings. Wren Blair of Minnesota met the WHA challenge head on, offering good contracts and losing only one player. The Rangers' brass, too, escalated the salary scale to the point of alienating most other teams' conservative managements. Major losses besides Parent were Toronto's Ricky Ley, New York's Jim Dorey, Montreal's J. C. Tremblay, California's Wayne Carleton, and Boston's Cheevers (who was moonlighting as an owner of fine horseflesh), McKenzie, and Green. The Bruins also lost Sanderson, but many felt that was no great loss. The flashy, flaky forward held out every year (not for money, so he says, but to avoid the exhibition tour) and had played as a resident of Massachusetts General Hospital through the 1972 season with colitis and a bad case of nerves.

The major loss, of course, the single signing that made the WHA a major league, was that of Bobby Hull. He was not only a superstar as a player but also a superimage as a personality. Thus the league supported Hatskin's attempt to woo the Golden Jet to the Winnipeg Jets. The deal was a million dollars front money for ten years' service to the league, $1 million for four years as player and coach at Winnipeg, and $100,000 a year for six additional years in Winnipeg's management. Hull would probably have stayed in Chicago for any kind of deal that included the magic figure with six zeroes, but the Hawk management was slow, reluctant, and skeptical. In the absence of what he could consider bargaining in good faith, Hull departed, with some sadness on his part, great outcry in Chicago, and new respectability for the WHA.

A year later Los Angeles lost Howell, St. Louis Brewer, Montreal Marc Tardif and Houle, Boston Walton, and Chicago Backstrom and Stapleton. And this time the biggest name in hockey went over. Gordie Howe came out of retirement to sign with the Houston Aeros along with his teenage sons Marty and Mark. When the NHL responded with a package offer, it was too little and too late. "In my scoring-title years and my Stanley Cup years," Howe said, "I had to take a summer job." He felt no debt of loyalty to the old league, and he so thoroughly enjoyed playing with his sons that he led the Aeros to the title as the league's MVP while son Mark was rookie of the year.

According to Gary Davidson, if the NHL "had gone at us full bore, they could have broken our backs. . . . We counted on the overconfidence of men who have had a monopoly for a long time, who have operated so arrogantly they could not conceive of anyone's being able to challenge them." The NHL fought the upstarts on many fronts: franchising in WHA target areas, creating difficulties over renting rinks, and suing to block jumping contract-breakers from playing. They also had the support of the CAHA and the AHAUS. WHA players were excluded from Team Canada's series against the Russians, and the new league could not get approval for a series against the reigning world champions from Czechoslovakia.

But the NHL failed to win the war because it was too slow to recognize the value of players in a competitive marketplace situation. In 1974 the two leagues signed a peace pact of mutual recognition. In 1976 Team Canada had players from both leagues. The WHA has yet to compete for the Stanley Cup, but its teams may soon. The WHA began 1977 with six teams each in two divisions: Quebec, Indianapolis, Cincinnati, Minnesota, New England, and Birmingham in the Eastern; Winnipeg, San Diego, Houston, Phoenix, Edmonton, and Calgary in the Western.

Skating for his last season in a Hawk uniform, Hull led Chicago to another first-place finish in the West. With ninety-three points, including fifty goals, he was sixth in scoring, the only representative of the division in the top ten. Esposito, the all-star goalie, shared the Vezina with Gary Smith, and Stapleton and Bill White were second all-star defensemen. Minnesota moved to second place with its first winning record, ahead of St. Louis and Pittsburgh, while Philadelphia joined California and Los Angeles out of the playoffs. It was hardly an auspicious debut for Fred Shero behind the Flyer bench. His team easily led the league in penalty minutes, but, tied with the Penguins in points with sixty-six, they were eliminated for fewer goals.

In the East, Detroit, led by Mickey Redmond's ninety-three points, moved back ahead of Buffalo and Vancouver, but failed to make the playoffs again. The first four repeated in order: Boston, New York, Montreal, Toronto. The low-scoring Leafs had played winning hockey for King Clancy, who took over as coach when John McLellan was hospitalized with ulcers, but managed only one overtime win against the Bruins in the playoffs. The Canadiens' second all-star goalie, Dryden, won the Calder, Cournoyer with eighty-three points was also second all-star, and Big M and Lemaire added ninety-six and eighty-one points. But the light-hitting Habs took the fewest penalty-minutes in the division, and the Rangers took them out of the playoffs in six games.

New York totaled 109 points again, raising their goals total to 317. Byng-winner Ratelle was the second all-star center and the league's third scorer with 109 points. Hadfield, with 106 points, was fourth and also second all-star. Gilbert, with 97 points, was fifth and first all-star, along with defenseman Park. In 257 power-play opportunities, the Rangers scored 60 goals (Park 8, Gilbert 6, Hadfield 23), while opponents got only 44 in 282 chances, with Walt Tkaczuk, Bill Fairbairn, Glen Sather, Bruce MacGregor, and Ron Stewart as the main penalty-killers. Stewart, back from a brief tour with Vancouver, had never recovered his top form after a scuffle with his roommate Terry Sawchuk resulted in the accidental death of Ukey in 1970.

Boston remained the powerhouse of the East. Bucyk was tied for eighth with 83 points. Esposito was first again, with 133. And Orr, who won the Hart, Norris, and Smythe trophies, was second with 117, including 80 assists. The Bruins led all teams with 330 goals and their division with 1,112 penalty minutes. They dominated the ice throughout the season and were determined not to falter again in the playoffs.

In the revamped format, the first-place teams played the fourth-place teams in their divisions, the winners then crossing over to play against winners of second-place versus third-place teams from the other divisions. While Chicago breezed by Pittsburgh in four straight, St. Louis kept coming back to beat Minnesota in seven games. Kevin O'Shea got the winning goal after ten minutes of overtime in the seventh game. Boston then blasted the Blues out, 10–2, 6–1, 7–2, and 5–3, while New York had things almost as easy against Chicago, winning 3–2, 5–3, 3–2, and 6–2.

During the season Boston had beaten New York five straight times. While

226

the line of Ratelle, Gilbert, and Hadfield scored almost two goals a game and devastated the league, they were dominated by Esposito, Cashman, and Hodge. And now Ratelle was injured, replaced on the line by Bobby Rousseau. Orr, on the other hand, was playing hurt on his bad left knee. Francis decided to play the shadow game, Tkaczuk on Esposito, and it worked—up to a point. Espo didn't have a goal in the six games, but his eight assists added up to the fact that the Ranger defense was weakened by having Walt, their best hitter, occupied with the big center.

Boston led, 5–1, on Hodge's hat trick in the first game, but New York came back, MacGregor finally tying it up. At 17:44, however, Garnet (inevitably "Ace") Bailey took passes from Walton and Westfall, got around Park, and beat Giacomin for the winner. Power-play goals by Bucyk and Hodge beat Villemure, 2–1, in the second game, but in New York the Rangers came back, winning 5–2 as Park and Gilbert scored twice each. Park knew that Orr was hurting, but in the fourth game he saw him score twice in the first period and assist Marcotte on the game-winner in the second, while Ted Irvine, Seiling, and Stemkowski teamed up for both Ranger goals.

In Boston two nights later, New York reversed the 3–2 decision on two third-period goals by Rousseau. But they would not score again. While Cheevers got his second shutout of the playoffs (Johnston had one, too), the Cup-winning goal was Orr's in the first period. He lured MacGregor into a lunge, wheeled in and beat Villemure low on the left side. That held up into the third period, when Cashman got a deflection goal off an Orr slap shot and added another for insurance just before the end. Wayne led the team in celebrating the second championship in three years, at one point being arrested for drunkenness. Allowed his constitutional single phone call, Cashman rang a Chinese restaurant to order a late supper delivered by cab.

While the WHA prepared to launch and the NHL tinkered with obstructive tactics, the hockey world was further enlivened by negotiations for a series between the Russian national team and an all-star team of professionals called Team Canada. In world amateur hockey play, Canada had been dominant into the fifties, winning fourteen of the eighteen championships contested through 1952. The exceptions were 1933 (USA), 1936 (Great Britain), and 1947 and 1949 (Czechoslovakia). But in the twenty years since, Canada had won only four times, USA and Czechoslovakia once each, Sweden three times, and the Soviet Union eleven times, including nine in a row from 1963 to 1971. Canadians had always dismissed that record by pointing out that the Russian teams were year-round professionals, while the best hockey players in the world, the NHL, were prohibited from the so-called amateur competition.

A series of eight games were arranged, four in Canada, four in Moscow, to take place before the NHL season began. Harry Sinden was named coach. He

Checking Back

requested John Ferguson as his assistant, and they chose a squad of thirty-five players including Bobby Hull, Sanderson, Cheevers, J. C. Tremblay, Giacomin, Tkaczuk, Dallas Smith, and Laperriere. The latter four declined for personal reasons. The former four were banned because they were jumping to the WHA. This was strictly an NHL operation. Some owners threatened to keep all their players out if any rebels played. The NHL pension fund was to get the major share of the profits. The loss of Hull was considered a national catastrophe, and Prime Minister Trudeau got into the act. But Alan Eagleson and Clarence Campbell, two of the prime movers in Hockey Canada, prevailed, and the WHA was locked out. Team Canada would also be without Bobby Orr, not fully recovered from knee surgery.

But the all-star squad was still formidable. Goalies were Dryden, Esposito, and Johnston. Defensemen were Park, White, Stapleton, Awrey, Seiling, Lapointe, Savard, Brian Glennie, and Gary Bergman. Forwards were Ratelle, Gilbert, Hadfield, Clarke, Ellis, Henderson, Esposito, Cournoyer, Berenson, Redmond, Dennis Hull, Perreault, Martin, Cashman, Parise, Goldsworthy, Mikita, the Mahovliches, Mariel Dionne, Dave Tallon, and Jocelyn Guevremont.

A summary of the series makes it sound quite exciting. The Canadians were shocked by the Russians in Montreal, 7–3, as Valeri Kharlamov was awesome and Vladislav Tretiak, the goalie, belied scouting reports about his weaknesses. In Toronto, Team Canada tied the series with a 4–1 win, Esposito replacing Dryden in goal and Cournoyer getting the game-winner. In Winnipeg they played a 4–4 tie, and in Vancouver Russia won, 5–3. The last four games were played in Moscow. The Canadians led, 4–1, but lost, 5–4, to put them down three games to one. Game 6 went to Canada, 3–2, Henderson scoring the game-winner; Dryden was excellent. It was Henderson again in game 7, a 4–3 win for Canada, setting up the last game as truly climactic. The Russians led, 5–3, after two periods. In the third, Phil Esposito, who had been effectively shadowed by Vladimir Petrov throughout the series, powered a shot past Tretiak. The Russians started backing up to protect the lead, and Team Canada found the ice opened up for their offense. Cournoyer tied the game at 12:56, and then in the last minute, Espo's shot was rebounded by Henderson, Tretiak saved again, but Henderson got another rebound and slid it home.

So much for the summary of Canada's triumph and Henderson's heroism. The significance and implications of the series went far beyond the won-lost record. The global superiority of Canadian professionals was no longer to be comfortably assumed. Team Canada was not as strong as it could have been, because of the exclusion of the WHA and Bobby Hull, because Orr had not sufficiently recovered from knee surgery to play, and because the series took place at a time when Canadian players were not in shape. They were at a further disadvantage because they played under international rules and with officials who took many opportunities to interpret those rules in favor of the USSR.

But those factors had all been taken into account beforehand, and Team Canada was expected to prevail anyway, simply on the strength of their superiority at *their* game. Yet they nearly lost the series, and they lost a great deal of respect along the way. There were defections: Hadfield, Martin, and Guevremont left Moscow without playing, Perrault after playing in Game 5. There was a constant stream of wailing from the Canadian camp about conditions, officiating, and dirty play. And during the games, Sinden led demonstrations of temper tantrums that could have set athletic diplomacy back to the Berlin Olympics in 1936. The Team Canada coach made Woody Hayes look like Dean Martin.

Team Canada won, beating the Russian team four games to three with one tie (and a tie in total goals). On the way to Moscow they beat Sweden, 4–1, and tied them, 4–4. On the way home they tied Czechoslovakia, the reigning world champions, 3–3. It was hardly a demonstration of absolute supremacy by an all-star NHL squad. Indeed, Sinden's team won the way Sinden's Bruins had won the Stanley Cup: by outhitting rather than outskating the opposition. The Europeans had played better classic hockey and their playmaking was much better to watch, but they could not finally withstand the heavy pressure of the Canadians' bodychecking.

Hockey had clearly become an international game. There was no doubt that players like Petrov, Aleksandr Ragulin, and Vladimir Lutchenko could play in the NHL. Aleksandr Yakushev could be a star, and Tretiak and Kharlamov probably all-stars. But the Europeans would all have had to learn several items in the NHL code: (1) skate with head up or get knocked off; (2) to vent anger, drop gloves and stick and fight, rather than using sticks and skates as weapons of aggression or revenge; and (3) forget showing off injuries to the crowd (and officials)—or risk the consequences of being a marked man. It is interesting that Sinden, in his account of the whole venture, singles out the second game in Sweden as the dirtiest, with the most vicious incident, but admits that "it wasn't as rough as many of the NHL games I've seen over the years." Nevertheless, NHL teams have tried to recruit European players. On NHL rosters in 1977—in addition to players born in out-of-the-way places like Denmark, Poland, Scotland, England, Germany, Finland, France, the Netherlands, Yugoslavia, Czechoslovakia, Italy, Paraguay, Venezuela, and Texas, but nurtured in college or junior amateur hockey in Canada—there are three players straight from Sweden, forwards Lars Bergman for Detroit and Inge Hammar-strom for Toronto, and the Maple Leafs' second all-star defenseman Borje Salming, considered by some to be the class of the league at his position.

The season that followed was anticlimactic to many and disappointing to more. Paul Henderson, briefly a national hero, had his worst year in a decade. The WHA inroads hurt some established teams but hurt the new expansion teams more by outbidding them for draft choices. The New York Islanders lost seven of their twenty picks, so that their ten-million-dollar investment (six for the franchise, four more for territorial rights to the Rangers) seemed rather extravagant. They won only twelve games and tied six, losing a record sixty. But one win was against the proud Bruins in Boston who—reeling from the loss of Cheevers, McKenzie, Sanderson, and young Ron Plumb to the WHA, West-fall in the draft to the Islanders, and goalie Don Bouchard in the draft to Atlanta—gave up nine goals to the sorry upstarts.

The new Atlanta Flames did better in the West, finishing ahead of California and only 11 points out of the playoffs. Chicago led the division again, Stapleton and second all-star White anchoring the defense in front of second all-star Esposito, and Jim Pappin and second all-star Dennis Hull leading the attack. They easily eliminated the Blues in five games in the first round. Meanwhile the Flyers were riding high. Bobby Clarke, second all-star center and second leading scorer in the league behind Espo, had emerged as a genuine superstar who won the Hart. Rick MacLeish, in his first full season, was fourth in the league with an even 50 goals and 50 assists. The Minnesota North Stars had played tough throughout the season, giving the West three teams over .500 for the first time, and extended Philadelphia to six games.

In the East the Bruins had lost their dominance. They still led the league in goals with 330. Esposito won the Ross with 130 points as first all-star, Orr won his sixth straight Norris and was third in scoring with 101 as first all-star, and Bucyk was tied for seventh with 93. But they were weaker on defense, in goal-tending, and in intimidation, as many other clubs adopted their tactics. So it came as no surprise when the third-place Rangers, led by second all-star Brad Park and the scoring of Ratelle, Gilbert, and Calder-winner Steve Vickers, knocked Boston out of the playoffs in five games.

The pennant had come back to Montreal after four years. Dryden played fifty-four games in goal and won the Vezina by a wide margin. He was joined as first all-star by Lapointe and the Big M, while Cournoyer, who was to win the Smythe, made the second team behind Detroit's Redmond, and Lemaire led the team with ninety-five points. The most significant change in the East, however, and a promising development for the future, was the fourth-place finish of Buffalo. It was the first time an expansion team made the playoffs in the old division, and they did it under coach Joe Crozier with a pattern of play that bucked the bruising Bruin trend—with speed and playmaking, especially by the line of Gil Perreault, Rick Martin, and Rene Robert, inevitably called the French Connection. Perreault, who had been the first choice in the expansion draft (Buffalo winning the toss from Vancouver) and nearly unanimous choice for the Calder in 1971 with a rookie-record thirty-eight goals, scored eighty-eight points and won the Byng with only ten minutes in penalties. Robert and Martin added eighty-three and seventy-three points.

The glimpse of things to come lasted only into the first round, as Montreal won in six fine games, but it provided an exciting impetus (along with the examples of the Russians and the Czechs) toward developing a new artistic style. The semis were both five-game affairs, Montreal over Philadelphia and Chicago over New York, setting up the expected series between the two pennant-winners—a host of experienced skaters on both sides and the league's two highest-regarded goaltenders.

Goaltending was hardly outstanding in the first game, as eleven goals were scored. The Hawks led, 3–2, at the close of one period on Pit Martin's second goal, but it was all Canadiens after that, Lemaire getting two, including the game-winner, and rookie Chuck Lefley two. Dryden held Chicago to one goal in the second game, while Cournoyer got two of Montreal's four including the winner. The slow ice of Chicago Stadium did not slow down the scoring in Game 3. The Hawks beat Dryden four times in the first period and led, 5–1, after two. The Frenchmen came back, Cournoyer, Lapointe, and Lemaire scoring, but when they skated a sixth man in the last minute, Chicago got two quick empty-net goals for a 7–4 win. Dryden then did another about-face. He shut out Chicago, and Montreal had a 4–0 win and a 3–1 lead in games.

The speedy ice of the Forum must have been too much for Esposito and Dryden after the Chicago mush, because neither one seemed to be able to get to a shot in Game 5. Frank Mahovlich scored and Dennis Hull tied it up. Mikita scored and Peter Mahovlich tied it. Larose scored and Dave Kryskow tied it. Larose again and Mikita again. Cournoyer and Pappin. When Len Frig, who had never played a regular-season NHL game, scored for Chicago, Pappin followed with his second and the Hawks led, 7–5, after two periods. Savard scored in the third to make it close, Angotti got the game-winner for Chicago, and Richard made the final score 8–7. Game 6 was not much better, as the Stadium ice could not slow up the scoring parade. Pit Martin's hat trick had the Hawks even, 4–4, after two periods, but Dryden settled down to shut them out in the third, Cournoyer got the Cup-winner on a rebound from Lemaire, and then the two of them assisted Marc Tardif for the clincher.

It had not been a vintage year. Continued expansion had further diluted the talent, and the disparity between the haves and have-nots continued. If there

Checking Back

was an approach to parity, it was because the WHA had taken some of the brightest stars, the very ones that made mediocre teams good or good teams excellent. The lesson of winning with intimidation was apparently the only one heeded, while the lessons of international play were apparently ignored. The Cup finals had lacked the characteristic intensity and flair of the past, were not persuasive advertisements of the best that hockey had to offer.

The 1974 season persisted in these alarming trends but ironically set the stage for the two developments essential to fulfilling the long-range hopes of the NHL. In the East, Boston surprised almost everyone when they were expected to continue the last year's slide. Harry Sinden took over as manager and, with Bep Guidolin as coach, drove the Bruins to the pennant. Chief Bucyk won his second Byng, but with 75 points he was only fifth among Boston scorers. Cashman with 89 was second all-star left wing; Hodge with 105 joined Espo and Orr as first all-stars. They were 1–2–3–4 in the league in scoring. Orr had 122 and his seventh Norris; Espo 145, his fifth Ross and second Hart. With 349 goals they won 52 games, and with Gilles Gilbert in goal for 54 games, they led the division in goals-against average. Montreal finished second, Cournoyer and the Mahovliches having good years, New York third, led by all-star Park, and Toronto fourth, led by Darryl Sittler. Buffalo was a disappointing fifth despite Martin's all-star performance, Detroit sixth, and the latecomers in Vancouver and Long Island dismal in seventh and eighth, despite Denis Potvin's Calder-winning performance in Nassau County.

Greater surprises were in the West. California was an expected eighth, and the slippage of St. Louis and Minnesota to sixth and seventh behind Pittsburgh (where Syl Apps, Jr., and Lowell MacDonald both had a big scoring year) was not entirely unexpected. But for the upstart Atlanta Flames to make the playoffs behind Los Angeles in just their second year of operation was shocking. And at the top, with Mikita still scoring well, White still a second all-star defenseman, and Tony Esposito earning a share of the Vezina, the Chicago Black Hawks were denied the pennant for the first time since their move to the new division. The winners and new champions were the hard-hitting, crowd-pleasing Philadelphia Flyers. Made in the image of the 1970 Bruins, the Flyers under Fred Shero outdid the old masters in intimidation and penalty minutes, making up for lack of finesse with a style that justified their nickname as Broad Street Bullies. Parent had returned from the WHA and earned a share of the Vezina as first all-star. Clarke and Barry Ashbee were on the second team. Clarke led the scorers, but MacLeish, Bill Barber, Ross Lonsberry, Gary Dornhoefer, Bill Flett, Orest Kindrachuk, and Don Saleski all made major contributions. In the bullying department, Dave Schultz was the egregious leader, followed by Andre Dupont, Saleski, Bob Kelly, Dornhoefer, and Ed Van Impe. Clarke, as feisty as he was fast and as competitive as he was skillful, himself had 113 penalty minutes, among Philadelphia's record-shattering total of 1,740, but he seemed to win 90 percent of the face-offs.

Those achievements, including the dubious ones, helped set the stage for the playoffs of 1974, a turning point in recent NHL history: Boston against Toronto, New York Rangers against Montreal, Philadelphia against Atlanta, and Chicago against Los Angeles. The results were hardly a step forward in terms of the way hockey can be played, but a backward step can sometimes be preparation for a great leap forward.

26

Parity and Beyond

A significant degree of competitive parity in the NHL was attained at great cost. The price was a brief reign of terror, and the reigning terrorizers were housed in the Spectrum in Philadelphia. Fred Shero's team was determined to prove that the pennant was not just a meaningless, regular-season aberration, and in the playoffs they checked—if possible—with even more determination. They dominated the Flames in two games in Philadelphia and then extinguished them in two more at the Omni. The fourth game was won in overtime when Bobby Clarke won a face-off, as he does with amazing consistency, and fed Dave Schultz at the goalmouth for a quick shot past Phil Myre. This game was won with assistant coach Mike Nykoluk, behind the bench, because Shero had been jumped by Atlanta fans after the third game and gone home to Philadelphia to nurse his wounds.

In other first-round action, Chicago whipped Los Angeles in five games and Boston swept Toronto in four, starting with a masterful 1–0 shutout by Gilles Gilbert in the opener. The other series in the East matched the high-priced Rangers against the poor-mouth Canadiens. Montreal had failed to meet Ken Dryden's salary demands, so their all-star goalie spent the season clerking in a law office, and it seemed that other Habs were not giving their all for the club. With the series even at two games each, New York won on an overtime goal by spare Ron Harris and then closed out the Canadiens with a 5–2 win.

Against the Rangers, the Flyers concentrated on their body-checking even more than usual because of the conventional wisdom that Emile Francis's men didn't care for that sort of thing. At center on the first line, however, they had a willing mixer in Walt Tkaczuk and the matchup with Clarke augured good theater. But in the opening round, as Clarke was engaging Tkaczuk low, Moose Dupont hit him high for a clean knockout. New York sagged after that, and Philadelphia gave Parent a 4–0 shutout. Tkaczuk came back to earn a draw with Clarke in game two, but the rest of the Rangers didn't fare as well. Kelly kayoed Jerry Butler with a characteristic quick flurry of punches, and

Lonsberry sent Stemkowski to the ice with a good check and on the play scored one of his two goals in the 5–2 win. Giacomin had apparently lost his poise under the Flyer assault: he was checked himself whenever possible under Shero's very physical game plan.

New York scrapped back at the Garden, winning 5–3 and then 2–1 on Gilbert's overtime goal, besides getting the only knockout when Dale Rolfe's shot caught Barry Ashbee in the right eye, ending his career. The teams then exchanged 4–1 wins on home ice, setting up the climactic seventh game at the Spectrum. Fairbairn scored first for New York, but MacLeish, Kindrachuk, and Dornhoefer got the puck past the embattled Giacomin. Vickers got the Rangers close, but only twelve seconds later Dornhoefer got another. Stemkowski's rebound shot made the final score 4–3, but the expansion Flyers had made history, winning a playoff series from an old, established NHL team.

In the other semis, Tony Esposito kept Chicago ahead of Boston for three games, making well over a hundred saves as the Hawks won the first, lost the second, and won the third in overtime. In Game 4 at the Stadium, however, the Bruin scoring machine got in gear again. Phil Esposito and linemates Hodge and Cashman each got a goal in a 5–2 win, and Espo got two past his brother in a 6–2 game in Boston. Gregg Sheppard got the series-winner in the 4–2 sixth game, and the Bruins went home to take on the Flyers.

Shero's strategy was based on the assumption that the Bruins could and would hit as hard as the Flyers but that they could not sustain it as long, particularly if Orr and Esposito could be treated as hittable mortals. Cashman and Sheppard gave Boston a lead, Kindrachuk and Clarke took it away, but Orr won the opener in the last minute. The second game repeated the pattern, up to a point. Cashman and Espo gave Boston a lead; Clarke and Dupont took it away, the tying goal coming with less than a minute to play and with Parent replaced by a forward. In overtime, the tireless Clarke won another face-off, rebounded his own shot, and put it past Gilbert and over the diving Terry O'Reilly. It was Philadelphia's first win at Boston Garden in over seven years.

In the Spectrum, Bucyk scored first, but Tom Bladon, playing in Ashbee's slot, tied it up. Spare Terry Crisp, hustling the puck away from Vadnais and Smith, got the winning goal in a 4–1 game, and the upstart Flyers took control of the series. Game 4 was 4–2, with Barber getting the winner, and they went back to Boston with a chance to clinch the Cup, despite injuries to Kelly, Dornhoefer, and Bill Clement. Game 5 was marred by six fights, a record forty-three penalties, and blood on the ice. Orr's two goals turned the game Boston's way. They won, 5–1, but were through for the season. Kate Smith belted out "God Bless America" in person at the Spectrum, and both teams responded with aroused, close-checking play. MacLeish scored on a give-and-go play from Dupont against the short-handed Bruins in the first period, and Parent made that lone goal stand up. The Stanley Cup, as likely a Philadelphia property as W. C. Fields, had gone to an expansion team.

The league celebrated by welcoming two new franchises in Washington and Kansas City with the poorest quality yet made available in drafts. There was a new alignment in four divisions and a new arrangement for the playoffs. The Charles F. Adams Division had Boston, Buffalo, Toronto, and California. The Lester Patrick had Philadelphia, Atlanta, and the two New Yorks, Washington was put in the James Norris with Montreal, Detroit, Pittsburgh, and Los Angeles; Kansas City in the Conn Smythe with Chicago, St. Louis, Minnesota, and Vancouver.

Each division would place the first three finishers in the playoffs, the winners to get first-round byes. The other eight were ranked according to points earned during the season, the best record against the worst and so forth, with the home-ice advantage in best-two-of-three series always going to the higher-ranked team. The survivors then were seeded against the pennant-winners to complete the tournament in four-out-of-seven matches. The system of seedings put new emphasis on regular-season play: the whole eighty-game schedule would have continued bearing on the match-ups in the playoffs.

The race in the Smythe turned out to be the closest. The Hawks had disappointing seasons by Martin, Hull, and Pappin, costly injuries to White, Tallon, and Magnuson, and a third-place finish barely over .500, but comfortably ahead of the North Stars and the tyro Scouts, who won only fifteen games. The surprising Blues were second, led by Garry Unger and Pierre Plante, just two points behind the more surprising Canucks, whose Andre Boudrias had 62 assists and Gary Smith six shutouts in goal.

In the Norris the new Capitals won only eight games, losing a record sixty-seven. Manager Milt Schmidt had drafted a team of big hitters; they didn't hit anybody and got progressively puny through the season. In Detroit, Marcel Dionne scored 121 points, won the Byng, and led the Wings nowhere as they finished far back in fourth. Pittsburgh was third with a wide-open attack and balanced scoring (and an outstanding rookie in Pierre Larouche) but not much defense. The name of the game was defense for Bob Pulford's Kings, and they played it well enough in front of second all-star Vachon to win 42 games and the highest second-place point total in the league. The Canadiens were first. All-star Lafleur was fourth in scoring, Peter Mahovlich fifth, Lemaire eleventh, and Lapointe second all-star defenseman. Moreover, they were building for the future with rookies Doug Risebrough, Mario Tremblay, and Yvon Lambert, while also acquiring veteran defenseman Don Awrey, and management had loosened the purse-strings to get Dryden back.

The Adams Division leaders were the Sabres, matching Montreal's 113 points and getting seeded second ahead of them with two more wins. Only the presence of the Seals in their division put the Leafs into the playoffs. California was beginning to assemble good young prospects (Larry Patey, Dave Hrechkosy, Al MacAdam), but Red Kelly's Toronto team had little behind second all-star Salming and forwards Sittler and Ellis. The Bruins were marking time and losing ground. Orr won the Norris and the Ross (135 points), Espo was second all-star center behind Clarke and second in scoring (127), and Bucyk and Sheppard scored well, but Boston clearly needed some shaking up. Buffalo had glided by them, the French Connection amassing 291 points with Martin first and Robert second all-star, and additional help coming from rookies Danny Gare and Peter McNab as well as defensemen Guevremont, Jerry Korab, and Jim Schoenfeld. Their goaltending was inconsistent, with veteran Roger Crozier and young Gary Bromley, but Gerry Desjardins returned from the WHA for nine games at the end of the season.

The champion Flyers led the Patrick and the league with 113 points and fifty-one wins, while their division-mates all had winning seasons. The Flames had the Calder-winner, Eric Vail, but found themselves gerrymandered out of the playoffs. The Islanders had all-star Denis Potvin at defense, rookie Clark Gillies at forward, and rookie Glenn Chico Resch and Billy Smith in goal. The Rangers got productive years from Gilbert, Ratelle, second all-star Vickers, and rookie Ron Greschner. But neither New York team was a match for Philadelphia, with Hart-winner Clarke backed up nicely by MacLeish and Leach in scoring; by Schultz, Dupont, and company in muscle; and by Parent (Vezina, all-star, twelve shutouts) in goal.

In the preliminary round of the playoffs, where the home-ice advantage should have been most decisive, it only held up in one of the four series as Pittsburgh took two straight from St. Louis. Chicago upset Boston in three, Toronto Los Angeles in three, and the Islanders the Rangers in three. The New York series saw every game won by the visiting team, a record fifty penalties called in Game 2, and an overtime win by Jean-Paul Parise against Giacomin in Game 3.

At least one of these teams would have to survive the quarterfinals (a new term for hockey), since the seedings matched the Penguins against the Islanders, both with better records than the Canucks. Pittsburgh beat Billy Smith in the first three games, but New York rallied in front of Resch to win the last four, the seventh game a 1–0 thriller won by Ed Westfall near the end. Vancouver, meanwhile, fell to Montreal in five games, Chicago to Buffalo in five, and Toronto to Philadelphia in four, justifying the seedings across the board.

The Islanders tried to repeat their come-from-behind heroics against the Flyers, losing three and then winning three, but fell short in the seventh game. Buffalo took two from Montreal, were bombarded, 7–0 and 8–2, in the

Forum, but regrouped to win in six. Again the seeds held up. Against Philadelphia, Desjardins was as nervous in the Buffalo goal as Parent was his laughing self at the other end. Ironically, Desjardins's odyssey to Imlach's Sabres had begun when Imlach underbid for him on behalf of the Leafs. He was rookie of the year in the AHL at Cleveland, but Montreal traded him to Los Angeles (the deal eventually brought them Steve Shutt) rather than lose him in the draft. He went to Chicago in a six-man deal, to the Islanders in the expansion draft, and to the WHA in the goldrush. And now he was at the top of his game for Buffalo.

For two periods Desjardins matched Parent save for save, but Clarke did a number on Perreault that bottled up the French Connection. Philadelphia's pressure paid off in the third period. Barber scored first and Lonsberry got the game-winner in the 4–1 opener. The second game was tighter, but Clarke got the winner for 2–1. The pattern changed in Game 3 in Buffalo. The Flyers led, 3–2, after one period, and Desjardins asked to be relieved. Crozier got credit for the win as the Sabres rallied to tie and Robert scored at 18:29 of overtime. Desjardins won the fourth, 4–2, without relief as Buffalo tied the series, but that was as close as they came. Philadelphia pounded out a 5–1 win at the Spectrum, and then Parent shut out the Sabres, 2–0, at the Aud, despite Crozier's fine goaltending. The Smythe Trophy went to Parent again as Philadelphia successfully defended its prized Stanley Cup.

The 1975 Flyers broke their own record in penalty minutes, nearing the 2,000 mark with 1,969, as Schultz broke his individual record with 472. But they were not a team of indiscriminate maulers. There was method to their mayhem. Fred Shero claimed to have learned from the Russians the lessons of positional hockey, so that no matter who was on the ice his teammates could expect him to be in a certain place. They checked close in center and defending zones, of course, but when they got the puck they attacked en masse with short passes. Not that their plays themselves were like the Russians'—far from it—but their positional discipline was. Their offensive pattern was simple, repetitious, intimidating, effective: get the puck into the corners, win the fight to dig it out, and then win the fight to send it home from in front.

What was significant, however, about the 1975 season, aside from the unusual number of outstanding rookies, was not the continued success of the Flyers, but the nature of the challengers. Of the other three semifinalists, none played Philadelphia-brand hockey. The Canadiens, the Islanders, and the Sabres all relied on speed as opposed to strength. Their coaches had learned lessons from the Russians, too, but Scotty Bowman, Al Arbour, and Floyd Smith found more value in the plays themselves than in the positional discipline. Thus, while all three teams occasionally loosed their individual speed in imitation of old-style rushes, for the most part they outmaneuvered their opposition. They could all check well, especially Montreal; they could all hit, especially New York; and they could all use their sticks to finesse most pugnacious teams, especially Buffalo. They all sought the right implementation of available talent. And they all bucked the trend to dump the puck into a corner at every opportunity. Teams that copied the Flyers or the older Bruins were brawlers but losers. And when they did so, it was a confession that they lacked the speed and other hockey skills to play the game. Philadelphia's model was excellently workable during a time of diminished or diluted skill, but as the NHL looked ahead toward a new day of hockey excellence, the days of the Flyers' dominance were numbered.

One vital side-effect of Philadelphia's back-to-back titles was a focus of attention on the violence in hockey. Nothing in sports draws the attention of fans and media alike quicker than winners. So the years of the Flyers' ascendancy have been marked with investigation, indignation, and prosecution. Jack Ludwig has neatly capsulized the prevalent attitude of the media:

> The hockey fan's concept of the game as a blood sport is helped by coaches, team and league officials, and that breed of hand-out publicity agent variously called public relations officer and/or sportswriter. A game like hockey, with its speed and body contact, is more likely to lead to fighting than almost any other sport. But hockey's becoming Show Biz has incorporated fighting into its attempt at "crowd-pleasing." A bloodthirsty fan is a loyal fan. So why cut off his enthusiasm, and his money?
>
> It's not then the *chance* fight spontaneously set up by a hit just a little too hard, or from the back, or clearly dangerous that one is concerned about. It's the staged roller derby-wrestling-Show Biz scrap league officials think is box office and just dandy. More: it's the fight *as intimidation*, a strategy to even things up when the other side is too talented, too fast, too good.

This all sounds reasonable, but it is unrealistic in any historical perspective.

Hockey is no more violent than it ever was. There is, if anything, proportionally less violence with intent to injure, less use of the available weapons. The media have drawn more attention to it, and the legal authorities have responded with appropriate knee-jerks, but there is a long (and always irresolute) tradition of criminal assault cases growing out of hockey incidents. The fighting itself—that is, with fists—is a safety valve for aggression, anger, and revenge. A ban on fighting would increase serious injuries in the course of play. Fake fighting is all too obvious and only serves to interrupt the flow of play. It is well to discourage this, but it is more important to penalize severely any excessive roughness in play that can lead to injury. And as for winning by intimidation, well, superior play will overcome excuses for excellence every time. The 1976 season demonstrated that very well.

Finally, much has been made of the increased taste for violence among the fans. The Nielsen ratings for TV shows seem to support this observation, and the media's focus on cheap shots, fouls, and beanings sharpens it. There is something very frightening about fans' more and more often becoming mobs on playing fields and courts, as North American spectators rival the involvement of our Latin neighbors with their *futbol*. But as long as hockey has attracted crowds, that danger has been present and felt. Again, in any historical perspective, what is out of proportion here is the suggestion of newly risen blood-lust among hockey fans.

In 1976, hockey fans had renewed excitement and saw some of the best hockey in years in the NHL. Early in the season, the perennially disappointing Rangers and the fading Bruins made a deal of extraordinary impact and implications. Boston sent Phil Esposito and Carol Vadnais to New York for Brad Park, Jean Ratelle, and Joe Zanussi. The Boston move was motivated by desperation over Orr: the knee was apparently just not going to hold up, and contract negotiations loomed menacingly. Their whole modus operandi was keyed to the dominant defenseman, and Park was the nearest thing they could see to Orr (with Potvin presumably untouchable). New York needed tough competitiveness and scoring punch at the same time, and Esposito was defined by those terms.

Park-for-Esposito would have been sensational enough, rather like the baseball trade of batting champion Harvey Kuenn for home-run champion Rocky Colavito, but holes at defense and center also had to be filled. The Rangers gave up their own veteran high-scoring center, a former Byng-winner, threw in a marginal defenseman, and got a steady journeyman defenseman in Vadnais. What made the trade especially interesting was what Park had said about Boston in his book: that the Garden was a shabby, grubby zoo; that players like Hodge and Cashman, who'd been peaceful in Chicago or placid in Toronto, turned fighters as Bruins; and that Espo, an extraordinary stick-handler and superb shooter, had no guts.

In the event, Park found a pleasant home in Boston. Ratelle found a new lease on life (his second Byng, sixth in scoring). The Bruins found that even without Orr they could play less like Flyers and more like Canadiens, and they finished strong to beat Buffalo in the Adams Division. Park, first all-star, was beaten in the Norris voting by Potvin. In the Patrick Division, Vadnais gave the Rangers a bit of muscle, but Esposito, never known for his skating and not really comfortable in the Ranger system, dropped to twentieth in scoring and New York dropped under .500 and out of the playoffs behind Atlanta. The Islanders got tougher: Chico Resch was second all-star and second in the voting for the Calder, while Potvin and Calder-winner Bryan Trottier were eleventh and twelfth in scoring. Philadelphia took the pennant again and appeared to be better, particularly as they modified their style somewhat with new speed and playmaking. Hart-winner Clarke had 119 points as all-star center, Barber 112 as all-star left wing, and Leach a league-leading sixty-one goals as second all-star right wing. They also had flashy rookie Mel Bridgman, the top pick in the amateur draft.

Washington had given up that pick for Bill Clement, who brought a new stability and some big-league quality to the Caps whenever he was on the ice, but could not bring them the points to get out of the cellar of the Norris Division. So he was dealt to Atlanta, and Milt Schmidt was replaced. Detroit had lost Dionne and gotten Dan Maloney. Walt McKechnie got them some goals, but they were still far from a playoff team. Los Angeles edged Pittsburgh, whose Pierre Larouche had 111 points, for second, but they were in another class than pennant-winning Montreal.

The Smythe Division still struggled. Minnesota was not much better than Kansas City. St. Louis, with consistent scoring from Lefley and Unger, finished third but without a winning record. Chicago and Vancouver were just barely over .500. In the playoff preliminaries, Vancouver went out meekly at the Islanders' hands, St. Louis won a game from Buffalo before successive overtime losses on goals by Danny Gare and Don Luce, and Chicago, drawing a bye into the quarters, got only three goals in a four-game sweep by the Canadiens.

Elsewhere, Los Angeles edged Atlanta in two games and then extended Boston to seven, winning twice in overtime on Butch Goring goals. Toronto, led by second all-star defenseman Salming and scorers Sittler and McDonald, won the three-game prelim with Pittsburgh on a Wayne Thomas shutout, and took the Flyers to a seventh game before losing. And in a fine series, the Islanders lost two games to the Sabres, as second all-stars Perreault and Martin scored well and Gare, who won the second in overtime, better; but then came on to take the next four in a row.

In the semis, the Bruins were weakened by injuries and could not withstand the Flyers, who lost the first game but could not be stopped after Leach won the second in overtime. The finest series of the year sent the Islanders against the Canadiens. At the Forum, Montreal won, 3–2 and 4–3. At the Coliseum, New York lost, 3–2, but won, 5–2. The last game went to the Canadiens, 5–2, at home, but all five had been well-played. The fourth was the only postseason game lost by Montreal. It was the hockey of the future that the more thoughtful expansionists had hoped for, and it was in the play of the young losers and the way they had built their challenging team—with draft choices trained in the style of skilled playmaking—that a model of hope's fulfillment could be found.

There was already a fulfillment of true excellence in the Montreal team. The Canadiens were awesome as they mowed down the Flyers in four straight for their nineteenth Stanley Cup. Only Reggie Leach, whose 19 goals in Philadelphia's sixteen-game playoffs won him the Smythe Trophy, prevented a total rout. In goal, Dryden had allowed only 25 goals in thirteen playoff games. He had already won the Vezina and the first all-star selection with a 2.03 average on the season. The defense was anchored by second all-star Guy Lapointe, but was solid throughout with Serge Savard, Larry Robinson, and Pierre Bouchard, with young Bill Nyrop and Rick Chartraw coming on to challenge Don Awrey. That crew helped cut the goals allowed considerably. The forwards were simply overwhelming, beginning with all-star Guy Lafleur, who won the Ross with 125 points, and including Steve Shutt, Peter Mahovlich, Yvan Cournoyer, Jacques Lemaire, Yvon Lambert, Jim Roberts, Bob Gainey, Doug Jarvis, Doug Risebrough, and Mario Tremblay. And if that weren't enough, Rejean Houle would be coming back from Quebec in the WHA for the 1977 season.

The gaps in quality from top to competent to mediocre to poor in the NHL, shrinking but still pronounced, made it hard sometimes to judge in noncompetitive competition, but in the eyes of many that Canadien team could rank with the great ones of the past. They made their case by dominating the other good teams with splendid skating and playmaking. And at times, with Cournoyer skating at right wing, it seemed like the ghost of the all-lefty Punch Line of the past.

One team they did not dominate in their single meeting was the Soviet Army team they played on New Year's Eve. The Russians had arranged a series of midseason exhibitions against the NHL, sending over two full squads. The Soviet Army beat the Rangers, 7–3, and the Moscow Wings beat the Penguins, 7–4, before the Army (with Tretiak in goal) tied Montreal, 3–3, at the Forum in a game in which the Canadiens looked a little ragged because they were unprepared for the Russians' patterns.

In the next game it was the Moscow Wings that looked ragged as Buffalo poured in the shots to win, 12–6. Thereafter, it was Moscow Wings 4–2 over the Black Hawks, the Soviet Army 5–2 over the Bruins, and the Wings 2–1 over the Islanders, before the Flyers beat the Army, 4–1. Only Fred Shero had taken the trouble to scout the Russians, study the films, and develop a game plan to stop them. It was the brains behind the brawny bullies that often made them winners.

Certain statistics from the 1976 and early 1977 seasons demonstrate the trend away from reliance on strength factors to reliance on skill factors. Statistics in hockey are not often illuminating. The impression that 90 percent of NHL players shoot left-handed, when checked, is reduced on a count of the 1977 rosters to exactly a 2 to 1 ratio. Basically that is a result of Canadian youngsters learning to control the stick naturally with the right hand high and power the shot with the other hand low. A better example is the plus-minus figure often used to measure individual value, but meaningless for that purpose because it is *always* determined by the combinations of other skaters on the ice. Again, the shots-on-goal figures are no measure of performance unless shots-*at*-goal are added, meaningless shots with automatic saves are subtracted, and goalies' percentages on meaningful shots are factored in.

An approach to a meaningful statistical evaluation of team performance (similar to the way professional basketball scouts and coaches, as opposed to PR or media people, do it) is to ask the essential question, How do teams get into position to score? How do they get to control the puck in the attacking zone? Setting aside opponents' failures to clear the puck and resultant fumbles or interceptions (to borrow analogous football terms for costly turnovers), there are four ways: from a face-off in the attacking end, from carrying the puck in on a solo dash, from taking it in on a play (at least two players, at least one pass), and from dumping it into a corner and digging it out. The next question is, How many shots does each way lead to (shots on or at, shots with reasonable expectation of success)? And finally, What is the degree of success for each way?

In the early days of expansion, most goals came from turnovers, and for later expansion clubs in their early years most goals were given up that way. With the approach to parity, those figures became relatively inconsequential, except that the excessive dumping-in of the puck which such lack of skill encouraged has not diminished in proportion. For the immediate purposes, however, offensive possessions, shots, and goals from turnovers have been omitted.

The Bruins-Flyers style of the championship years was to dump the puck in on one third to nearly half of their possessions. The would-be power teams followed suit. Finesse teams and their imitators cut the figure to one fourth. And yet the number of meaningful shots from that type of possession has never been as high proportionally. The Canadiens-Sabres style uses plays to set up offensive possessions better than one fourth of the time. Shots from plays are also proportionately small, but the percentage of *goals* when shots result from plays is the highest (the Russians give good support to those figures).

Neither the good power teams nor the good finesse teams bother much with the solo dash for offensive possession. The weak finesse teams do, and there is a high percentage of shots resulting from this, in the 25 percent range. But it produces the lowest percentage of goals from the shots. Most of the shots are straight in from long range and merely add to goalies' saves. Offensive possessions produced from face-offs are a constant 20–25 percent for all styles. They produce a high percentage of shots (more at than on), often accounting for 30–35 percent of the total, but very few goals.

Checking Back

The play of the champion Canadiens could serve as a paradigm for these figures in action. They disdain the solo dash that yields the easy save by a goalie or block by a checking defenseman. They use the corners to forecheck opponents into errors or to change lines on the fly, but not as a basic offensive play. They shoot off a draw whenever a quick opening is there, but often pass to set up a play to relieve defensive congestion and produce a better shot. And mainly they make plays, playing hockey as best it can be played, with grace and speed and spontaneity with precision as a team game.

The Canadiens were, if anything, even more dominant in the 1977 season. But they were far from the whole story in the NHL. Beginning on January 3, the league produced its own Monday night "game of the week" for TV without benefit of a network contract. The first game was a splendid one, Montreal beating Philadelphia but making the Flyers compete on their level, setting a high standard for future games in both production and play.

The greatest disappointment was in the Smythe Division where all five teams were below .500. St. Louis was first, with a veteran team; Minnesota second, featuring a rookie line of Roland Eriksson, Steve Jensen, and Alex Pirus. Chicago, with Bobby Orr playing in only twenty games, barely edged Vancouver for a playoff spot. Colorado, transplanted from Kansas City, was far back, despite an outstanding rookie in Paul Gardner, and hoping that the franchise would not melt away when springtime came to the Rockies.

In the Patrick Division, the Rangers showed late-season signs of renascence and a promising rookie in Don Murdoch, but finished last. Atlanta was led into the playoffs by Tom Lysiak, Eric Vail, and Calder-winning, Paraguay-born Willi Plett. The Islanders fought Philadelphia most of the way, led by second all-star Denis Potvin and Masterson Trophy–winner Eddie Westfall, but fell 6 points short of the Flyers' 112. MacLeish was fourth in the league in scoring, Clarke tenth.

An even better race came down to the last day in the Adams Division, where Boston had to beat Buffalo, the Islanders, and Toronto in their last three games to beat the Sabres by two points. Jean Ratelle scored his one-thousandth NHL point in the last game, as he, Peter McNab, Gregg Sheppard, Brad Park, and Terry O'Reilly brought new hope to the Orr-less Bruins. Buffalo was led, as usual, by second all-star center Gil Perreault who was fifth in the league in scoring and tied Shutt with nine game-winning goals.

Toronto took the other playoff spot, nearly by default, as the troubled Cleveland team finished out of sight amid reports that the franchise, never successful in California, might fold in Ohio. The Leafs were an erratic team all season, with high-scoring Lanny McDonald (second all-star) and Darryl Sittler backed up by a record-breaking pair of scoring defensemen, Ian Turnbull, who scored five times in a single game, and first all-star Borje Salming. They also had a rookie goalie in Mike Palmeteer and a champion penalty-earner in Dave Williams, who drew more attention to the unnecessary violence in the game than the Paul Newman movie *Slap Shot,* an amusing burlesque of minor-league hockey that appeared during the season.

The Norris Division, like the whole league, was dominated by Montreal. Their team records were 132 points, sixty wins, twenty-seven road wins, a thirty-four–game unbeaten streak at home, only one loss at home, and only eight losses in a minimum seventy-game schedule. Ken Dryden (ten shutouts, forty-one wins, first all-star) and Michel Larocque (four shutouts, league-leading 2.09 average) won the Vezina. Larry Robinson won the Norris, while Guy Lapointe was second all-star defenseman. Steve Shutt was a unanimous first all-star selection, with sixty goals and 105 points, but his linemate Guy Lafleur was even better. Le Demon Blond, a.k.a. Superfleur, scored eighty assists and fifty-six goals to win the Ross and the Hart Trophies, later adding the Smythe as playoff MVP. Scotty Bowman, who seemed to have the easiest job in hockey, was Coach of the Year.

Los Angeles edged Pittsburgh for second place in the division. Second all-star Vachon had a fine season in sixty-eight games in goal, and first all-star center Marcel Dionne had fifty-three goals and 122 points while winning the Lady Byng Trophy. Washington, in fourth place, was easily the most-improved team in the league, as Coach Tommy McVie had the Caps in condition and in contention in most games. They went from 32 to 62 points, finished over .500 at home, won seasonal series from five clubs including three that made the playoffs, and got outstanding individual play from Gerry Meehan and Guy Charron.

Detroit went from bad to the league's worst. They lost not only fifty-five games but a chance to bring Gordie Howe back into the Red Wing fold along with his sons. They did bring Ted Lindsay back to manage and did manage one triumph (other than the first draft selection) when one of their executives, lawyer John Ziegler, was deemed acceptable throughout the league to succeed Clarence Campbell as president.

In the playoffs, Buffalo eliminated Minnesota easily in two games, with Jim Lorentz scoring a hat trick in the second. The Islanders took Chicago out in two games, scoring four third-period goals in the first and winning 2–1 in the second game, which was not played in the stadium because of a Led Zeppelin concert.

The visiting team won each game in the Toronto-Pittsburgh series, Mc-Donald scoring three goals to win the rubber match in Palmeteer's first playoff start. The Leafs then extended their streak to four straight on the road by winning twice in the Spectrum, only to have the Flyers take the next four. The third game was won by MacLeish in overtime, the fourth by Leach in overtime, despite four goals and an assist by McDonald. Leach had the only two goals as Stephenson shut out Toronto in the fifth game, and Jim Watson scored the winner in the 4–3 sixth game, despite two more by McDonald.

Los Angeles won in the first round over Atlanta, though the Flames had their first playoff win ever, when Butch Goring's hat trick helped win the third game 4–2. Then the Kings extended the Bruins to six games. Bobby Schmautz had a hat trick in the first period to pace an 8–3 Boston win in the first game, then scored the winner in Game 2 and two more goals in a 7–6 Boston win in Game 3, Stan Jonathan getting the winner with thirteen seconds left. Dionne got the winning goal as Los Angeles took Game 4, and Vachon had thirty-nine saves to hold off the Bruins 3–1 in the fifth. Boston wound up the series on a Sheppard goal in Game 6. Shortly thereafter Bob Pulford resigned from the Kings' organization and soon was hired to pilot the Black Hawks.

St. Louis got only four goals in four games as Montreal swept them easily 7–2, 3–0, 5–1, 4–1. Dryden played all four games but was rarely challenged as Lafleur all but settled the issue in the first game with three goals and three assists. Playing for the right to challenge the Canadiens, the Islanders swept the Sabres 4–2, 4–2, 4–3, 4–3. Gillies had the game-winner in the first three games, making four in a row, Billy MacMillan in the fourth. Billy Smith was in goal in all four games, as injured Chico Resch hoped to be back for the semis.

It was Smith in the Forum, however, as Bill Harris's hat trick fell short of upsetting Montreal. Shutt had the winner in the 4–3 opener. Dryden then shut out New York 3–0, Jim Roberts scoring the winning goal while Montreal was short-handed. Back home in Nassau County, New York won 5–3 as Denis Potvin scored twice and Andre St. Laurent got the game-winner, but in Game 4 Dryden got another shutout, his seventh in playoff competition, his third in eight games. Shutt scored twice, including the winner, and assisted once. Resch, who returned to the ice in Game 4, played all of Game 5 and won it 4–3 as Harris scored in overtime. Then he played brilliantly in Game 6 only to lose 2–1 as Bob Gainey scored twice, even though Lafleur was shut out of the scoring for the first time in thirty-eight games since January 30.

Boston, meanwhile, swept Philadelphia 4–3, 5–4, 2–1, and 3–0. The Flyers scored three times in the third period to tie the first game, but Rick Middleton won it in overtime. O'Reilly won the second in overtime. And it was all Cheevers after that, the shutout being his seventh in playoff competition. Mike Milbury and Ratelle had the game-winners and Don Marcotte scored twice in the final game.

This should have set the stage for a splendid Cup series, since Boston was the only team to have beaten Montreal in the Forum all season. But it turned out to be a dreary affair, swept by the Canadiens 7–3, 3–0, 4–2, 2–1. Even the fourth game, which went into overtime before Lafleur fed Jacques Lemaire for the Cup-winner, provided little excitement as Boston never got a shot on goal in the four-and-a-half extra minutes. As great a team as these Canadiens were, with no weakness throughout the squad and the whole system for that matter, they were capable of lackluster play because they had little competition.

The hoped-for improvement in play across the board was perhaps assured but perhaps postponed by postseason developments. The WHA seemed ready to disband. The Minnesota franchise folded during the season, Phoenix at the end, and Indianapolis shortly thereafter. Of the remaining nine, several were prepared to apply for membership in the NHL, including the champion Quebec Nordiques, Cincinnati, and Edmonton. New England was in a solid position for a bid after signing Gordie, Marty, Mark, and Colleen Howe. Birmingham, Houston, and Winnipeg would also be considered, with only Calgary and San Diego as totally unlikely prospects.

With elements of expansion and of merger, this anticipated move would resemble the consolidation of pro basketball. All the best players in North America would be in the same league, but there would be further dilution of talent and greater disparity from top to bottom, even if the new teams were all grouped in a new division. The financially troubled NHL franchises might benefit from expansion fees, but their gate attractions would not likely be improved. In time, perhaps, there would be natural attrition and the number of big-league teams would approach a stable norm, at least until expansion reaches out to another hemisphere.

In any event, with Campbell's retirement at seventy-two and with *some* kind of realignment a certainty, the NHL as it approached its sixtieth birthday had to look at 1977 as the end of an era. With many good young players coming up, with renewed recognition of the virtues of wrist shots over slapshots, and with management recognizing the practical advantages (on ice, in crowd appeal, in potential TV attractiveness) of a style that exposes the limitations of the dump-and-hit game, the National Hockey League was skating toward a bright new age.

Index

Index

Index

(continued)

Index

Index

Index